1975

THE EPIC QUEST

THE EPIC QUEST

STUDIES IN
FOUR OLD FRENCH
Chansons de Geste

WILLIAM CALIN

THE JOHNS HOPKINS PRESS
BALTIMORE

Library of Congress Catalog Card Number 66–16042

For H. C.

Acknowledgments

Without a fellowship from the John Simon Guggenheim Memorial Foundation and a grant-in-aid from the American Council of Learned Societies, both of which enabled me to devote much of the academic year 1963–64 to writing and research, this book could not have been completed. I should like to thank the following persons: Professor Daniel Poirion of Grenoble, whose course on the *chanson de geste* at Yale University in 1958 greatly benefited this study, especially in light of the chapter on *Aymeri de Narbonne;* Professor Alfred Adler of the City University of New York, who sent me a manuscript copy of his *Rückzug in epischer Parade* several months prior to its publication and submitted wise counsel in the United States and Paris; Professor John Lapp of Stanford University, who, having read the manuscript of the present volume, made it better. Encouragement and advice of the warmest, most humane sort came from Professors Pierre Le Gentil and Jean Frappier of the Sorbonne, Ronald Walpole of the University of California at Berkeley, and Robert Cohn of Stanford. To my graduate students over the past years—Geraldine Berman, George Diller, Jack Dixon, David Gardner, Elwood Hartman, Gerald Herman, Edward Killen, Marshall Metcalf, Elizabeth Taylor, Earl Walpole—go thanks for stimulating term-papers and many an hour of seminar discussion. From time to time, they will recognize an allusion or turn of phrase of their own making.

Contents

THE EPIC QUEST

Introduction

A well-established tradition holds that of the one hundred or so *chansons de geste* which have come down to us, only the *Song of Roland* is a masterpiece worthy of serious study. This view has long been enshrined in standard works of vulgarization, in the writings of some distinguished men of letters, and is restated from time to time by the scholar.[1] However, a steadily increasing number of medievalists have, since the last war, written excellent literary criticism of *chansons* other than the *Roland*, emphasizing their aesthetic value and right to a place in the canon of French literature.[2]

[1] For example, Jean Boorsch in *The Encyclopedia Americana*, 1963 ed., XI, 684a: "Most epic poems are tediously long, ill composed and, for us, readable only in excerpts; yet the exalted heroism of *The Roland Song* can still be felt today"; André Gide, *Anthologie de la poésie française* (Paris, 1949), p. xiv: "Pour s'intéresser à nos 'chansons de geste,' aux vastes épopées qui du XIème au XIVème siècle encombrent notre littérature (fût-ce à la célèbre *Chanson de Roland* qui surnage un peu dans ce grand naufrage et que, de nos jours, on cherche à renflouer), il faut effort et complaisance"; Jean Rychner, *La chanson de geste: Essai sur l'art épique des jongleurs* (Geneva-Lille, 1955), pp. 124–25, 154; C. M. Bowra, *Heroic Poetry* (London, 1952), pp. v–vi.

[2] Among others should be included such names as Adler, Bezzola, Curtius, Foulon, Frappier, Horrent, Jonin, Le Gentil, Neuschäfer, Nichols, Panvini, De Riquer, Walpole, and Woledge; William Calin, *The Old French Epic of Revolt: Raoul de Cambrai, Renaud de Montauban, Gormond et Isembard* (Geneva, 1962), treats three poems of the feudal cycle as literature; for detailed references, consult the usual bibliographical aids and the issues of the *Bulletin bibliographique de la Société Rencesvals* as they appear.

The present volume contains essays on four epics; each essay is preceded by a brief plot résumé of the *chanson* in question. The poems do not treat a common theme. They resemble each other only in that they were composed at about the same moment in time, the generation extending roughly from 1190 to 1230 (which approximates the reign of Philip Augustus), and that all diverge from the heroic pattern of earlier *chansons de geste.*

The *trouvères* of this generation were in search of new material; they introduced new forces into traditional literary currents. We shall discuss certain of these forces—romance, comedy, religion—as they were embodied in literary form. The concluding essay will then touch on some broader issues and seek to justify the aesthetic criteria we have used. Literary characters set out in quest of honor and adventure; medieval poets search for new ways of appealing to their public; and we the moderns seek the literary essence of poems written hundreds of years ago.

Chapter I

THE QUEST FOR THE WOMAN AND THE CITY
Aymeri de Narbonne

Returning from the Battle of Roncevaux, Charlemagne's army comes upon the city of Narbonne, fallen into Saracen hands. The emperor offers Narbonne to twelve of his greatest barons. All refuse. The thirteenth, Ernaut de Beaulande, also declines but designates his son Aymeri in his place. The young man accepts and, in a series of engagements, captures the fortress. Charles leaves it to Aymeri, who is now Count of Narbonne.

Aymeri's counselors urge him to marry. He refuses obdurately until Hugues de Barcelone suggests Ermengarde, sister to King Boniface of the Lombards. Aymeri sends an expedition, led by Hugues, to seek Ermengarde's hand. These messengers quarrel with a band of Germans encountered en route; the German leader, Savari, also wishes to marry Ermengarde. Although outnumbered, the Frenchmen defeat their rivals.

In Pavia, Boniface's capital, the messengers prove to be wealthier and more generous than their hosts. Disdaining Boniface's hospitality, they manage to live luxuriously in spite of various obstacles the king places in their way (raising prices, forbidding the sale of firewood). Boniface is forced to listen to, and favorably consider, the Frenchmen's suit.

Ermengarde accepts with joy the husband proposed for her.

Ten of the messengers return to France with the news and tell Aymeri he may claim his bride in person. On the way they are ambushed by Savari; Hugues de Barcelone escapes and rides full speed to Narbonne. Having set out with an army, Aymeri rescues his men and takes Savari prisoner. He receives Ermengarde from the hands of her brother.

Meanwhile, a Saracen host has been raised in the young count's absence and is in the process of besieging his city. A messenger, Fouques, escapes from battle with the news. He discovers Aymeri and Ermengarde on the road. The Frenchmen increase their speed of march and, with the help of Aymeri's uncle, Girard de Vienne, defeat the invaders. Aymeri marries Ermengarde and retakes possession of Narbonne.

*   *   *

One of the few examples of pertinent literary criticism devoted to *Aymeri de Narbonne*[1] is by Hans Weiske.[2] Weiske claims that those scenes dealing with the seizure and defense of Narbonne (*Die Eroberung Narbonnes*) have no direct connection to the scenes recounting Aymeri's search for a wife (*Die Braut-fahrtsage*). In fact, the two themes, originating separately, would have been brought together only by the very last poet working on the text, Bertrand de Bar-sur-Aube.[3] Other scholars, while not

---

[1] Ed. Louis Demaison (2 vols.; Paris, 1887); subsequent references to the poem will be from this edition.

[2] "Quellengeschichtliches zu Aimeri de Narbonne," *Archiv für das Studium der neueren Sprachen*, CVII (1901), 129–34.

[3] *Aymeri de Narbonne*, I, lxxiii–xcii, discusses the very sound arguments, agreed to by most scholars, indicating that the epic was composed in the early years of the thirteenth century by Bertrand de Bar-sur-Aube, the author of *Girard de Vienne*; against this opinion, see Philipp August Becker, *Das Werden der Wilhelm- und der Aimerigeste* (Leipzig, 1939), chap. 5. Becker claims that the two epics were written by different authors and

necessarily proposing extreme theories as to the poem's origins, agree that *La Chanson d'Aymeri* suffers from the gratuitous juxtaposition of disparate elements which correspond to Weiske's *Eroberung* and *Brautfahrt*.[4] These reveal a fundamental ambiguity in the poem's structure and tone. For the rest of this chapter we shall concentrate on this problem. Does there exist, in fact, a contradiction, opposition, or imbalance between the elements of love and war in *Aymeri de Narbonne?* If not, from whence arises the feeling of ambivalence noted by so many readers? And how has the poet overcome the various structural and thematic problems inherent in his material to create a work of art?[5]

*   *   *

An important theme of section one, the *Eroberung*, is service to God. The battle for Narbonne is not a common, mundane war, the quest for a fief or dispute over a city. It is a crusade, and the Saracens are depicted as wicked, ungodly people who must be attacked and destroyed. At the beginning of his poem, in a kind of exordium, Bertrand speaks of Aymeri as a Saracen-killer (vss. 18–22). At the very end this theme is repeated (vss. 4698–704). And in the narrative itself the hero's very first speech contains a threat against the pagans (vss. 687–91).

On several occasions Aymeri and Charlemagne give vent to similar expressions of hostility. One scene illustrating the hero's impetuousness occurs when he breaks off a conversation with his

---

that *Aymeri* can be dated at approximately 1170. However, his dating has been contested and, in our opinion, refuted by Ferdinand Lot, "Encore la légende de Girart de Roussillon. A propos d'un livre récent," *Romania,* LXX (1948–49), 192–233, 355–96, and Ernst Robert Curtius, Über die altfranzösische Epik V. 3. Girart de Vienne," *Zeitschrift für romanische Philologie,* LXVIII (1952), 183–95.

[4] *Aymeri de Narbonne,* I, xcii–xcvii; Joseph Bédier, *Les Légendes épiques* (Paris, 1908), I, 30–31; Friedrich Schürr, *Das altfranzösische Epos. Zur Stilgeschichte und inneren Form der Gotik* (Munich, 1926), p. 466.

[5] Parts of this chapter have appeared in *Romance Notes,* VIII, and *Neophilologus,* L.

uncle Girard, cuts short the thanks he owes the Lord of Vienne
for having rescued him, lest some of the enemy escape:

> "Biaus niés," fet il, "estes vos en santé?"
> "Oïl, biaus oncles, la merci Damedé!
> Mès s'un petit eussiez plus esté,
> Je sai de voir, mal me fust encontré,
> Or tost, biaus oncles, n'i ait plus demoré,
> Gardez paien ne soient eschapé!
> Or tost après, trop avons sejorné!"[6]   (vs. 4322)

Aymeri is convinced that God on high will bring him victory
(vss. 762–69), a belief that Charles himself has enunciated twenty
lines before (vss. 740–44). When Charlemagne orders a knightly
diversion, a tilt at the quintain in Aymeri's honor, the youth
refuses to waste his time on such trivial matters. Instead he lies
in wait to ambush those Saracens who will come out from
Narbonne, attracted by the commotion. Later, when the enemy
city is captured, Aymeri treats the two Saracen kings in an unusually cruel manner (they are kept in a dungeon till they die).
We cannot help noticing the difference between their fate and
that of Savari, the Count of Narbonne's wicked personal enemy,
who is permitted ransom. Finally, it should be noted that both
Charles and Aymeri are conspicuously generous to the Church.
The former builds the Cathedral of Saint Paul in Narbonne,
donates relics, and appoints an archbishop; the latter builds an
abbey where masses are said for the souls of his departed parents.

Thus the doctrinal orientation of *Aymeri de Narbonne* is
strongly religious. Aymeri's military victory is a triumph of good
over evil, of Christ over antichrist. The capture of Narbonne is a
tangible sign of this victory. One more city, one more piece of
land, has been regained from the enemy. The founding of a
cathedral, the appointment of an archbishop, the importation of

---

[6] "Good nephew," he says, "are you safe and sound?" "Yes, good
uncle, thank God! But I am certain that if you had waited just a little
longer, harm would have befallen me. Now quickly, good uncle, no more
delay, see that the pagans do not escape! Now after them quickly; we have
been dallying too long!"

relics—these are acts of purification, of symbolic regeneration, which permit life—Western, Christian, French—to begin anew.

Aymeri's triumph stands for something else. It is a reaffirmation of the heroic life, in defense of God, country, and crown—in other words, heroism in the tradition of the *Song of Roland.* The martyr of Roncevaux is, in fact, mentioned in the poem ten times by name and on other occasions is cited indirectly. He remains an obsession for more than one major character. The narrative action begins with the French army returning from the south. A mixed tonality pervades these opening scenes: on the one hand, joy over the victories in Spain; on the other, sadness over Roland's demise. Charlemagne personally regrets his loss again and again (vss. 134–42, 543–46, 586–92). The emperor's grief stems from political as well as personal reasons. Of course, Charles loved Roland deeply; he regrets the death of a beloved nephew and friend. But even more agonizing to him is the loss of the *miles Christi.* All of Spain would have been conquered, says the author, had Roland lived (vss. 107–12). Nor would Charles have had any difficulties seizing Narbonne had his nephew been at hand (vss. 586–92). In fact, one reason for the "procession of barons"— Charles's offer of the city to different chieftains, and their refusal—is to point up the greatness of the disaster at Roncevaux, the immeasurable loss to France occasioned by Roland's death.

A natural reaction on the Frenchmen's part is to seek revenge. Both Charles and Aymeri speak of vengeance: against Ganelon, once the army returns to France; against the Saracens here and now. Aymeri himself will make them pay for it:

> "Car se Dex done que j'en soie fievez,
> Molt chier vendré as paiens desfaez
> La mort Rollant. ..."[7]   (vs. 683)

Even the Saracens interpret the siege of Narbonne in this light (vss. 979–84). The city's capture appears as a final administering of justice, the last act in the drama of Roncevaux, the ultimate

---

[7] "For if God grants that the fief [Narbonne] is bestowed on me, I will make the miscreant pagans pay dearly for the death of Roland. . . ."

punishment for one of the gravest iniquities of history. The battle won, Charles admits that he feels better, that much of his grief has been lightened by Aymeri's triumph (vss. 794–801). In fact, the hero of Narbonne proclaims that, for love of Roland, he will continue to fight for Charles in the future (vss. 1270ff.). The capture of Narbonne was made possible only because a young hero was willing and able to do Roland's job. Thus Aymeri replaces Roland, becomes a new Roland, in the world's eyes and in his own. He will defend France and Christianity in Charles's stead, be his *avoé* (vs. 3547) as Roland would have been. Because of him the good work will proceed.

To "become" Roland, Aymeri must enter into a special relationship with Charlemagne—one similar to Roland's. Not related to the emperor by blood or marriage, at least he will maintain with Charles the same tight feudal bond portrayed in Turold's masterpiece.[8] Normally the vassal owes his lord fidelity, aid, and counsel. Aymeri fulfills all three conditions; he even defends his city as much for Charles as for himself. The Saracen messenger points out (in a verbal projection, vss. 3564–580, anticipating Picrochole's counselors in *Gargantua*) that once Narbonne is captured all of Western Europe, from Paris to Aachen to Rome, will fall. Aymeri commands the outer defenses of Christendom, one of the most important bulwarks to enemy attack. Charles likewise agrees to protect his vassal in kind. He grants him Narbonne, leaves him 1,000 knights to occupy the city, abandons to him all spoils won in future action, and volunteers to come to his aid when needed.

The fact that Charles does not come to Aymeri's defense in this poem (he is not called upon) in no way changes our conception of their relationship. At all times the two men treat each other in exemplary fashion. The one is a gracious lord, the other a loyal, upright vassal. No conflict exists between them. Whereas in so many epics of the Guillaume cycle the emperor is portrayed in less than flattering colors, here his dignity is scarcely questioned. True, Charles appears more poignant than glorious in the open-

---

[8] Did Turold write the *Song of Roland?* We adhere to Pierre Le Gentil's point of view, *La Chanson de Roland* (Paris, 1955), pp. 32–35.

ing scenes. But the theme of his weakness, already introduced in the *Roland*, is merely being embroidered here. As in the earlier poem, the emperor's suffering adds beauty, a warm, human trait to his character. On the strong side, the pagan messenger praises Charles openly (vss. 3560–563); the enemy rightly fears his coming (vss. 3731–734). And not a word of criticism or reproach is uttered against him by anyone in the Christian camp. Quite the contrary. Girard points out, for example, that the emperor will be pleased by Aymeri's conquests and the use he makes of them. Indeed, lord and vassal are mentioned in the same breath. Hugues de Barcelone states that Aymeri must be placed after Charles in glory, but that, otherwise, he is the finest knight in the world (vss. 2343–351). The author goes even further by claiming that these two alone, without distinction, are responsible for victory in the holy war (vss. 62–71). Roland lives on in Aymeri; Charles lives on in his own person. The two can be measured against each other but surpass everyone else. They triumph together against all obstacles.

The question quite legitimately arises as to what relationship Aymeri's newfound glory—as crusader, loyal vassal of his emperor, and second Roland—bears to the second of the epic's themes, the bride quest. The connection appears, at first sight, remote. We must grant, however, that if Aymeri's absence from Narbonne during the bride quest is a direct cause of the pagan counterattack, this diversion provides the necessary reinforcements to set matters aright. The happy couple sets out from Pavia accompanied by Aymeri's French army and 1,000 Lombard knights. Five hundred of the latter participate in the fight for Narbonne. They fight well; without their services the battle might never have been won. Ermengarde herself, by no means a pale, lilywhite heroine of romance, contributes directly to the victory. She suggests that aid be sought from Girard de Vienne; then, having carried the message to Girard, she accompanies him to Narbonne. Their arrival, at a crucial moment, saves the day. Girard's wife also joins the rescue party. She too proffers good advice: that Aymeri and Ermengarde's wedding feast should take place on the field of battle, and that from his own landholdings the Lord of Narbonne should grant his bride a dowry worthy of her. Although the idea of wedding feast and dowry has already occurred to the men, the Countess of Vienne shows spunk and good sense. Thus she participates, if only a little, in the action.

Ermengarde contributes more to Aymeri's cause than a few reinforcements, money for the troops, and wise counsel. Most of all, she offers him the glory of love. If Aymeri is to replace Roland, someone must be found to parallel Aude, the fallen hero's fiancée. One of Roland's greatest claims to glory was that this beautiful girl loved him so much that she could not survive him:

> "O est Rollant le catanie
> Ki me jurat cume sa per a prendre?"   (vs. 3709)

> "... Ne place Deu ne ses seinz ne ses angles
> Après Rollant que jo vive remaigne!"[9]   (vs. 3718)

So too for the heroes of *Raoul de Cambrai* and *Garin le Lorrain.* Ermengarde certainly demonstrates a like passion for Aymeri. She had already heard of him and was predisposed in his favor, reports Hugues de Barcelone, when the latter first met her in Pavia on returning from a pilgrimage (vss. 1378–380). Later she declares how much she loves the victor of Narbonne, that if she cannot have him she will marry no one (vss. 2432–436, 2443–446). But since, unlike Roland, Raoul, Garin, and Bègues, Aymeri himself does not fall in combat, neither is his fiancée obliged to perish. Instead, resembling Berthe in *Girard de Roussillon* and Clarisse in *Les Quatre Fils Aymon*, she marries the hero and will devote her life to serving and honoring him, associated with but most of all contributing to his glory.

An important aspect of feudal honor concerns the family. Only through Ermengarde can Aymeri found a dynasty, the family of the Guillaume cycle. Already in the exordium the poet speaks of Aymeri's sons (vss. 23–31). Thinking of his lineage in battle (vss. 839–41), the hero is spurred on to greater valor. The people

---

[9] "Where is the captain Roland, who swore he would take me to wife? . . ." "May it not please God, his saints, nor his angels that I outlive Roland!"

urge the Lord of Narbonne to take a wife: only through marriage
will he bear sons to continue the good fight after he is dead
(vss. 1335–340). In reply Aymeri observes that the finest, noblest
girls, those worthy of him and who could attract him, are already
in the family! But the right girl is found. Ermengarde and Aymeri
are married, and she gives birth to twelve children—seven sons,
five daughters—who themselves with their issue will surround
Aymeri, succor and defend him (in *Les Narbonnais, Les Enfances
Guillaume, La Mort Aymeri*, etc.). The holy war will be maintained by future generations till the enemy are overcome.

The notion of lineage contributes directly to the action. Girard
de Vienne, Aymeri's uncle, rescues him at Narbonne. It is significant that whereas the Saracens expect the beleaguered garrison to seek help from Charlemagne, help comes from Aymeri
himself and his uncle. Further examples of "keeping within the
clan": When Charles offers the city of Narbonne to Ernaut de
Beaulande, the old man, like his twelve predecessors, is obliged
to decline; unlike them, however, he has a strong, willing son.
By nominating him for the task, Ernaut preserves the family's
honor. Later in the poem (during the bride quest) we find the
motif of succession repeated. During Savari's first ambush of the
messengers, Count Aymer de Lausanne falls. His nephew replaces
him in battle and in life:

> "D'Aymer est la perte recovrée,
> Le bon vassal qui la vie a finée.
> Cist est ses niés, fiz sa seror l'ainnée;
> Bien doit tenir la terre et la contrée
> Qui fu son oncle a la chiere menbrée.
> Mal ait par cui il an perdra denrée,
> Q'an lui ert bien tout par droit asenée."[10] (vs. 1831)

We perceive that love and war are not Bertrand's sole major
themes. The call of the family is every bit as significant as that

[10] "The loss of Aymer, the valiant warrior who died, has been recovered.
Here is his nephew, son of his older sister; it is the young man's right to
hold the lands which belonged to his uncle of the renowned [mighty?] face.
May evil befall him who causes the nephew to lose a penny's worth of the
fief, for by rights all of it will be awarded to him."

of France or Christendom; indeed the epic matter serves at every turn to emphasize the concept of lineage. Aymeri is a fine, loyal vassal, faithful to his king yet capable of maintaining personal integrity. He fights Saracens, captures a city, seeks a wife. In all this he closely resembles his son Guillaume, hero of *La Chanson de Guillaume, Aliscans, Le Charroi de Nîmes,* and *La Prise d'Orange.* The poet of *Aymeri de Narbonne,* who lived and worked at least one generation after the major epics of the Guillaume cycle had become part of the literary heritage, naturally patterned his protagonist on Guillaume. Yet even in the unique poetic world of *La Chanson d'Aymeri* the hero cannot stand alone, abstracted from his illustrious model. Nor did the medieval public conceive of Aymeri apart from his sons, of his destiny separate from theirs. For generations the family struggles against the Saracen onslaught, sometimes united, sometimes apart, but always as one. Aymeri begins the fight that will be brought to fruition, as it were, by Guillaume. So whenever we come upon Aymeri, we think of Guillaume too. The Count of Narbonne not only resembles his son but prefigures him. Every heroic act committed by Aymeri will be repeated, enhanced, fulfilled by Guillaume. The family contains an aura extending beyond the individual member. The hero of these poems is the family, the poem's message an exaltation of the family—not a real family, of course, but a stylized representation embodying the heroic-feudal ideal. And the idealized lineage will enrich each hero's *persona* in equal measure. Such must be the case when historical events are transformed into legends—legends which give rise to poetry, which in turn creates new myths or reinforces the old.

Aymeri begins his career not as a patriarch surrounded by numerous progeny but as a young man only recently knighted, lacking wealth and power. Except for a few adventures recounted in *Girard de Vienne,* this is his jumping-off point in the heroic life. Ernst Robert Curtius has brilliantly analyzed the exaltation of youth in *Gui de Bourgogne.*[11] In that epic the veterans of

---

[11] "Über die altfranzösische Epik II. 2. Gui de Bourgogne," *Romanische Forschungen,* LXI (1948), 437–47; Alfred Adler, *Rückzug in epischer Parade* (Frankfort on the Main, 1963), *passim.*

Roncevaux are unable to continue the fight. A troop of young French warriors comes to the rescue. They treat their elders with disdain, refuse to greet them, and on one occasion seize an enemy stronghold more or less for the fun of it, without Charles's permission and when he is in serious need of help.

Although the conflict between youth and age is not as pronounced in *Aymeri de Narbonne*, the opening scenes of the epic do recall the principal theme of *Gui de Bourgogne*. Charles's barons decline the offer of Narbonne. Their reasons are many: the city is impregnable, they have already served their time in Spain, they are tired, they have lands elsewhere, they must repel invaders or rebellions at home, their families await, they are poor, they would be obliged to fight alone, they are too old. This last reason, though it is applied only to Ernaut de Beaulande, includes the others since the other excuses are all, in one form or another, manifestations of old age or rationalizations for it. Ernaut himself is eminently aware of this fact. He cannot fight for he is too old ("Vieuz sui et freilles," vs. 565). Charles has need of a younger man ("A un danzel fort et juenne et legier / Vos covendroit la cité a baillier," vs. 572–73). And Aymeri accepts the challenge in part because he is young. He supplies new blood to invigorate Charlemagne's tired, anemic forces. He replaces the lost, young hero Roland and conquers.

Further manifestations of the succession theme in *Aymeri de Narbonne* are the following: As Aymeri supersedes Ernaut, so too, as we have shown before, the messenger Aymer gives way to his young nephew. The squire inherits Aymer's lands and honors; his presence restores the group's homogeneity.

If, in the Christian camp, Charlemagne and Ernaut represent age, so does the famous Duke Naimes, the Nestor of the Old French epic. Naimes fulfills his usual role of wise counselor. After the victory he accompanies the emperor on the journey northward; we discover later on in the poem that he has left behind his nephew Hélinant. The "young Naimes" is one of those charged by Aymeri to guard Narbonne in his absence. Hélinant resembles Naimes in his ability to proffer good advice (to seek help), but he will also urge his comrades to come out from behind the city walls and help Aymeri in the field. His youthful enthusiasm contributes to the final victory.

Especially in matters of love, the peculiar domain of the bride quest, youth scores a triumph. Ermengarde refuses three suitors because they are too old. Even if he is rich, the feeble, ugly, elderly man cannot make a good husband, she says. The match may well lead to dishonor (courtly love, adultery?). She will never accept such a man! "Si m'eist Dex qui tot a en baillie, / Je n'avrai ja viel home" (vss. 2480–481). Interestingly enough, Savari the German ("a la barbe florie") is one of the graybeards Ermengarde will not marry. Presumably, a key factor for Aymeri's victory over him on the field of battle and in the girl's heart is the difference in their respective ages.

Although the feudal period was not the only time in world history to exalt the ideal of youth, it did manifest an extraordinary predilection for the young. One need think only of the various Children's Crusades with their ideal of the child (*pre-electa juventus*) as sacrificial victim and victorious warrior. Jeanne Lods has demonstrated how this ideal is expressed in the *chanson de geste*.[12] The young hero may be physically weak and unable to resist hunger and thirst; he may be brash, even insolent to his elders. But his heart is in the right place. His is the drive, the enthusiasm, the purity inherent in the crusade, essential to its successful outcome. The child is the true hero, chosen of God; older men are worthy to participate in the cause only to the extent that they retain the peculiar traits of youth. Now the *Aymeri* poet develops an interesting variation on the theme. For older men not only participate in, but are invigorated by, contact with the young. Of the sixty messengers sent to Pavia, twenty are patriarchs with flowing white beards. One of these, the leader of the troop (Hugues de Barcelone), gives a rousing account of himself in the fray. Still more to the point is the story of Girard de Roussillon. He was one of those weary barons who refused the gift of Narbonne. Now, serving Aymeri, he kills Germans in

[12] "Le thème de l'enfance dans l'épopée française," *Cahiers de civilisation médiévale*, III (1960), 58–62.

heroic fashion. Even Ermengarde's cowardly brother Boniface is transformed on contact with the hero. In *Aymeri de Narbonne,* as in so much of world literature, age stands as an image of death, decay, defeat, tragedy; youth represents birth, growth, triumph, happy ending. Our hero and heroine actualize the latter traits, rejecting the former, but they succeed in incorporating the best of the old world too.

Opposition between youth and age may be thought of in a different way, as the traditional dichotomy between *fortitudo* and *sapientia.*[13] The young hero possesses the strength, bravery, and enthusiasm necessary for committing great deeds. Although the older hero or wise companion lacks prowess, he compensates by demonstrating the virtues of prudence or wisdom not to be found in the young man. Ideally the perfect warrior possesses both strength and wisdom. But since the reality of life is otherwise, this disparity between the ideal and the actual forms the underlying conflict on which so much epic action is based.

It is true that in *Aymeri de Narbonne,* as in *Gui de Bourgogne, fortitudo* triumphs over *sapientia.* The poet's sympathies lie obviously with the impetuous hero and his young friends. But if the old men's prudence is condemned, we are not permitted to ignore what at least appears to be the hero's lack of wisdom and the difficulties into which he falls because of it.

Aymeri declines to tilt at the quintain, even though the game was instituted in his honor. Instead, he ambushes Saracens without Charles's permission, an action for which the emperor reproves him.

In a humorous speech he naïvely demands that the Saracens surrender Narbonne, their city, at once, because it has been given by Charlemagne to him!

> "Nerbone!" escrie, "moie est ceste cité!
> Fil a putain, fel glouton desfaé,
> Randez moi tost la mestre fermeté,

---

[13] For a study of this topic, see Curtius, *Europäische Literatur und lateinisches Mittelalter* (Bern, 1948), chap. 9; also Calin, *The Old French Epic of Revolt,* chaps. 3 and 4.

> Car Charlemaine m'en a le don doné!
> Se vos nel faites, tuit seroiz desmenbré,
> Ou ars en feu, ou au vant encroé,
>   Car la citez est moie!"[14]   (vs. 932)

As soon as Ermengarde's name is mentioned, Aymeri insists that she be given to him in marriage or he will destroy all of northern Italy. Hugues de Barcelone must cool Aymeri's ardor by insisting that an embassy first be sent to seek the girl's hand.

Yet the very same delegation, captained by Hugues, representing Aymeri and responsible for his honor, refuses to dine at King Boniface's table. They prefer to buy provisions in the city and hold open house for the poor. Boniface is quite naturally incensed at having his hospitality spurned: "Avis li est que c'est granz reproviers" (vs. 2116). A slur has been cast upon his honor; he and the author refer several times to the French as acting with *grant fierté*, (vss. 2168, 2183, 2390, 2403). The word is certainly meant to be taken in a pejorative sense. The Frenchmen's act of *desmesure* is the immediate cause for what amounts to a serious strain in diplomatic relations. Boniface retaliates as best he can, and soon a price war is wreaking havoc with the Lombard economy.

We must not take too seriously such departures from the most punctilious decorum. True, the emperor first upbraids Aymeri for disobedience at the quintain. But we know he does so only in fun. In reality he is pleased by Aymeri's deeds ("Grant joie en a li emperere eu," vs. 947). Once the young man explains his conduct (hatred for the enemy), Charles laughs and forgives him openly. The poet is telling us that his hero's foolishness is in fact a kind of superior wisdom, that his naïveté masks a finer comprehension of the situation than that displayed by his elders. If we must consider the youth's excessive enthusiasm a fault, it is a

---

[14] "Narbonne!" he cries, "this city is mine! You sons of whores, treacherous miscreant wretches, turn over to me the inner keep at once, for Charlemagne has given it to me. If you don't, you will all be torn limb from limb, or burned at the stake, or hanged from a gibbet, for the city is mine!"

mild one, whose chief effect is to excite a good-humored response in the public—laughter at his social foibles, coupled with
admiration for the very real virtues which go hand in hand with
them.

So too for the other examples of folly mentioned above. With
reference to the economic struggle at Pavia, the *fiertez* (violence,
audacity, prowess, fierceness, ferociousness)[15] displayed by
Hugues and his men may be, under different circumstances, a
stunning virtue. The word will characterize Charlemagne himself
in his fight against the Saracens (vss. 670, 860). Moreover, if
the French are guilty of shaming Boniface, he reacts in kind.
He seeks to dishonor them, and significantly the verb *reprover*
is used also in this context. It signifies how the messengers will
be reproached as a result of Boniface's actions:

> "... or nos fet grant vilté
> Rois Boniface qui ce a comendé.
> Mengier char crue n'avons pas ausé.
> Se la menjons, ce sera lascheté;
> En noz pais nos sera reprové."[16]   (vs. 2202)

The Frenchmen originally decline the king's hospitality as a sign
of independence, a tribute to their lord Aymeri's honor. Fulfilling
a boast or wager is a traditional way of maintaining honor in
heroic poetry. Of course it also challenges Boniface. But the dare
is not a blow of open defiance nor a manifestation of deep-
seated hostility; rather, it is the first stage in a kind of potlatch
ritual. The messengers claim to be wealthier and more generous
than their host. Boniface is not obliged to pick up the gauntlet.
By so doing, he chooses to enter into a contest with heroes; he
must lose and the responsibility for defeat rests on his own

[15] For an interpretation of *fiers*, see George Fenwick Jones, "Roland's
Lament—A Divergent Interpretation," *Romanic Review*, LIII (1962), 3–15;
"The *Chanson de Roland* and Semantic Change," *Modern Language Quarterly*, XXIII (1962), 46–52; *The Ethos of the Song of Roland* (Baltimore,
1963), pp. 65–7.

[16] ". . . King Boniface, by ordering this, has covered us with shame.
It is not our custom to eat raw meat. Eating it will be an act of cowardice
for which we shall be reproached back home."

shoulders. In terms of the epic, the contest can neither be blamed nor praised. The men responsible for instigating it, if it is in a good cause, also should not be blamed. The loser alone must pay the price; there is no justification as final as success, no condemnation as ultimate as failure. Thus the story falls into a large group of tales, one subdivision of which has traditionally been designated the *trompeur trompé*. Boniface hopes to deceive and humiliate his guests through a financial squeeze, but his city is forced to capitulate first. The Frenchmen, unlike Boniface, can *afford* to be foolish, to rush to excess. In this sense they are only profiting from natural superiority, living up to native ingrained capacity, transforming potentiality into actuality. Boniface and Savari, on the other hand, cannot afford to offer challenges, since they lack both the financial and physical resources to back them up. Although Aymeri and his men commit *desmesure,* unlike Roland's theirs is a good excess, an outburst of natural animal spirits and not defiance of the gods. The epic has come a long way from the *Chanson de Roland* and *Gormond et Isembard.* In the world of *Aymeri de Narbonne* the hero can do little if any wrong. Immeasurably superior to all possible competitors, he is permitted to indulge in whatever game may strike his fancy. The contest at Pavia generates a tone of frolic and good humor. Boniface may be ridiculous, but he can excite neither our hatred nor our sympathy, neither terror nor pity.

In support of this thesis it can be demonstrated that the Frenchmen quite often stand out in striking contrast to their opponents because of *sagesse.* In Pavia, for example, it would have been only natural for the messengers to execute a *coup de force.* Clear military superiority lay on their side. But when such a proposal is made (the French having discovered Boniface's ban on the sale of firewood), Girard de Roussillon insists on the rule of law, not might (vss. 2215–218). As he had proclaimed earlier (vss. 2077–79), his men have come in a spirit of peace, not war. Even when facing a more serious provocation, Girard replies in gentlemanly, measured tones to Savari's taunts (vss. 1669–682).

Aymeri himself is a shrewd captain in war and a skillful lover at court. For all his enthusiasm, the Lord of Narbonne seeks Ermengarde's consent before taking her. Were she to express disapproval, Aymeri would not marry her against her will. For this action he is referred to by the epithet *sages:* vss. 3302, 3310. We see, then, that Aymeri combines cool-headedness with enthusiasm, wisdom with youth. It is obvious that the author, when composing his work, was influenced not only by the *fortitudo-sapientia* topic; his hero also bears analogies to the *puer senex*, exemplifying the theme of the boy who possesses the wisdom of an old man.[17] These two conceptions of the hero are not entirely compatible in the same person. We notice the tension, the ambiguity, in Aymeri's character. But such a tension is not unattractive in a literary *persona* who is not only a *persona* but, to some extent, a mimesis of real human beings. After all, the psyches of "real people" contain even greater contradictions without falling apart. And, we must repeat, from the *trouvère's* point of view, the two conceptions (*fortitudo et sapientia, puer-senex*) go hand in hand. True wisdom contains, is even identical to, enthusiasm; *sapientia* should not be confused with an old man's cowardice. Even in Turold's masterpiece it is Roland, not Oliver, who attains the highest place in God's kingdom.[18] Not yet ready to die, Aymeri at least will attain the highest place in this world.

The tensions we have ascribed to the Count of Narbonne are not to be found in his bride. Ermengarde is referred to as *sage* (vs. 3862) and *doutrinée* (vs. 2545). She very properly declines to return to Narbonne with the French ambassadors, honor requiring that Aymeri fetch her in person. Meanwhile, fifty of the messengers are to stay in Pavia to guarantee the contract, in case a rival should arrive with sufficient funds to corrupt Boniface. Later she counsels that military aid be sought from Girard de Vienne and sets off in person on that mission. In fact, the Lombard princess stands as a Guibourg figure (Guillaume's wife in the epic cycle), as much a prefiguration of the daughter-in-law as Aymeri is of the son. In one significant respect, however, the

---

[17] Curtius, *Europäische Literatur*, pp. 106–9.
[18] Le Gentil, *La Chanson de Roland*, p. 131.

two women differ: Guillaume's consort appears a hardened matron, twice married and mother of several children, while Ermengarde is a young girl, a virgin, inexperienced in the ways of the world. She is a *puella senex*,[19] a maiden with the wisdom of an old woman. As such, she is the perfect match for Aymeri. It is most appropriate, in the structure of our poem, that the two protagonists should be young and old at the same time. As creators of a city they are young; as founders of a great feudal line, which will reach an apotheosis in the stalwart Guillaume, they are old. The dual nature of their mission is reflected symbolically in the psychology with which they have been endowed.

Aymeri's having been deemed worthy to found a dynasty implies that he has risen beyond the state in which we found him at the poem's beginning. No longer the anonymous raw youth, one of a multitude in Charlemagne's host, he has become a man of great honor. First of all, and very important for a hero of *geste*, he has triumphed in feats of arms. When the most famous knights of Christendom are afraid, Ernaut's son, of his own free will, seeks the privilege of fighting for Narbonne. As a reward, Charles creates a tournament in his honor where he may tilt first at the quintain. Instead, Aymeri defeats a pagan force. Later he leads the attack proper on Narbonne, enters the city and castle ahead of the others, and personally raises his own flag over the newly conquered fief. As Charles avows (vss. 1188–189), Aymeri fully deserves to reign in Narbonne; the city is rightfully his.

Nor is valor without significance to the protagonist's love life (the bride quest). Ermengarde has fallen in love with him from afar because of his reputation as a Saracen-killer (vss. 2436–442). The themes of love and war are thematically united in our poem. Without military victories Aymeri would not have been loved by Ermengarde; without her aid (a gift of love) he could not have regained his city. Yet before either the Lombards or

---

[19] Curtius, *Europäische Literatur*, pp. 109–13; Alfred Adler's stimulating article, "Eneas and Lavine: *Puer et Puella Senes*," *Romanische Forschungen*, LXXI (1959), 73–91.

Girard de Vienne enter the fray, Aymeri commits one more act of heroism. He enters the Saracen camp alone, proceeds to the emir's tent, defies him, then kills him and three other kings; this deed sows panic in the host and gives the signal for his own men to attack. At the summit of his career Aymeri commits deeds of superhuman prowess. Because of their epic exaggeration they prove him worthy of entering the company of those other great semimythical heroes—Roland, Renaud, Guillaume, Girard, Ogier.

Wealth, riches, abundance—these contribute to Aymeri's glory. Narbonne is a place of great splendor, a near-impregnable fortress and active port, whose ships carry goods in all directions. The city's wealth is indeed one of its chief attractions, the lure *par excellence* for Charles's weary, impoverished host. Ernaut urges his son to accept the challenge by promising him the spoils: "Bien sai q'ancore seroiz riches clamez" (vs. 677). Aymeri makes a like boast after he has been invested with the city: "Se de l'avoir ont la paienne gent, / Nos en avrons, par le mien escient" (vss. 768–69). Indeed, once the French have triumphed they discover a profusion of luxuries they soon make their own. In the *Song of Roland* the Christian host's motivation is national and religious; in *Aymeri de Narbonne* desire for spoils also plays a role. The heroes are rewarded not only by the complete annihilation of the enemy troops but also by the no less complete confiscation of their goods.

Without his newly acquired spoils, Aymeri would not have been able to marry Ermengarde. Because of wealth, the Lord of Narbonne can afford a delegation of ambassadors mighty in arms, attired in the most sumptuous manner with princely accouterments. Their squires present a no less striking appearance. Obviously, Aymeri sends such a delegation not merely out of vanity. If the Lombards are impressed by the strangers' appearance, they will be more likely to grant Aymeri's suit. Such indeed is the case. Boniface is terrified by the warlike exterior of these people he thought to be pilgrims. But outer show will not suffice to convince the Lombards. Since force has been renounced, the French make use of their wealth. The motivating force behind their challenge is a need to convince Boniface of Aymeri's glory.

This is why the Frenchmen refuse to dine at the king's table, why they purchase food at exorbitant cost, why when kindling has been denied them they purchase supplies of *hanaps* and nuts instead, why finally they leave their cloaks on the benches where they have sat, for as Gui says,

> "N'est pas reson en ce nostre pais
> Que cuens ne dus ne princes ne marchis
> Enport le siege sor coi il avra sis."[20]   (vs. 2672)

After all, did not Girard de Roussillon himself proclaim that, for him and his men, spending a thousand marks means nothing? They will do what Aymeri has ordered, that his honor may be upheld (vss. 2224–229). Because of such largess (as well as the always latent threat of force) Ermengarde herself is favorably disposed toward the visitors, and Boniface agrees to the marriage.

The term *largess* is particularly appropriate to Aymeri. Although the Count of Narbonne acquires great wealth (a sign of honor), he spends it no less quickly. One reason for the messengers' declining Boniface's hospitality is their desire to hold open house for the poor people in town, an act Boniface is incapable of and which horrifies the avaricious Lombard bourgeoisie. The cloaks, too, are left as a present to servants in Boniface's castle. Later, after the second ambush, Savari's ransom is turned over to a *vavassor* who had aided the messengers. During the final battle Aymeri promises that spoils will be distributed among the soldiers in his army. After the Frenchmen have conquered, a wedding banquet will be held on the field of battle, one of the reasons being that in this way every man in the army may participate in the festivities and benefit from the distribution of gifts proper to the occasion. We have already noted that a sumptuous dowry is provided for Ermengarde by Aymeri himself; it includes the cities of Narbonne and Beaulande and the country around the latter (a fief attributed to the count's father, Ernaut). Nor should we forget that Girard's wife persuades

---

[20] "In our country it is not right that a count, duke, prince, or marquis take with him the seat on which he has been sitting."

Aymeri to offer the dowry on the grounds that Ermengarde will *love* him all the more because of it (vss. 4435–437).

Aymeri acquires riches, then spends them. But, given the laws of epic narrative, his largess serves to amass still more money. If vast sums are thrown away in Pavia, the result is a princely marriage to the king's sister. She brings treasures to Narbonne which will further increase her husband's honor. Then, with the help of Ermengarde's and Girard's troops, he recovers not only his city but the riches the pagans brought from Babylon. The banquet in the field is Aymeri's final act of triumph. He has conquered. As a symbol of victory, he indulges in the greatest possible display of wealth, thus giving expression to glory and his right to command.

The nuptial feast is of course sanctioned by the entire army, the hero's honor not being complete until it is recognized and participated in by all of society. This need for social approbation explains in part the importance accorded the messengers in our poem. Sixty ambassadors are sent, not one; each is attended, not by one squire but five. Some of the noblest figures in epic legend are included in their number: Thierri de Lorraine (Metz), Geoffroi d'Anjou, Girard de Roussillon. No doubt the *trouvère* is enhancing Aymeri's glory by demonstrating the esteem in which he is held by his peers, by claiming that even the greatest lords of the earth fear and obey him. Hugues de Barcelone claims that none of Aymeri's vassals, however noble, would refuse to act as his messenger (vss. 1417–422). The sixty knights are divided into three equal groups according to age: one section for graybeards, another for the middle-aged, the last for raw youths. Symbolically these men are not only representative of the hero's own class, exteriorizations of himself, but also members of the human race as a whole. All of society participates in Aymeri's quest. As human beings and as doubles of the hero, participating both in his heroic world and the day-to-day world of ordinary mortals, they serve as a bridge between protagonist and public, between art and reality.

To give the messenger corps greater impact the poet raises two or three figures above the group, endowing them with individual character traits and a specific role in the narrative. Hugues de Barcelone is perhaps the most impressive of these figures. He launches the bride quest. Having made Ermengarde's acquaintance on his return from a pilgrimage, he mentions her name to Aymeri but then must dampen his lord's enthusiasm by insisting that ambassadors be sent before war is declared. As leader of the detachment, Hugues formally asks for the maiden's hand, skillfully praising Aymeri to Ermengarde in order to win her favor. In battle he fights well, almost killing Savari in each of the two engagements and capturing his horse in the second one. He also advises his men to arm on the return trip (a wise move since Savari had hoped to catch them unawares) and suggests they retreat to the *vavassor*'s tower. Then he repairs to Narbonne to seek help and, the battle won, turns over Savari's ransom money to the *vavassor*. Hugues's last appearance is to ride in with the messenger corps during the final battle for Narbonne. His character is in every way exemplary. He is praised by Aymeri (vss. 1437–441), referred to often as *li preuz et li senez*. A good fighter, Hugues stands out even more as a wise counselor and ambassador. In fact, he stands as a Naimes figure, fulfilling the same role in Aymeri's court that the Duke of Bavaria holds in Charlemagne's. Hugues even goes beyond Naimes; whereas the latter had twice declined the offer of Narbonne, thereby proving himself one of the aged, Aymeri's counselor accepts the most perilous tasks, willingly and without fear. He proves himself to be a young man at heart, worthy of sharing Aymeri's glory. Conversely, it is the greatest possible tribute to the Count of Narbonne that he should be served by such a man. In this respect at least, Aymeri rises above Charlemagne.

Second only to Hugues in importance is Girard de Roussillon. In battle he kills a German knight, Goniot, and gives his horse to Gui de Montpensier. Then, after killing other Germans, Girard is knocked from his own horse, but is rescued by Gui. Like the Count of Barcelone he acts in the capacities of fighter and leader, as *preux* and *sage*. It is Girard who talks with Savari before the first ambush, who negotiates with King Boniface that the messengers may enter Pavia, who discourages Gui's inciting to violence within the city, who suggests the ruse of using nuts and *hanaps* for kindling. In each case Girard adopts a position of conciliation. As he declares to the Lombard king:

> "Mesagier somes, ne vos covient douter:
> Pès et amor vos venons aporter,
> N'avons talant de guerre demener. ..."[21] (vs. 2077)

Of course we recognize that Girard's salient traits were not invented by Bertrand de Bar-sur-Aube. The hero of *La Chanson de Girard de Roussillon* was known to be a valiant warrior and innocent victim, forced into rebellion against his lord yet ever seeking a reconciliation and the cessation of hostilities. So he acts, for instance, in *Renaud de Montauban*. But in our *chanson* he is not a rebel. The heroic traits employed for evil purposes in other works here are used for good. Girard, one of the barons who refused Charles's gift, now serves Aymeri in love and war. His great name, the aura of his legend, adds further glory to the Lord of Narbonne.

The third messenger to receive individual treatment is Gui de Montpensier. This worthy speaks insultingly to Savari, then gives the order to attack, seizes Goniot's horse, rescues Girard, and kills several Germans. At Pavia he suggests a violent course of action which is rejected; in the end he explains why the messengers leave their cloaks behind. Presumably he embodies the spirit of largess inherent in the French army. Even more, Gui's actions are immediate, personal manifestations of bravery. A valiant warrior himself, he urges strong action—against Savari and Boniface. His advice is accepted in the one instance, declined in the other. It may be posited that Gui contains within himself that *menos* or active strength native to the hero, good in itself but which must be tempered with Hugues's and Girard's prudence. Along with Hugues and Girard he belongs to a particular group, a corps of soldier-statesmen whose assignment is to win a bride for Aymeri. Like the two others, his *persona* is given a degree of individuality; his character, words, and deeds

---

[21] "We are messengers, you need not be afraid: we come bringing peace and love; we have no desire to wage war. . . ."

stand out from those of the others. He possesses a name. But, like the others, his role in the narrative is to enhance the hero's honor. He is a member of that feudal society in which the Lord of Narbonne not only finds a place but reaches a position of glory second only to Charlemagne's.

We suggest that *La Chanson d'Aymeri* contains a theme, a unifying principle which dominates otherwise conflicting elements and provides for synthesis. This is the hero's quest for and attainment of honor, manifested by victories in battle, the love of a woman, accumulation of riches, and the esteem of his fellow men. Aymeri's adventures may be defined as a series of ordeals. Each one accomplished, he arrives at a more advanced stage of knightly development; each ordeal leads inevitably to another until the final victory is won. The following analysis (which summarizes material covered earlier in the chapter) will help indicate how these ordeals are organized into a graded pattern leading to a climax.

1) Narbonne appears on the crusaders' route. This fortress of incalculable wealth and power stands as a challenge—for Charlemagne and every man in his army. Aymeri alone accepts the challenge, even demands it (vss. 678–82). He conquers; his flag is raised over the Castle of Narbonne. The city belongs to him.

2) Aymeri seeks a wife. The only maiden in the world who is beautiful, noble, and good enough to marry him is Ermengarde. If he cannot have her, he will marry no one; "se ge ne l'ai, n'avrai ouan moillier." (vs. 1474)

3) In order to win a maiden, the hero must traditionally compete with rivals. In our case the rival is Savari the German, who has declared that he alone will marry the girl. The messengers, projections of Aymeri, give battle for him, in his stead and in his name (vss. 1703–707). Their triumph, against heavy odds (five to one), is Aymeri's triumph.

4) So too is the ordeal in Pavia. Since force will not do, Hugues and Girard enter into a battle of wits against Boniface. Three times he hopes to force them to capitulate: inviting them to his table, raising the price of food, banning the sale of firewood. Each time the Lombard is defeated.

5) The second mission, led by Aymeri in person, must vanquish obstacles in love and war. The Germans are defeated again. (The odds against the returning messengers were ten to one this time.) At Pavia Aymeri must convince not only King Boniface but the prospective bride herself. In a scene suffused with ritual gesture, Ermengarde first seeks to *recognize* her suitor. The presentation made, Aymeri formally asks her hand, stipulating that, despite Boniface's promise, the marriage will take place only if it is agreeable to her. Ermengarde openly declares her love, "Car plus vos aim que home qui soit nez" (vs. 3323).

6) Aymeri has passed the test of love, but the ultimate military ordeal lies before him—giving battle to an immense Saracen army come to besiege his city. Alone, he enters the enemy camp, kills the emir and four other potentates, then leads his men to victory. He is the chosen hero, the only man who can maintain civilization and God's law in the south. This final ordeal, greater than the others, provides a climax to the hero's activity; it contains an inner gradation corresponding to the broad general pattern of the epic as a whole. For, as Aymeri struggles on the field of battle, people come to his rescue: first the messenger Fouques (alone); then the ambassadors to Pavia (60 men); then the besieged garrison inside Narbonne (approximately 500 men); finally Girard de Vienne (with 10,000 men). Each wave is greater than the preceding; only the last suffices to turn back the enemy.

The hero's ordeals are more than physical. They also serve to test his character. In another form of epic, the epic of revolt, the protagonist himself undergoes spiritual transformation. He may, like Girard de Roussillon or Renaud de Montauban, atone for past sins; he may, like Raoul de Cambrai or Fromont de Lenz, descend to the very pit of degradation. *Aymeri de Narbonne,* however, is a poem of a different stamp. The hero's character does not evolve at all. His virtues are present from the beginning, are part of him because he is Ernaut's son and a member of the clan of Garin de Monglane. An ideal crusader, warrior, and lover, he fuses within himself qualities often found to be contradictory in other men. The one failing, youthful impetuosity, is,

as we have noted, either curbed by advisers or adjudged to be
a superior wisdom. Thus Aymeri inspires admiration. He is the
magnanimous man *par excellence,* an ideal figure, archetype of
manly virtue. And a social archetype as well as an individual one.
The hero does not stand alone: he is the representative of a fictional society in the epic and the ideal of a real one in thirteenth-
century France. He embodies social and moral virtues necessary
for the proper functioning of the community. What transformation Aymeri does undergo is not of soul but status, not of character but condition. He does not *become* great but is slowly and
surely recognized to *be* so. Thus from a lad in the troops, the
past son of Ernaut and future father of Guillaume becomes in
the present an ideal champion, then an ideal ruler. At the end
he has achieved the greatest of honors, sovereignty. He has
proved his right to command—in love and war, a woman and a
city.

The woman and the city—these are the tangible signs of
achievement. They are emphasized stylistically. Consider, for
instance, the isolated six-syllable line which concludes the *laisse*
in our poem and in so many epics of the Guillaume cycle. The
city of Narbonne is mentioned in fifteen concluding lines (*laisses*
12, 20, 22, 32, 34, 37, 43, 69, 74, 75, 94, 99, 100, 108, 115). The
city or the land, without being specifically named (such as
"Maudite soit tel terre!" vs. 539 or "Car la citez est moie!" vs.
938), appears in ten other strophes (11, 16, 17, 18, 19, 21, 23, 29,
35, 68). Ermengarde, the sought-after bride, is the subject of ten
concluding lines (*laisses* 39, 40, 41, 46, 48, 61, 70, 71, 87, 98).
If the four strophes alluding to Ermengarde's city, Pavia (45, 47,
59, 65), are included, we discover that approximately one third
of all the *laisses* end with a reference to the woman or the city.
Whatever our views on the origins of the *Kurzvers,*[22] it resembles

----

[22] Philipp August Becker, "Die Kurzverslaisse," *Zeitschrift für französische Sprache,* LXV (1943–44), 257–77; Aurelio Roncaglia, "Petit vers et
refrain dans les chansons de geste," in *La Technique littéraire des Chansons de Geste. Actes du Colloque de Liège (septembre, 1957)* (Paris,
1959), pp. 141–57; the discussion at the Poitiers Meeting of the Société
Rencesvals as recorded in the *Bulletin bibliographique de la Société Rencesvals,* II (Paris, 1960), 99–104.

a refrain in aesthetic effect. As the concluding line of each strophe, differing from all other lines in length and assonance, whatever it says or implies is given prominence, underlined in a manner of speaking. We think of Ermengarde and Narbonne, concentrate on them; they crystallize our emotional and artistic awareness. They play the same role, have the same functional value in this poem as the time refrain in *La Chanson de Guillaume* or the recitation of Gormond's feats in *Gormond et Isembard*.

Effects of style are never gratuitous; they can never be separated from the thematic and psychological lines of force they help create. As we said before, the city appears almost miraculously on the crusaders' path, an object of immeasurable strength and beauty. It is not only a challenge to the Frenchmen, a measure of their worth, but an archetypal figure of all cities and communities, reflecting, perhaps, the splendors of the *Civitas Dei*. Not in vain does a magic carbuncle shine from the palace (vss. 175–81), revealing one of the few manifestations of the supernatural in this poem. No wonder Charles is overcome with desire to capture Narbonne, a desire verging on obsession. No wonder he forbids his siege experts to level the walls. The city must be captured intact (vss. 1106–111).

Ermengarde too is an extraordinary figure. She alone in the world is considered worthy of Aymeri. Her beauty will outshine all others ("De tel biauté l'ot Dex enluminée / Que puis ne fu si bele dame née," vss. 2537–538), its glory falling on the husband as well. The barons cry out that no one, king, duke, or count, will have so beautiful a wife (vss. 2541–544). Ermengarde is the ideal figure of a young woman. Pure, noble, beautiful, wise, a kind of Proserpina figure, she symbolizes the virtues of youth and spring. Aymeri loves her from afar and performs deeds (himself or by proxy), by no means inferior to those called forth at Narbonne, to win her. She will marry the hero and live happily ever after, as true a wife as she was a pure maiden. At the poem's end, the woman and city appear together, as one. Aymeri and Ermengarde are married in Narbonne; the nuptials are celebrated on the field of battle, in the enemy camp, at the very spot where they fought so hard. The marriage is a token of victory, a reward for struggle, a ritual gesture guaranteeing the possession of both woman and city, ensuring a happy ending.

The two images are symbolic of the hero's progress, of his newly acquired status in society. Within the epic the hero and his people are one; they stand together. A hero is known by his city (Guillaume d'Orange, Raoul de Cambrai); without it he cannot exist, cannot participate in the heroic life. Without the woman he cannot participate fully in the social life, her love ensuring his glory in another sphere and his arrival at manhood. Only with a woman can he hope to found a dynasty to perpetuate his name. Both she and the city provide an opportunity and an inspiration for heroism, when the hero first conquers them and again, whenever he must fight to keep them. They are the two motivating forces in his life, indissolubly bound to each other, the cause of and spur to greatness.

The woman and the city, the dominant images of this epic, archimages around which the epic action turns,[23] have had more than a slight impact in Western literature. In the oldest and greatest of Western epics the troops of Argos seek to capture a city (Troy) and a woman (Helen). Within this host the honor of chieftains is measured by prowess in battle and the possession of beautiful women, Briseis among others. In the *Odyssey*, a group of villains struggle for the hand of a woman (Penelope) and for sovereignty over a community (Ithaca) belonging to the hero. The fact that the hero is distracted by other women (Circe, Calypso) and their false kingdoms provides grounds for conflict. Again in the *Aeneid*, a woman and a city are the hero's ultimate goals, the reward for *pietas*. Conflict centers on the fact that Aeneas is not permitted to enjoy Creusa-Troy or Dido-Carthage, false goals, but must renounce them in favor of sovereignty over Lavinia-Rome. In medieval France the tradition lives on. In addition to *Aymeri de Narbonne*, such poems as *La Prise d'Orange*, *Le Siège de Barbastre*, *Guibert d'Andrenas*, and *Foucon de Candie* tell of a young hero who conquers an enemy stronghold

[23] For the concept of archimage, Thomas Greene, "The Norms of Epic," *Comparative Literature*, XIII (1961), 193–207.

and wins a bride. In *Girard de Roussillon* the theme is treated with greater complexity. Girard, having inherited his city, is about to marry the perfect bride. The girl's beauty excites envy in the king, who takes her for himself, but must in return free Girard of his feudal bonds. Then the king becomes jealous of his ex-vassal's remaining emblem of sovereignty, the city of Roussillon. A similar pattern of jealousy is evoked in *Garin le Lorrain*, this time complicated by the intervention of a third party, a rival feudal house. We do not mean to imply that the medieval *trouvère* knew Virgil or had ever heard of the stories of Troy and Rome, though he may well have. Nor should the differences between *chanson de geste* and classical epos be ignored; the woman-city theme, treated in a highly sophisticated way, is only one facet of the *Iliad* or *Aeneid*. We consider the woman and the city not in terms of a formal literary tradition (Curtius' *topoi*) but as archetypes, in Maud Bodkin's words: "themes having a particular form or pattern which persists amid variation from age to age, and which corresponds to a pattern or configuration of emotional tendencies in the minds of those who are stirred by the theme."[24] They will appear to men in all times and places, in widely different cultural matrices, reflecting the most elemental experiences of the human unconscious, giving expression to the collective emotions and activities of the group.

Aymeri de Narbonne can be divided structurally into four narrative blocks of about equal length.

   I. First battle for Narbonne, vss. 1–1294.
  II. First Pavia expedition and first ambush, vss. 1295–2591.
 III. Second Pavia expedition and second ambush, vss. 2592–3460.
 IV. Second battle for Narbonne, vss. 3461–4708.

We do not force the narrative to underscore the parallelism between Parts I and IV and between Parts II and III. A sym-

---

[24] *Archetypal Patterns in Poetry* (2nd ed., London, 1948), p. 4; also Northrop Frye, *Anatomy of Criticism* (Princeton, New Jersey, 1957), pp. 95–115.

metrical pattern is established: two wars, two embassies, two minor battles against Savari, two confrontations in Pavia.[25] Equally important, and complementary to the parallelism, is an antithesis between the larger groupings I–IV and II–III. Parts I and IV deal with full-scale pitched battles, while II and III recount smaller engagements depending on surprise and movement; I and IV are carried on against pagans, II and III against Christians; I and IV preclude parley and quarter, while negotiation is a major element in Parts II and III. Most of all, Parts I and IV are concerned primarily with winning the city, II and III with the woman; the pairs oppose and complement each other structurally as do the woman and the city in Aymeri's career.

In all four parts is to be found an opposition between a small effort and a greater one, the two also forming a gradation which contributes to the poem's development: Part I, a skirmish at the quintain followed by the siege of Narbonne; Part II, Savari's ambush followed by the greater ordeal of the potlatch; Part III, 10 knights against the Germans (defeat) followed by 500 knights against the Germans (victory); Part IV, the Saracens attacked by Aymeri, then by his entire army. In Parts II and III Savari assaults the French twice. The first time he is defeated but escapes; the second time he appears to win but gives Aymeri time to gather an army and wipe him out. In Parts I and IV both pagans and Christians seek reinforcements. The Saracen reserves do not come in time to save Narbonne; when they do arrive, they are routed by Aymeri's reinforcements. Thus the epic is studded with parallelism and antithesis, symmetry and gradation. What some scholars have interpreted as disunity or incoherence is the result of a traditionally grounded narrative pattern.

An essential feature of the structure of *Aymeri de Narbonne* remains to be taken into account: the factor of space. We have mentioned other *chansons de geste*, particularly of the Guillaume cycle, which deal with the woman-city archetype. *La Chanson d'Aymeri* differs from these in that the hero's two goals (fortress

[25] Weiske, "Quellengeschichtliches," claims that the parallelism in embassies is evidence for the existence of two original bride quest stories later combined by a *remanieur*. In our opinion it is only a manifestation of jongleuresque technique, demonstrating the poet's skill as an artist.

and bride) are located in different countries (France and Italy). Aymeri, his messengers, and Ermengarde travel from one locus to the other, and important events (Savari's ambushes) occur in an intermediate region between the two. If Ermengarde did not dwell in Pavia there would be no reason for Aymeri's leaving Narbonne, hence no reason for the Saracen invasion and second battle. The spatial factor in turn gives rise to a temporal one. The necessity for speed, for a rapid voyage, becomes manifest—for one messenger to report Savari's ambush, for another to report the pagan attack, for Ermengarde to seek help in Vienne, and, of course, for Aymeri and Girard to send expeditions in response to these calls. Space provides an area in which to maneuver, a dynamic continuum propitious for dramatic action. Time forces the hero to act quickly, provides tension—the opposition against which he must struggle. As in *Le Couronnement de Louis,* the epic's plot is based on presence and absence, and the protagonist is tested as to his capacity to act simultaneously on several fronts, this (given Aymeri's supreme heroic traits) being the only way of providing conflict without recourse to the supernatural or the incredible.

Since the hero is to progress physically in space, he must set out from a fixed spot; if he is to progress metaphorically up the hierarchical ladder, he must set out from, and act according to, a resolution. For both the physical and spiritual aspects of his journey, the jumping-off point is the council scene before Narbonne. Here Charles offers the city, with its dangers and rewards. Only Aymeri is willing to confront these dangers, overcome them if possible, and reap the subsequent glory. He takes a stand in favor of the heroic life and the ideas embodied in it. The remainder of the poem will demonstrate his adherence to these ideals, the actualization of his resolution. In the *chanson de geste,* essence precedes existence. The hero's potentiality is disclosed early; we observe its transformation into actuality in the course of the narrative.[26] Although the hero does not himself develop,

---

[26] This pattern is manifested in other poems of the Guillaume cycle: *Le Couronnement de Louis, Le Charroi de Nîmes,* etc. The idea was suggested to me by Professor Daniel Poirion of Grenoble.

is not transformed from sinner to saint or vice versa, our view of him is one of transformation. To the other characters and to the public, he proves his right to a position in society, he advances in the eyes of his fellow men.

A static affirmation of principles is followed by a dynamic effort to put them into practice; the first state is represented by the city of Narbonne, the second by the open road from Narbonne to Pavia. The setting is dramatic and symbolic at the same time—symbolic of the hero's resources, of his putting them into action, and of the two major strands of the plot, the winning of a city and the winning of a bride.

At the poem's end the protagonists abandon the road and return to Narbonne. Aymeri soundly defeats the enemy, recaptures his city, marries his bride. This finale is celebrated by a magnificent victory feast. Near the poem's end, as at the beginning, we find a major static scene, a moment of repose, spectacle, ritual. The return in space—to Narbonne—corresponds to a return in time and mood—to the moment of harmony at the beginning. (This is not the only return to Narbonne, of course. Hugues seeks help from Aymeri after the second ambush. But Hugues's return is not definitive; it occurs at a moment of great tension and launches an immediate departure. It is a false return.) Nor does our hypothesis conflict with that provisory four-part schema suggested above, two expeditions (for the woman) encompassed by two great battle scenes (for the city). We are led to ask whether the key to the returning and encompassing structure of *Aymeri de Narbonne* does not lie in a circular pattern (or figure eight, counting the false return). Working it out, we arrive at the following schema:

> Narbonne: Saracens
> The Road: Germans
> Pavia: Lombards
> The Road: Germans
> (Narbonne: regroupment)
> The Road: Germans
> Pavia: Lombards
> The Road: (Vienne)
> Narbonne: Saracens

The epic's structural pattern is conceived as spatial—geography reflecting narrative action, movement in space corresponding to movement in time. Viewed in this way, certain structural factors, otherwise inexplicable, fit into place. There is some question as to why Bertrand de Bar-sur-Aube gives a list of Aymeri's children, seven sons and five daughters, at the poem's end: perhaps, critics have said, as a preparation for later poems in the cycle, *Les Enfances Guillaume* for instance. This may well be the case. But the list also serves as a pendant to the list of twelve barons who, in the beginning, refused the offer of Narbonne.[27] The first group failed in their duty to king, country, and God; they will be replaced by a new race, the clan of Monglane, which will maintain French presence in the south. Also worthy of scrutiny is the *département* of Aymeri's sons, hinted at in the last four lines. This setting out in quest of adventure, love, war, and riches stands again in contrast to the opening journey, the French army's lamentable retreat from Spain.

From every point of view—list, journey, battle, ritual—the relationship of beginning to end is one of antithesis or fulfillment rather than identical correspondence. There is a progression in the narrative action and the moral situation. Aymeri is initiated into the heroic life. Overcoming obstacles, he proves his greatness as a man and his fitness to continue the Monglane line, to sire other heroes of the cycle. Potentiality has been actualized; the feast at the end consecrates achievements and values absent from the French army at the beginning but which Aymeri has restored to his people. He and his family achieve a place in society which will endure.

*   *   *

We have discussed certain aspects of *Aymeri de Narbonne:* problems of structure and ethos, *forme* and *fond*. The *chanson*

---

[27] Although at one point in the narrative the *trouvère* refers to the thirteen counts who declined Charles's offer (vss. 1305–306), we must remember that one of the thirteen is Aymeri's father, Ernaut, who on all counts must be distinguished from the other twelve. Or the poet may have been including Naimes twice. Charlemagne asks him on two separate occasions; the Duke of Bavaria declines each time.

also manifests atmosphere or tone, which, differing in varying respects from other epics, early and late, gives rise to a new form of ambiguity. Consider, for instance, Bertrand's treatment of the crusades.

Crusading is central to the *Song of Roland's* dramatic action and doctrinal message. Roland is guilty of *hubris* because he places personal and family considerations ahead of the crusade, then is vindicated for having immolated himself and the entire pagan host in atonement. The poem's *raison d'être* is grounded in the notion of an apocalyptic struggle between Christ and antichrist. Christ triumphs. But the poem's ultimate beauty lies not in victory but defeat—in the personal loss, tears, and sacrifice undergone in an interminable war of the soul as well as the body: " 'Deus', dist li reis, 'si penuse est ma vie!' /Pluret des oilz, sa barbe blanche tiret."

La Chanson de Guillaume evokes *lacrimae rerum* even more poignantly. Guillaume too must undergo an eternity of unequal struggles against invading Saracen armies. Unlike Roland, he cannot rely upon aid from a central authority; the crown will not assist him. He must struggle alone, against superior odds, winning battles now and then but with never a hope for final victory or peace in his old age.

Although the crusade theme is an important motivating force in *Aymeri de Narbonne,* pathos is all but completely absent from this poem. The hero joins battle with the pagans twice, admittedly under difficult circumstances, but the outcome is never doubtful. Aymeri is personally too valiant, his army too strong, his family too numerous to permit a catastrophe comparable to Roncevaux or L'Archamp. He triumphs with ease. How can it be otherwise when God, who is all-powerful, will sustain his men, when a small group of heroes can readily overcome a vastly superior enemy? The Christian cause, if well defended, is unbeatable; since it is unbeatable, real conflict, dramatic or psychological, is reduced to a minimum. Without conflict the crusade theme diminishes in artistic significance. In fact, the holy war, for all its external importance, and despite the author's protestations, no longer serves as a justification for life; it has become a pretext for other, secular motivations.

Historically, the shift in tone from *Roland* or *Guillaume* to *Aymeri de Narbonne* is to be explained by a transformation of the crusade ethos during the twelfth and thirteenth centuries.[28] The *Militia Christi*, the *via Hierosolymitana* considered as penance and the way to an eschatological experience in the Promised Land, the rite of purification, the consciousness of mission and sacrifice—these hallmarks of the primitive crusade mentality have evolved a long way by the time of Philip Augustus. A divergence based on class distinctions may be observed. The masses, as eager to crusade as ever, are set in motion by the same idealistic, fanatical motives as before, but the princes either hesitate to act or they participate for other reasons. They may wish to establish personal and political hegemony, punish heretics or secular enemies (the Byzantines), obtain spoils, discover relics, or take part in a pilgrimage. The crusade has become a social gesture, part of the behavior expected of a gentleman; it has lost its original fervor, the preeminent hold it had on the total social consciousness a hundred years earlier. Religious spirit has been diverted into other channels. Preoccupations of a worldly nature—among them the attainment of a more civilized, refined, cultured way of life (which includes the rise of vernacular literature)—have come to enrich the emerging French world view. Most of all, the very existence of a significant vernacular current results in a stylized, literary treatment of social and political reality. Even the most vital of society's preoccupations will become matter for ornament in the hands of a poet.

What we have said of the crusades applies equally well to the more immediate problems of the feudal bond within France. The twelfth century is the time of the "second feudal epoch,"[29] a period of crisis within the body politic. The barons were in the process of losing much of their power to the king. This struggle between vassal and monarch forms the subject of the feudal cycle or epics of revolt. Such works as *Raoul de Cambrai*,

[28] The standard work on the ideological-psychological background of the crusades is Paul Alphandéry and Alphonse Dupront, *La Chrétienté et l'idée de Croisade* (2 vols.; Paris, 1954–59).

[29] According to Marc Bloch, *La Société féodale* (2 vols.; Paris, 1939–40).

Renaud de Montauban, Girard de Roussillon, come to grips directly with the problem and try to offer a solution.[30] The Guillaume cycle is equally concerned with the role of the proud, lonely baron in society. Although the Monglane clan never enters into open rebellion, its relations with the monarchy are strained. Because King Louis will not come to Guillaume's assistance, the latter learns to fend for himself. He wards off the enemy alone, by force of his strong right arm. In fact, in such works as *Le Couronnement de Louis* he fights not only his own battles but the king's as well. If it weren't for Guillaume, the Carolingian heritage would be engulfed; his good will alone stands between Louis and the innumerable enemies assailing him on all sides.

Aymeri de Narbonne seems immune to these tendencies. The action takes place not in the reign of Louis the Debonair but during the lifetime of his great father, Carolus Magnus. Charles retains the aura of his legend. No conflict arises between lord and vassal; it may well be asked if conflict, aside from the time factor, exists in the poem at all. Only Boniface and Savari remain as foils to the hero. The king of the Lombards provides no real opposition; the French, who are richer and more intelligent than he, do not even resort to arms. Savari alone presents the traditional attributes of a traitor. His two sneak attacks on the messengers resemble acts of felony in *Garin le Lorrain, Renaud de Montauban,* and *Gaydon.* But, differing from the traitors in these other poems, he is a foreigner, not French, he does not hold a pre-eminent position at court from which to influence the king, he has under his command only a small contingent, and he (and his Germans) show cowardice in battle. The presence of evil is concentrated in and reduced to a minor character who holds little influence and still less importance. The poet's response to the socio-juridical problems of his world is to ignore them.

We find no pathos, no tension, no conflict, in *Aymeri de Narbonne.* Instead, the author recounts the story of his hero's initiation into the heroic life. In keeping with this subject matter,

[30] See Calin, *The Old French Epic of Revolt,* chap. 3.

Aymeri's is not the cruel, bleak world of Raoul, Garin, or the aging Guillaume. The Count of Narbonne leads a gracious, courtly existence, which takes cognizance of life's amenities. Charles's first act in the battle for Narbonne is to institute a sort of tournament, the tilt at the quintain. War is more than a ferocious will to annihilate; it can be transformed into a sport, an art, a pageant, to be cultivated and enjoyed for its own sake.

The ambassadors are not sent just to deliver a message and return. Handsomely dressed and equipped, they symbolize the wealth and power to which Aymeri has attained. They also represent the magnificence of his class and countrymen. The more elegant, late twelfth-century society is exalted in this picture of a refined courtier at work.

Other examples of splendor are the almost supernatural aura of Narbonne (ships, battlements, a magic carbuncle shining from the palace, the palace gardens), Aymeri's spoils, the food purchased by the messengers, a magic organ in Babylon, Aymeri's and Ermengarde's personal beauty, and the largess displayed at their wedding feast. Bertrand has a special predilection for effects of light, color, sheen, texture. In this respect he partakes of an aesthetic tradition that was very strong in the Middle Ages.[31] But the tradition is adapted to an individual work, to create an aura of wealth and luxury proper to the hero and his world.

Ladies now have a place in the epic scheme. Aymeri is drawn by the renown of Boniface's sister. He actively seeks her hand; for all the passion she bears the Count of Narbonne, Ermengarde does not somehow fall into his arms (as in *Roland, Raoul*) or make the advances (as in *Aiol, Ami et Amile*). Nor will the sending of messengers suffice to win her. As Ermengarde herself points out, it behooves Aymeri to come for her in person (vss. 2598–616).

Aymeri responds in kind. Although he resembles the hero of the Guillaume poems, we must be careful to distinguish between

[31] See Edgar de Bruyne, *Etudes d'Esthétique médiévale* (Bruges, 1946), I, 79–80; II, 25–26; III, 3–29, etc.

the two. The Lord of Narbonne eschews the roughness, the gross
humor, the buffoonery inherent in his distinguished prototype.
With the exception of one or two moments of exaltation, he is
sages et enparlés (vs. 3302), a speaker in council, one who knows
how to *doneier*. Not only does Aymeri woo Ermengarde; he
insists on her right to refuse his suit. He will take her only on
the basis of mutual love. Thus courtliness penetrates the *chanson
de geste*. Politeness, graciousness, adherence to ceremony and
strict rules of breeding—these set the tone for a new epic style.

If *Aymeri de Narbonne* takes on a festive almost courtly air,
in our opinion the poet compensates by a premeditated striving
for effects of realism. The question of realism in medieval literature is a complex one. Many of the criteria locating a work of
art in the realistic tradition, many of the traits of realism discussed with such penetration by Auerbach,[32] are entirely absent
from *Aymeri de Narbonne*. Members of the lower classes play no
greater role in this poem than in other *chansons de geste*. The
language is at least as formal and stylized as in other works. The
intrigue is rather complicated. And, unlike so many monuments
of the Guillaume and rebel cycles, this poem fails to explore
the vital problems of the feudal world, the feudal tensions existing within France itself. Nonetheless, as there are many ways of
telling a story, so too a poet will use many techniques to create
the necessary air of credibility without which, in all times and
all places, his work would be repudiated by the public.

One such technique open to the poet is a negative one: to
relinquish indiscriminate use of the supernatural. In *La Chanson
d'Aymeri* only three examples are to be found: the magic carbuncle of Narbonne (vss. 175–81); various wonders of the emir's
palace at Babylon (vss. 3507–528); the extraordinary potion,
concocted by a Saracen doctor, which heals Aymeri's wounds
(vss. 4412–419).[33] These are not many. Other late epics, *Raoul*

[32] Erich Auerbach, *Mimesis: dargestellte Wirklichkeit in der abend-
ländischen Literatur* (Bern, 1946).

[33] Adolphe Jacques Dickman, *Le rôle du surnaturel dans les chansons de
geste* (Paris, 1926), index, includes the first two items under several different headings. Dickman also lists the subterranean passage leading out of

de Cambrai and *Garin le Lorrain,* for instance, are also relatively free from the supernatural. The fact that several poems, by different authors and evolving independently of each other, demonstrate a turning away from such effects (in the very heyday of Arthurian romance) is then all the more significant. Disparate traditions exist concurrently in literature; realism, in Auerbach's terms, is applicable to some medieval epics.

Another feature is the poet's conception of war. In early *chansons—Roland, Guillaume, Isembard—*war is conceived as a pitched battle between immense armies, fought largely on horseback in an open plain. The outcome is determined, at least symbolically, by the success or failure of the leaders. In a sense these heroes oppose only each other. The prowess of Charlemagne defeating Baligant, of Louis overcoming Gormond, is far more important than the actions of the several thousand "extras" who also happen to be on the field. The extras exist to be cut down by the heroes. More important still, epic melees admit little or no question of tactics or strategy. Pincer movements, flank attacks, surprise sorties, an opportune withdrawal to a better position— these are inconceivable in the worlds of Roncevaux and L'Archamp. Epic action hinges on the fact that it is considered dishonorable for Roland to call for reinforcements, even when ambushed, and for Vivien to retreat, even when betrayed by his allies.

This highly stylized representation of warfare has been modified, in the later *chanson de geste,* to conform more closely to the reality of medieval life. Of the many engagements described in *Aymeri de Narbonne,* only one (the last) is an open melee in the Rolandian tradition. The first battle of Narbonne is composed of a brief skirmish, followed by the formal siege of a stronghold. Savari twice ambushes a small contingent of messengers; the second time, he besieges them in a tower but is forced to yield upon the arrival of reinforcements. Even the final

---

Narbonne, the pagans' fear that the French are sorcerers, and the Frenchmen's belief in God's power—examples which, in our opinion, cannot be thought of as serious manifestations of the supernatural.

battle is preceded by a Saracen ambush of the garrison defending
Narbonne.

The *trouvère* paints a picture of several small battles determining a war's outcome and a hero's military career. This pattern—a
continuity of engagements—resembles far more closely the
actuality of medieval warfare than the single decisive battles of
Roland or *Isembard.* Equally important is the emphasis on control of strong points (Narbonne, Pavia, the *vavassor's* tower),
routes of communication (the road from one strong point to
another), and the factor of time: whether or not reinforcements
can be brought from one point to another (from Babylon or
Vienne to Narbonne, from Narbonne to the tower) before the
objective has fallen.

Most of all, tactics enter into the conduct of war. We have
already noticed the enemy's proclivity for sneak attack: Savari
ambushes Hugues on the return from Pavia; the pagans ambush
those Frenchmen left in charge of Narbonne. In the latter
instance the emir hides two thousand men in a wood near the
French city, then releases beasts of burden charged with provisions. Hélinant's garrison, having come out from behind the
outer walls to seize the provisions, is crushed by the army in the
wood. Further examples of enemy cleverness are the subterranean
passage leading out of Narbonne, an escape hatch which permits
the garrison to seek reinforcements early in the war, and Agolant's
suggestion that, of the four kings, only two should go to Babylon
for help, while the other two remain to defend their city (vss.
986–93).

Enemy cleverness! But these are deeds of villains—Saracens or
Germans. The hero, strong and pure, at grips with a crafty, more
intelligent opponent, is a commonplace in traditional literature.
Even in *La Chanson de Roland* the enemy attacks in full strength
only a segment of the French expeditionary force, and attacks
without warning. The ambush at Roncevaux does not differ essentially from the ambushes at Narbonne and in the Piedmont. It is
a fact, however, that in *La Chanson d'Aymeri* the French employ
strategy, even trickery, every bit as much as their opponents.
(1) Aymeri's victory at the quintain is an ambush, anticipating

the emir's deception of Hélinant. The young Christian knight lies in wait with his men and routs a Saracen force lured out from behind the walls by the jousting. (2) On the return from Pavia, Hugues advises his men to arm; he fears trouble en route (vss. 2725–736). (3) Sure enough, Savari attacks. On the point of annihilation, Hugues perceives a tower. He and the other messengers see no dishonor in retreating to this stronghold to save their lives. (4) Hugues seeks help from Narbonne. When he and Aymeri arrive at the tower, the old warrior advises his men to surprise the Germans (who are occupied entirely by the messengers within, vss. 3114–121). (5) On receiving notice of the Saracen invasion, Ermengarde suggests seeking help from Girard de Vienne. Aymeri by no means disdains his fiancée's prudent counsel. On the contrary, he provides her with a strong escort. (6) Before the battle at Narbonne, Aymeri exhorts his men to give the cry *Montjoie!* so that the pagans will think Charlemagne himself has come to relieve the city (vss. 3943–951). (7) Aymeri announces his plan: to enter the Saracen camp (pretending to be an ambassador) and kill the emir; without their leader the enemy will be helpless (vss. 3992–4001). (8) Once this coup has been brought off, panic sweeps the host. Aymeri does not hesitate to defy chivalric procedure by cutting down as many of the surprised, unarmed Saracens as he can find (vss. 4060–75). In such ways has the notion of heroism evolved in the late epic. Warfare is no longer conceived only in terms of feats of arms between particulars; it no longer suffices for the leader to exhort his men and provide good example. The new heroes (Aymeri, Hugues) are captains and leaders of men as well as the strongest warriors in the field. They will organize a carefully thought-out plan of campaign, resorting if need be to methods which the older generation of heroes would never have condoned. And they glory in the newfound source of victories.

War is a necessity, a sport, an art—and a technique. The day of the knight on horseback as sole combatant has passed. There exist many ways, many levels of fighting: at each level are to be found specialists. Late epics such as *Aymeri de Narbonne* (other examples are *Guibert d'Andrenas, Fierabras, La Destruction de*

Rome, and *La Chevalerie Ogier*) concentrate on the siege operations involved in the capturing of cities. Charlemagne calls before him military engineers (Morant, Savari, Jordan) who are to build siege engines (vss. 1030–36). Carpenters set to work constructing the *berfroi* or siege tower and *perriere* or catapult. Our author recounts with glee how the Saracens recoil before the engines as if they were an enchantment, crying "Molt sont François sachant!" (vs. 1046). At the moment of assault, Frenchmen fill the castle moats with trees cut from neighboring woods; with picks and axes they batter the walls, later the portals. Meanwhile, archers and arbalesters send a rain of missiles onto the walls to subdue those Saracen defenders dropping stones on the assault teams. Later in the narrative Christians too drop rocks on an advancing enemy. The inhabitants of Vercelli (vs. 1965) and Hugues's men in the tower (vs. 2974) employ this tactic against Savari. The Saracens, however, are endowed with one weapon unknown to the French—Greek fire—which they hope to use in the second battle for Narbonne (vs. 4020).[34]

A final example of realism in military matters concerns the numbers of troops said to participate in each campaign. No one can forget the gigantic armies involved in the *Chanson de Roland, Aspremont, Girard de Roussillon,* yet the exact size of the hosts is often left in doubt. When a figure is given, it can be justified only on poetic grounds, as symbolic of an encounter which, in the poet's mind, attains apocalyptic proportions. *Aymeri de Narbonne* partakes of a different tradition.

In the first battle for Narbonne 20,000 Moslems are said to be behind the walls; no figures are given for the Christians. The French army is presumably immense, having just returned from Spain. Although the poet cannot deny the Rolandian tradition, he may have wished to avoid specific allusions to it. We are given the details of Aymeri's skirmish at the quintain, however. One hundred imprudent Saracens are surprised by 500 French youths;

---

[34] Note also, though non-military in character, the list of tradesmen in Pavia: bakers, smiths, tavern keepers, chandlers, fishmongers, hay and oats dealers, butchers, mercers, furriers, shoemakers (vss. 2122–128).

less than 40 pagans return to Narbonne. Also, 100 Frenchmen hack away at the city gates, 20 with axes. When the battle is over, Charles leaves 1,000 knights to help Aymeri guard his prize. Hugues's "ambassadorial suite" of 60 knights is attacked by a party of 300 Germans. Although 13 of the enemy fall in the first shock, 100 in all, the day is saved only when the 300 French squires join battle on their masters' behalf.

On the return from Pavia, Savari attacks the 10 messengers, plus their 10 squires, with 100 men. The squires perish; their masters would have fallen too but for Hugues's discovery of the tower.

Having left 400 knights and 1,000 sergeants to guard Narbonne, Aymeri takes 4,000 men with him to Pavia; on the way he uses only 500 to wipe out Savari. Hearing of the Saracen invasion (of 10,000 men), Hélinant leads a sortie of 1,000. He kills 1,000 pagans, then is surprised by the 2,000 men the emir had ordered to lie in ambush. Another 1,000 of the enemy are slaughtered, but only 500 Christians return to Narbonne alive, one-half of these wounded. Meanwhile, Aymeri leaves Narbonne with his own men plus 1,000 Lombards; of the latter, 500 escort Ermengarde to Vienne. Aymeri is joined by 20 counts in leading the assault on the pagan army; of these, 10 are made prisoner but later released. The combined Franco-Italian force would have been overcome by 4,000 enemy reinforcements but for the arrival of Girard de Vienne's 10,000-man host. Then, once the issue is decided, 2 Saracen kings escape in a boat with 30 attendants.

The author extends numerical precision to the most minute details of the narrative. Twenty towers, plus one in the middle, create the Narbonne skyline. The moat is wide and deep by twenty *toises*. Aymeri had been knighted two years and four months before the great council scene. Hugues reports having seen Ermengarde with fifteen maidens. He says the messengers will require only two weeks to reach Pavia, that Aymeri will have the princess in Narbonne within two months. Meanwhile, it takes a month for the messengers, after being summoned, to come to Narbonne. Savari claims that Ermengarde was promised to him two and a half years ago. Boniface has thirty attendants in his

train. The messengers wait for twenty days before seeing the
king. Ermengarde insists that fifty of them remain with her, leaving ten to carry the news to Aymeri. After Hugues has left, the
ten ambassadors, says the author, are reduced to nine. Upon
Aymeri's arrival in Pavia, one thousand Lombards await his
entrance to the palace. Four counts accompany Ermengarde to
Vienne. The Saracen host needed only fifteen days to sail from
the East. The wedding festivities last eight days and break up
on the ninth. Aymeri and Ermengarde produce seven sons and
five daughters, who are contrasted with the twelve nobles who
had originally refused the gift of Narbonne; the eldest daughter
in turn gives birth to four sons, the third daughter to five sons.[35]

Sixty messengers had been sent by Aymeri to ask for Ermengarde's hand. They are depicted as a unified group, a team whose
existence hinges on the preservation of its exact numerical identity. Although one French knight is killed in the first ambush,
a nephew takes his place. Now, say the ambassadors, our group
is restored to its original number: "Or est la nostre conpangne
restorée, / Or resomes .lx." (vss. 1888–889). Later, when Hugues
returns to Narbonne seeking help, Aymeri demands to know
what has happened to the others. The emotive quality in his
speech resides largely in its numerical overtones:

> "Hugues," fait it, "com avez esploitié?
> Ou sont remés li bon conte proisié,
> Tuit li .lx. que j'avoie envoié,
> Qant ge n'en voi fors que vos reperié?
> Ou en avez .lix. lessié?"[36]   (vs. 3000)

---

[35] Admittedly, the text reveals inconsistencies. Of the more than 5,000
knights assembled in Narbonne, Aymeri puts Hélinant in charge of 400
(with 1,000 sergeants) and leads the remainder to Pavia (vss. 3068–81).
But the poem also says that Hélinant leads not 400 or 1,400 but exactly
1,000 men on a sortie (vs. 3709), that Aymeri has 4,000 (not 3,600 or
4,600) men in his bride quest procession (vs. 3787). These disparities
may have been due to the hazards of oral recitation or dictation, the
caprice of *remanieur* or scribe. In addition we may note, first of all, that
if we correct the text in only one place (vss. 3080–81, 1,000 knights and
no sergeants to remain in Narbonne), all further discrepancies vanish;

No less significant is the author's presentation of the messengers in the first place. In a series of four *laisses* (vss. 1490–1560) each of the sixty is named and most of the first forty referred to by number. Here is a sample:

> Hugues ira et Garin le lancier,
> Fouques de Fors et Acharz de Vivier,
> Li quinz Bernarz, et li sistes Gontier,
> Raoul li semes, li huitiemes Braier,
> Herchanbaut .ix., et .x. a Engelier,
> A Girart .xj., et .xij. a Berengier,
> A Huon .xiij., et .xiiij. a Bruier,
> A Milon .xv., .xvj. erent a Renier,
> Et .xvij. a Buevon le guerrier,
> Et .xviij. esteront a Garnier,
> Et .xx. seront a Tierri et Fouchier.
> C'est la tierce partie.[37]   (vs. 1491)

Each man's being named is, of course, a *tour de force* (cf., however, with the *Song of Roland*, vss. 3214–264) designed by the author to convince the public of his own expert knowledge of the *geste*. At the same time he is aware that the mention of heroes, names already famous in epic legend, will enrich his poem with literary overtones. Girard de Roussillon is brought into the story as Aymeri's messenger. Other names on the list—

---

secondly, if the poet commits errors, he is led to do so by a quite apparent personal intoxication with numbers and the ideal of precision in the recounting of military affairs.

[36] "Hugues," he says, "what have you accomplished? Where are the valiant, esteemed counts, all sixty whom I sent, when I see none but you returned? Where have you left the other fifty-nine?" All in all, the band is referred to by the number *sixty* fourteen times: vss. 1411, 1452, 1459, 1476, 1555, 1562, 1729, 1889, 1895, 2130, 2427, 2446, 3002, 4203.

[37] Hugues will go and Garin the lance-bearer, Fouques de Fors and Achard de Vivier, the fifth will be Bernard and the sixth Gontier, Raoul the seventh, the eighth Braier, Herchambaut number nine and Engelier ten, Girard eleven and Berenger twelve, Huon thirteen and Bruier fourteen, Milon fifteen, Renier will be sixteen, and Beuves the warrior seventeen, and Garnier will be eighteen, and Thierri and Fouchier will make up the twenty. This is the third group.

Gaydon, Thierri de Lorraine, Geoffroi d'Anjou—are probably to be identified with characters famous in other works. Even those members of the expedition bordering on anonymity, whose names are the most common in the Old French epic—Gontier, Engelier, Renier, Milon, Beuves,[38] to name some from the passage we have quoted above—even they may refer to men of glory: that is, respectively, (1) Louis's standard-bearer in *Gormond et Isembard*, (2) one of the peers who fell at Roncevaux, (3) Oliver's and Aude's father, (4) Renier's father, (5) Renaud de Montauban's uncle. We do not suggest that these identifications should be insisted upon within the context of the poem itself, that either the poet or his public were consciously aware of and could agree upon any one identity chosen. Nonetheless the name remains, sign of precision and veracity, and also evokes poetic overtones.

Having chosen to list sixty names, the author faces difficulties. How can he render a sense of individuality, variety, and credibility, while at the same time avoiding an overly long digression which would try his audience's patience? Bertrand chose to risk monotony for the sake of brevity. All sixty messengers are named in a total of seventy lines. But he makes an effort to differentiate his characters, to create the illusion that they are more than just names. For some, he mentions their fief or country (Fouques de Fors, Mauduit l'Espangnois, Loihier de Genois, Ors de Valbeton, "Alori / Qui tint Estanpes avec Monleheri"); for others, position, title, or office in the hierarchy is the distinguishing mark (Henri the chastelain, Guerri the seneschal, Aliaume the standard-bearer); for still others, some physical or moral trait ("Buevon le guerrier," "Jociaume as crins blois"). Although the poet has a limited stock of names in his repertory, when he does repeat a name—Garin, Fouques, Bernard, Girard, Gui, Geoffroi—he changes the fief or epithet. Granted that the modern reader may reproach Bertrand for pedantry and lack of imagination, the total effect on the medieval public must have been different. He

[38] Ernest Langlois, *Table des noms propres de toute nature compris dans les chansons de geste imprimées* (Paris, 1904): Gontier, thirteen references; Engelier, ten references; Renier, sixty-five references; Milon, sixty references; Beuves, twenty-three references.

probably succeeded in infusing a sense of authenticity and credibility (maintaining the public's trust in the veracity of the *geste*) while at the same time invoking a feeling for the exotic. The messengers are shown to be a group of men of more than common strength and courage, rich in literary affinities.

A similar ambiguity conditions the problem of intercultural tensions. Bertrand de Bar-sur-Aube sketches widely differing portraits of the major national or ethnic groups peopling his epic. The two primary groups—the Frenchmen and the Saracens—are depicted in traditional manner:[39] the French are strong, brave, generous, light-hearted, pious, loyal, proud, victorious; their adversaries are certainly wealthy enough and may fight bravely but are seen to be ugly, idolatrous, grotesque, ridiculous, fanatical, and prone to failure. The Frenchman is endowed with all possible manly virtues, while the Saracen, a Satan figure, the natural enemy, is assumed to partake of the corresponding vice. The *trouvères* deal with a stereotyped world of romance. Collective psychology is the rule, realism in the domain of national character (as we know it today) impossible. However, the two other ethnic groups appearing in the *chanson,* the Germans and Italians, stand in a far different light.

Savari's Teutonic warriors, though Christians, and, like the French, subject to Charlemagne's rule, differ from Aymeri's men in most respects. (1) The poet indicates that the newcomers speak a language different from his own but of which he has some precise knowledge. When surprised, angered, or aroused, the Germans cry *Godehelpe!* (vss. 1635, 2821) or *Godeherre!* (vs. 1734). Bertrand is aware that the first of these exclamations may be translated by *Dex aiue!* (vs. 1808). He is equally aware of the difficulties of communication between the two national groups. Savari speaks French, however ("Mès Savaris qui ot la barbe lée, / Parla romanz, que la terre ot usée," vss. 1636–637),

---

[39] See Julius Malsch, *Die Charakteristik der Völker im altfranzösischen, nationalen Epos* (Heidelberg, 1912); for the Saracens in particular, W. W. Comfort, "The Literary Rôle of the Saracens in the French Epic," *PMLA,* LV (1940), 628–59, and C. Meredith Jones, "The Conventional Saracen of the Songs of Geste," *Speculum,* XVII (1942), 201–25.

thus permitting him to converse with Hugues, Girard, and Gui. (2) The Germans are dressed and accoutered in a manner strikingly different from Aymeri's men (vss. 1622–632). (3) The Germans are extremely impolite. They insult the French troops and answer in a haughty manner. (4) They are called felons (vs. 2766) and traitors (vs. 3208). (5) They also display cowardice. Savari hopes to run away from both battles, and his troops hardly put on a better performance.

Is Bertrand's portrayal of the Germans an example of realism? Certainly his attention to problems of language is significant. As Lord Raglan has pointed out, characters in primitive drama and epic all speak the same tongue (the poet's). When in an Irish text the Celtic protagonist is surprised to hear his foreign adversary speak Irish, Raglan points out that the recorder possessed "the rudiments of a critical faculty" rare in such literature.[40] Bertrand too possesses this faculty. Though relatively uncommon, however, it is not unique in the *chanson de geste*. Several epics demonstrate some knowledge of or concern with differences between the speech of Frenchmen and Germans.[41] Furthermore, we have no certainty that Bertrand had any first-hand acquaintance with Germany or had ever met a German. His knowledge of the language is limited to two words, both exclamations. Now it is eminently possible for a twentieth-century American or Englishman to write an anti-Russian spy novel, dropping in such terms as *Tovaritch, sputnik, Russki, nyet*, without possessing any more than the grossest misconceptions about the Soviet Union. Nor should it be forgotten that the contemporaries of Jeanne d'Arc and Alain Chartier knew the English solely by an expletive, the famous *Bigod*, not unlike *Godeherre*. It was presumably the most used expression among the invading soldiery and thus penetrated more easily into the native consciousness.

The other traits attributed to the Germans do not fare any better under scrutiny. That the denizens of the east bank of the

[40] Lord Raglan, *The Hero. A Study in Tradition, Myth, and Drama* (New York, 1937), p. 236.

[41] Max Remppis, *Die Vorstellungen von Deutschland im altfranzösischen Heldenepos und Roman und ihre Quellen* (Halle, 1911), pp. 51–53.

Rhine differ from Frenchmen in regard to dress and customs is believable enough. The northern peoples, lagging behind in matters
of refinement, culture, civilization, might well appear somewhat
grotesque to a twelfth-century French poet. But the absurd
characteristics ascribed to Savari's men—wearing broad tunics
and jupes furred with lambskin, carrying excessively long
swords, riding to battle on mutilated or deformed nags, or even
mares—have no possible connection with reality. And it is un-
likely that anyone but an irrational Germanophobe would claim
the Teutonic people to be cowards, even in the twelfth century.
The poet obviously dislikes Germans. He depicts them much as
many of his fellow writers picture the Saracens—opposite from
and inferior to his own people in every respect.

But why this Germanophobia? One scholar claims that the role
given the Germans, "unique in the literature of the Chansons de
Geste,"[42] was caused by a rise in national feeling after the Battle
of Bouvines. In reality, hatred or contempt for Germans, though
rare in the Old French epic, is by no means unique. One need
only peruse *Les Narbonnais* or *Les Saisnes* to find similar por-
trayals.[43] The problem seems to be one of temporal progression. In
the early epics, Germans appear for the most part in a good light.
They are faithful subjects of Charlemagne, aiding in the common
fight against Islam; Naimes of Bavaria is the most striking example
of the "good German." Yet as neighbors enter more into contact,
they find reasons to dislike each other. Capetian monarchs, under
the impulsion of Suger and others, denied all claims to imperial
hegemony, insisting that the king of France, in his own kingdom,
was subject only to God. The notion of military and/or intellectual superiority became a part of the French cultural matrix.

A like prejudice acts in respect to the Lombards (Italians). On
the one hand, they are shown to be avaricious. Although their

[42] Alexander Haggerty Krappe, "Bertrand de Bar-sur-Aube and *Aymeri
de Narbonne*," *Modern Philology*, XVI (1918–19), 151–58, esp. 154.

[43] Karl Zimmermann, "Die Beurteilung der Deutschen in der franzö-
sischen Literatur des Mittelalters mit besonderer Berücksichtigung der chansons de geste," *Romanische Forschungen*, XXIX (1911), 222–316, esp.
284–89.

merchants are eager enough to raise prices when the ambassadors
come to town, once these measures backfire they complain
bitterly (vss. 2269–276). Ermengarde herself berates Boniface
because he seeks to marry her to an unworthy husband for the
sake of money; she further intimates that he would accept a
bribe from one of the other suitors, even after his word has been
given to Aymeri. Finally, when the ambassadors bestow their
cloaks on Boniface's servants, the latter observe that never has
their master shown such generosity (vss. 2678–680). The
Lombards marvel at this demonstration of largess, as does Boniface. But in his heart Boniface holds the French to be fools, "Car
il n'a pas tele despanse apris" (vs. 2686).

His people have never learned to do much fighting either, it
seems. From the moment Aymeri's messengers come into sight,
the Lombards feel one emotion above all others—fear. On per-
ceiving the sheen of their arms, pennants, shields, Boniface
orders the city gates closed ("Tel poor ot, tout a le sans mué,"
vs. 2008). When the French ultimatum is delivered (marriage or
war), the Lombards plead fervently that Ermengarde take the
Count of Narbonne as her husband, "Car des François avoient
poor grant." (vs. 2507). Boniface then offers to send 1,000 men
as a gift to his prospective brother-in-law; Aymeri will need
them in his Saracen wars! The men involved are furious. Aymeri
is a born fighter, they muse; he likes war better than food or
drink. Not one of them will return alive (vss. 3431–436)! Boniface himself recognizes that his men are cowards. He advises
the Lord of Narbonne to put them in the front ranks; under fire
they will do well, he says (vss. 3422–424, 3439–447). On the
field of battle the Lombards have displayed such lack of enthusiasm for the fray that Aymeri not only places them in the
van but orders his men to cut down any who turn and run.

Although Bertrand's portrait of the northern Italians is hardly
flattering, they do fare better than the Germans. For one thing,
Ermengarde, wife of Aymeri, mother of Guillaume, is herself a
Lombard from Pavia. Secondly, the Lombards, though ridiculous,
even contemptible, are never shown to be wicked. They may
seek to humiliate the messengers; they would never betray or

kill them. And in the end they improve. Aymeri's 500 Italians, enrolled in the front ranks, fall on the enemy like leopards. Aymeri proclaims that they have regained his love (vss. 4148–151). In one important respect, however, this national portrait is similar to that of the Germans: they are both stereotypes. Not the old stereotype of brave Christian warriors massed under Charlemagne's banner. No, the *chanson de geste,* in its later stages, has become cognizant of rising national differences. It seeks to take on an air of realism, by differentiating between countries, by dealing in concrete terms with the problem of intercultural tensions. Nor can it be denied that a certain, if ever so small, grain of truth lies behind Bertrand's prejudice. At the end of the twelfth century, German knights were perhaps less refined than their French counterparts, and Italian burghers (i.e., those a Frenchman might encounter inside France) were less warlike and more preoccupied with money matters than either Frenchmen or Germans. But the *trouvère,* in order to express this grain of truth, this perception of and interest in reality, creates new stereotypes: the vulgar, cowardly German; the greedy, cowardly Italian. The new stereotypes provide variety, but they are little more *real* than the old.

Inherent in the texture of *Aymeri de Narbonne* is a tension between illusion and reality. The poet strives for a more concrete, believable representation of reality in several domains: the conduct of war, numerical precision and credibility, the naming of messengers, the presence of foreigners. In some areas he succeeds better than in others. But in each we find along with nascent realism a corresponding stylization. He seeks to represent reality in a form which itself implies an artistic re-creation of life and can properly be termed artificial.

The poet, in creating his work, does not write in a vacuum. He must please a specific public located in space and time. French society in the second half of the twelfth century underwent a process of expansion, movement, vitality. Cultural life was in a process of ferment. New, more subtle art forms came into being: the ogival structure, the polyphonic organum, the courtly romance, and the late *chanson de geste.* In the special domain of literature, the public insisted on a more sophisticated presentation of narrative; emphasis on local color, detail, credibility, became *de rigueur*. Yet this very concern for sophistication, this interest in expanding horizons, leads to a penchant for the strange, the exotic, the unusual. Society was in a state of upheaval. Some poets, choosing to strike at the heart of the matter, to treat the struggles of their time, composed *Raoul de Cambrai, Garin le Lorrain, La Mort Artu*. Others chose to avoid these issues. The author of *Aymeri de Narbonne,* flattering his public's need for local color and an elegant outer sheen, creates a rigidly stylized, hierarchical world where evil does not stand a chance. In other words, he composes a poem of escape, a romance.[44]

Such a work of art is every bit as valid as the most intense effort, à la Sartre, to face the issues of the day. Marivaux's theater is in no sense inferior to, say, Beaumarchais's. But the author of romance is obliged to make the public accept the credibility of his narrative. The listener or reader insists upon some degree of realism, that the story presented him could have happened. This bare minimum of credibility is the indispensable condition without which the public cannot be maintained in a temporary "suspension of disbelief." In romance, because of the extraordinary demands made on the reader's credibility, those requirements often are higher than in other genres: *Le Petit Jean de Saintré* and *Jean de Paris* in the fifteenth century or the prose endeavors of Sue and Hugo in the nineteenth. Archetype and realism do not necessarily enter into conflict. Without descriptive detail Bertrand's archetypal world would appear incredible; without an aura of romance the lists of siege implements, foods, and trades would appear sterile. Each is necessary to make the

[44] By the term *romance* we refer not to any one specific literary genre which may have had a direct influence on *Aymeri,* i.e., the *roman arthurien,* but to Northrop Frye's much broader concept of romance as mode or mythos. He defines romance as the "mythos of literature concerned primarily with an idealized world" (*Anatomy of Criticism,* p. 367) and writes: "The mode of romance presents an idealized world: in romance heroes are brave, heroines beautiful, villains villainous, and the frustrations, ambiguities, and embarrassments of ordinary life are made little of" (p. 151).

other acceptable to the literary public. Furthermore, realism and stylization, at least in our *chanson,* come from the same poetic temperament and reflect an identical creative need. Realism in *Aymeri* is impressionistic: observation of details, lists of traits, quantities. The stylization, the romantic aura, is in part an exaltation of material luxury, exemplified by the observation of details, lists of traits, quantities. With both factors an interest in sheen, color, adornment is to be observed—in other words, the external world of surfaces. This world of surfaces in turn contributes to and is given meaning by an external, escapist view of life— Aymeri's formal, ritualistic, external progression in the feudal order. Hence we find reality and illusion, the down-to-earth and the exotic, in the same poem. A certain ambiguity is inherent in *Aymeri de Narbonne.* But it creates the epic's tonality, is eminently appropriate to the work as we know it. Otherwise, the poem would not exist as it does, would be a totally different (and not necessarily superior) work of art.

Behind every work of literature stands finally a poet, whether known to us or not, who has given it form. In *Aymeri de Narbonne,* more than in most Old French epics, we find evidence of a creator and some indication of his attitude toward life and art. Manfred Gsteiger has written very informative remarks on the epic *préambule.*[45] It is precisely in the opening sequence that the *Aymeri* poet's presence is revealed. In conformity with tradition he does not name himself, nor does he specifically denounce inept competitors, as does, for example, the author of *Le Couronnement de Louis.*[46] But in the extraordinarily long introduction (ninety-one lines) we find claims for the integrity and superiority of his work. Our *trouvère* maintains his epic's didactic importance. In it the public will find *sens, essenple,* and *reson;* the poet himself is a master of *escience.* In fact, the telling of the

[45] "Note sur les préambules des chansons de geste," *Cahiers de civilisation médiévale,* II (1959), 213–20.
[46] Jean Frappier, "Remarques sur le Prologue du Couronnement de Louis (v. 1–11)," in *Studies...Albert Croll Baugh* (Philadelphia, 1961), pp. 159–67; also *Les Chansons de Geste du Cycle de Guillaume d'Orange* (Paris, 1965), II, 59–68.

story is justified in the manner traditional to medieval aesthetics—
that he who is learned and wise, who knows the *sens,* is morally
obliged to teach others; refusal to do so *fet trop a reprendre*
(vs. 4). Furthermore, the telling of this story demands a special
public. Cowards and wretches, flatterers, rabble, and lackeys
should not be permitted in the audience. Knights and barons,
counts and kings, all men of good name who are capable of
understanding its *reson*—these make up an elite literary public,
the happy few, for whom the *trouvère* writes. They alone are
presumed worthy of appreciating the poem. The bard defends his
work: it should be heard in all places and seasons. The clergy
may condemn other vernacular writing, but the bard's epic tells
of heroism and the crusade. It is worthy of the best reception:

> En abaie et en religion
> Doit en oir d'Aymeri la chançon.
> Ja ne la doit deffandre sages hon,
> Car en toz tans escouter la doit on,
> Et an caresme et en tote sesson.[47]   (vs. 54)

Thus does the author working within the rhetorical tradition of
captatio benevolentiae lay claim to our respect, thus does he display the consciousness of a poet and teacher. It is fitting that, as
is not the case for so many *chansons de geste, Aymeri de Narbonne's* author has been identified with some certainty. But
whether or not he is Bertrand de Bar-sur-Aube, the "gentle
clerk" of Champagne who wrote *La Chanson de Girard de
Vienne,* we will always treasure his work, as the ultimate source
for a story which was to find a place in Hugo's *Légende des
Siècles*—and as an important epic poem in its own right.

---

[47] *La Chanson d'Aymeri* should be heard in abbeys and monasteries. No
wise man should forbid it, for it should be heard at all times, in Lent and
at all seasons of the year.

Chapter II

THE QUEST
FOR THE ABSOLUTE:
Ami et Amile

*Ami and Amile, two young nobles, are conceived the same
night and the pope of Rome baptizes them the same day.
From infancy they resemble each other so closely that no one
can tell them apart. At the age of fifteen each leaves home to
find the other. They meet; a pact of eternal friendship is
sworn.*

*They help the emperor Charlemagne repel Breton and
Burgundian invasions. Hardré, the seneschal, becomes jealous of their feats. He instigates a sneak attack by the
Burgundians, hoping that Ami and Amile will be killed. But
the plot is foiled. Once Charles is on the verge of discovering Hardré's machinations, the latter escapes by offering his
niece Lubias in marriage, first to Amile, then to Ami. The
latter accepts, marries Lubias, and dwells with her in the
city of Blaye.*

*The king's daughter Belissant falls in love with Amile. She
comes to his room at night and, pretending to be a chambermaid, tricks him into sleeping with her. Having overheard
the night's adventures, Hardré denounces Amile to the king.
A judicial combat is arranged between accuser and accused.
Amile finds himself in a critical situation; since Hardré's accusation is true, he must be condemned. He sets out to take*

counsel of Ami. The friends decide to change places: Ami will fight Hardré, Amile will await the outcome in Blaye. Thus the former is telling the truth when he swears that he has not seduced Belissant. The judgment is in his favor; Hardré falls. Meanwhile, Amile has slept with a drawn sword between himself and Lubias, thus preserving his friend's honor. Eventually the two couples are sorted out. Amile and Belissant, happily married, leave to occupy the city of Rivière.

Ami is stricken with leprosy. Disgusted by her husband's physical appearance, Lubias persecutes him terribly. She forces him to leave the city (over the Bishop of Blaye's protests) and eventually agrees to his permanent exile. When their son Girard tries to help his father, he too is persecuted. Accompanied by two faithful serfs, Ami visits his godfather the pope, is turned away by his own brothers, and, after an adventure at sea, seeks out his friend at Rivière. Amile welcomes the leper with joy and makes a home for him. One night an angel announces that Ami can only be cured by having his body smeared with the blood of children. Amile insists on performing the sacrifice. He beheads his own sons and Ami is cured, but a miracle occurs; the two boys have been restored to life.

Ami returns to Blaye, establishes his son, and forgives his wife. He and Amile undertake a pilgrimage to Jerusalem. They die on the return voyage near Mortara in Lombardy.

*   *   *

One approach to *La Chanson d'Ami et Amile*[1] is through the study of folklore; scholars have for a long time been aware of analogies between *Ami et Amile* and certain folk tales. The

[1] *Amis et Amiles*, ed. Konrad Hofmann (2nd ed.; Erlangen, 1882), poem written *ca.* 1200; subsequent references to the poem will be from this edition. Other important versions of the legend are: (1) Radulfus Tortarius' poem in Latin distichs, *Epistola ad Bernardum* (before 1114), ed. Angelo Monteverdi, "Rodolfo Tortario e la sua epistola *Ad Bernardum*," *Studj*

specialists are divided roughly into two camps, however; those who, positing the folkloric nature of *Ami et Amile,* maintain that the legend in its medieval, Christian form is the combination (and perhaps corruption) of traditions going back to the ancient Germans or Celts, to Egypt, Greece, or India,[2] and those who insist on the legend's uniquely clerical, feudal, and medieval aspects, each version being presumably the work of an individual poet.[3] What renders our problem unusually complex is the fact that professional folklorists, for all the advances made in their science during the last fifty years, have never agreed among themselves as to the exact nature of folkloric transmission or the relationship between the folk tale and literature. Nor, for that matter, have literary critics.[4] There is even some question as to

---

Romanzi, XIX (1928), 7–45; (2) a twelfth-century *Vita Sanctorum Amici et Amelii Carissimorum,* in *Amis and Amiloun, zugleich mit der altfranzösischen Quelle,* ed. Eugen Kölbing (Heilbronn, 1884); (3) a thirteenth-century Anglo-Norman *Amis e Amilun,* ed. Kölbing; and (4) its English adaptation *Amis and Amiloun,* ed. Kölbing, and *Amis and Amiloun,* ed. MacEdward Leach (London, 1937); (5) a fourteenth-century French miracle play, ed. Gaston Paris and Ulysse Robert, *Miracles de Nostre Dame* (Paris, 1879), IV.

[2] Most interesting are M. A. Potter, "*Ami et Amile,*" *PMLA,* XXIII (1908), 471–85; Gédéon Huet, "Ami et Amile: les origines de la légende," *Moyen Age,* XXX (1919), 162–86; A. H. Krappe, "The Legend of Amicus and Amelius," *Modern Language Review,* XVIII (1923), 152–61; *Amis and Amiloun,* ed. Leach. Leach's work is probably the most valuable.

[3] Joseph Bédier, *Les Légendes épiques,* II, 170–96; Francis Bar, *Les épîtres latines de Raoul le Tourtier (Etude de Sources. La Légende d'Ami et Amile)* (Paris, 1937), pp. 27–108; J. A. Asher, *Amis et Amiles. An Exploratory Survey* (Auckland University College, Bulletin No. 39, Modern Languages Series No. 1, 1952), has attempted a compromise between the two positions. Asher is one of the very few scholars to appreciate *Ami* as poetry. Unfortunately, as late as 1950, he was unaware of Bar's very important essay.

[4] For divergence of opinion between folklorists with specific reference to *Ami et Amile,* see Erich Rösch, *Der getreue Johannes* (Helsinki, 1928), pp. 161–73, and Kaarle Krohn, *Übersicht über einige Resultate der Märchenforschung* (Helsinki, 1931), pp. 82–89. The general nature of the problem is exemplified by the more recent "debate" between Roger Sherman Loomis, "Arthurian Tradition and Folklore," *Folklore,* LXIX (1958), 1–25, and Francis Lee Utley, "Arthurian Romance and International Folktale Method," *Romance Philology,* XVII (1963–64), 596–607.

whether *Ami et Amile* itself should be considered a folk tale. Utley's definition of folklore, "the literature produced and carried by oral tradition, oral transmission" (p. 600), might well include *La Chanson d'Ami* in its final version and, for that matter, all other *chansons de geste*. But does he take into account the artistic, literary aspect of medieval narrative? And if we accept his definition, would not searching for folkloric elements or origins in a piece of folklore be itself futile and/or trivial?

We shall begin by isolating from the *chanson* those elements which correspond to folkloric motifs. According to Stith Thompson, "a *motif* is the smallest element in a tale having a power to persist in tradition. In order to have this power it must have something unusual and striking about it."[5] Each item in our list will be designated by the epic's plot element, followed by the corresponding motif in Thompson's *Motif-Index of Folk-Literature*.[6]

1. An angel announces the heroes' births. A 182.3. *God (angel) speaks to mortal*. M 369.8. *Prophecies about children born at the same time*.

2. They are conceived, born, and baptized at the same moment. P 311.4. *Friends born at same moment*.

3. They grow up identical in appearance. F 577.1. *Friends identical in appearance*.

4. Ami and Amile are able to find each other because they look alike. H 20. *Recognition by resemblance*.

5. They pledge the closest friendship. P 311. *Sworn brethren*. Friends take an oath of lasting brotherhood.

6. Hardré severs the heads of two enemy soldiers, slain by someone else, as proof of his own valor. H 105.1.1. *False dragonhead proof*. Impostor cuts off dragon heads . . . and attempts to use them as proof of slaying the dragon.

---

[5] *The Folktale* (New York, 1946), p. 415.

[6] (Second ed. rev., 6 vols.; Bloomington, Indiana, 1955–58). Thompson never refers directly to our poem, seldom to the *Ami* tradition in any of its forms.

7. He then seeks to occupy Ami and Amile's posts at court. K 1932. *Impostors claim reward (prize) earned by hero.*

8. Amile meets Belissant, Charlemagne's daughter. T 31.1. *Lovers' meeting: hero in service of lady's father.*

9. Ami warns his friend against an affair with Belissant. M 340.5. *Prediction of danger.*

10. Belissant falls in love with Amile. T 91.6.4. *Princess falls in love with lowly boy.*

11. She declares her love for him. T 55.1. *Princess declares her love for lowly hero.*

12. She seduces him. T 338. *Virtuous man seduced by woman.*

13. Amile is held accountable. C 110. *Tabu: sexual intercourse.* C 567.1. *Tabu: eloping with king's daughter.*

14. A judicial combat is arranged between Amile and Hardré. H 218. *Trial by combat. Guilt or innocence established in judicial combat.*

15. Ami will take his friend's place in the ordeal. K 528. *Substitute in ordeal. An ordeal . . . is escaped by deceptively providing a substitute.*

16. The adversaries swear on relics. M 114.4. *Swearing on sacred relics.*

17. Pretending to be Amile, Ami claims he has not made love to Belissant. K 1840. *Deception by substitution.* M110.1. *Swearing while one knows that his oath is rendered valueless.*

18. He satisfies the letter of the law. J 1161. *Literal pleading: letter of law has been met.*

19. Ami promises to marry Belissant. C 94.2. *Tabu: false and profane swearing of oath.*

20. An angel blames Ami and threatens him. A 182.3.2. *God rebukes mortal.* C 905. *Supernatural being punishes break of tabu.*

21. Meanwhile Amile takes Ami's place in Blaye. K 1311.1. *Husband's twin brother mistaken by woman for her husband.* K 1844. *Husband deceives wife with substituted bedmate.*

22. To ensure his friend's honor, he places a sword between himself and Lubias in bed. T 351. *Sword of chastity. A two-edged sword is laid between the couple sleeping together.*

23. Lubias accuses both men of carnal infidelity. K 2114. *Man falsely accused of infidelity.*

24. Yet her accusations are not given credence. P 317.1. *Refusal to believe that a friend will harm one.*

25. Amile marries Belissant. L 161. *Lowly hero marries princess.*

26. Ami contracts leprosy. L 112.7.1. *Leper hero.*

27. He is being tested or punished. A 185.13. *God puts mortal to test.* C 941.1. *Leprosy from breaking tabu.*

28. Lubias persecutes the leper. K 2213. *Treacherous wife.*

29. His brothers refuse to help him. W 158. *Inhospitality.*

30. In Rivière he attracts Amile's attention and finally makes himself known to him. H 151. *Attention drawn and recognition follows.*

31. A goblet, one of a pair given to the twins by the pope, is involved in the recognition scene. H 121. *Identification by cup.*

32. An angel visits Ami. A 185.17. *God visits sick mortal.* V 235. *Mortal visited by angel.*

33. He tells the leper how he may be cured. V 246. *Angel counsels mortal.* D 1810.5. *Magic knowledge from angel.*

34. Ami must wash himself in the blood of a child. D 1502.4.2.1. *Blood of children (innocent maidens) as cure for leprosy.*

35. Amile comes to his friend's aid. D 2161.5.6. *Cure by surviving twin.*

36. He sacrifices his own children to provide the blood. S 268. *Child sacrificed to provide blood for cure of friend.* P 361.3. *Faithful servant sacrifices sons to save life of king.*

37. The children come back to life. E 1. *Person comes to life.*

38. Ami returns to Blaye in triumph. L 111.1. *Exile returns and succeeds.*

39. He punishes Lubias. Q 261.2. *Treacherous wife punished.*

40. She is condemned to live in the same hovel where she exiled Ami. Q 581. *Villain nemesis.* Person condemned to punishment he has suggested for others.

41. The friends undertake a pilgrimage to Jerusalem. V 531. *Pilgrimage to Holy Land.*

Quite an accumulation of motifs! In one form or another they include much of the plot of *Ami et Amile*. Unfortunately, no matter how rich a work of literature may be in folk motifs, their presence does not in and of itself prove an individual folk tale or tales to have been sources for the poem. The writer, in any age, is endowed with a certain amount of sophistication. He may combine motifs from different tales. He may utilize works of literature containing folk motifs borrowed directly from the tradition or from other works of literature. Several motifs (sword of chastity, false dragon-head proof, impostor claims reward, judicial deception, recognition token, nuptial taboos, treacherous wife) are to be found, for example, in the Tristan story; others (*compagnonage*, prediction of danger, judicial combat, swearing on relics, a pilgrimage) are native to the *chanson de geste* considered as a literary genre. Scholars have shown that much folklore permeating the Old French epic (the magic properties of plants, water, stones, animals) was transmitted to the *trouvères* directly by clerics or indirectly through a semilearned tradition in which scientific texts written in Latin played a large role; they have also shown that a blood cure for sickness (not death or turning to stone) belongs indeed to medieval folklore but was derived initially from the Bible. Our poet may also have gone directly to Scripture for the theme. Marriage-substitution motifs, though present in the *Motif-Index*, are nonetheless rare in that work and in world folklore; thus a folkloric tradition does not suffice to explain their presence in the French epic or its epigones.[7] Finally, the author is capable of re-creating, of "inventing" motifs himself, without the benefit of a conscious or unconscious source. The doctrine of polygenesis, applied to folk tale motifs, is quite tenable. As A. H. Krappe has pointed out, "There is nothing improbable in the fact that certain motives, sufficiently simple as they are, may have arisen independently

---

[7] Stefan Hofer, "Der Folk-lore des Mittelalters im franz. Volksepos," *Zeitschrift für französische Sprache*, XLVII (1925), 409–22; Paul Rémy, "La lèpre, thème littéraire au moyen âge," *Moyen Age*, LII (1946), 195–242, esp. 210–33; Francis Bar, "Le 'mabinogi' de *Pwyll, prince de Dyvet*, et la légende d'Ami et Amile," *Romania*, LXVIII (1944–45), 168–72.

in different places and in different epochs."[8] In fact, the folk motif, so common to people of all races and times, running so deep in the human unconscious, may be closely approximated to the Jungian archetype which we examined in *Aymeri de Narbonne* (Chapter I).

To "prove" a source for *Ami et Amile* we are obliged to go beyond the motif to a form necessarily having a genetic relationship—the folk tale itself or folk type. "A type is a traditional tale that has an independent existence. It may be told as a complete narrative and does not depend for its meaning on any other tale." ". . . A given type, composed as it is of a variety of motives in logical and fixed sequence, can have been composed only once, in a definite locality, in a definite time, the product of one individual mind."[9] The folk types most analogous to our epic are *The Two Brothers* (plus *The Dragon Slayer*)[10] and *Faithful John*. Scholars have been aware of the analogy for many years and have used the two *Märchen* to prove the epic's folkloric origins. But in summarizing or describing them, these scholars generally emphasize only the similarities. A rather different view is to be had if we examine the tale in its entirety, as it has been handed down in tradition. We cite therefore the relevant items as they are transcribed in the Aarne-Thompson *Types of the Folktale:*[11]

303. The Twins or Blood Brothers . . .

I. *The Twins' Origin.* (a) A magic fish, which a man has returned to the water twice, when caught the third time tells the man to cut him up and give parts of it to his wife, his dog, and his mare to eat; each of these bears twins;—or

---

[8] *The Science of Folk-Lore* (London, 1930), p. 46.

[9] Thompson, *The Folktale*, p. 415; Krappe, *The Science of Folk-Lore*, p. 2.

[10] Thompson, *The Folktale*, p. 24: "The Two Brothers, as a regular part of its construction, contains almost the whole of The Dragon Slayer, so that it is necessary to study the two tales together if one is to secure an accurate picture of their mutual relationships, and of the history of the two stories, both when they are merged together and when they exist separately."

[11] (Second ed. rev.; Helsinki, 1961), pp. 88, 95–96, 183.

(b) they are born after their mother has drunk a magic water or (c) eaten an apple or (d) in other magic fashion. (e) A mother of a child finds another identical and adopts him. (f) Magic swords and trees for each of the brothers. (g) The twins mature miraculously.

II. *The Life-Tokens.* As the boys leave on their adventures at a cross-roads, each with his dog and horse, they set up a life-token which will in the case of trouble to one notify the other; sometimes (a) a knife in a tree which will become rusty, (b) a track which will fill with blood.

III. *The Transformation by Witch.* Having rescued and married a princess (as in Type 300 [see below]), the first brother (a) goes hunting or, (b) goes in search of another princess, or (c) follows a fire which on his bridal evening he sees out the window. (d) He falls into the power of a witch who turns him into stone.

IV. *The Chaste Brother.* (a) When the second brother sees from the life-token that the first is in trouble he seeks him and (b) is greeted by the brother's wife as her husband. (c) At night he lays a naked sword between himself and her.

V. *Disenchantment.* (a) He disenchants his brother. (b) The first brother is jealous and kills his rescuer but when he finds the truth, he kills the witch and (c) resuscitates him with magic roots received from animals.

300. The Dragon Slayer ...

I. *The Hero and his Dogs.* (a) A shepherd, (b) with a sister who afterwards proves to be faithless, or (c) other hero (d) acquires helpful dogs, (e) through exchange or (f) because they were born with the hero; or (g) through kindness he receives the help of animals; (h) he also receives a magic stick or sword.

II. *The Sacrifice.* (a) A princess is demanded as a sacrifice and (b) exposed to a dragon. She is offered to her rescuer in marriage.

III. *The Dragon* (a) breathes fire and (b) has seven heads (c) which magically return when cut off.

IV. *The Fight.* (a) While waiting for the dragon, the hero is [de]loused by the princess and (b) falls into a magic sleep. (c) She awakens him by (d) cutting off a finger or (e) letting a tear fall on him. (f) In the fight, the hero is assisted by his dogs, or (g) his horse.

V. *The Tongues.* (a) The hero cuts out the tongues of the dragon and keeps them as proof of the rescue. (b) An impostor cuts off the dragon's heads, which he later seeks to use as proof.

VI. *Impostor.* (a) The hero leaves the princess (b) with an injunction of silence as to his identity; or (c) he is murdered and (d) resuscitated by his dogs. (e) The impostor forces an oath of secrecy from the princess.

VII. *Recognition.* (a) The hero intercepts the impostor on the wedding day, when he secures recognition (b) through the theft of the wedding cake by his dogs, or the presentation of (c) the dragon tongues, (d) of a ring, or (e) of another token.

516. Faithful John . . .

I. *The Prince Falls in Love.* (a) A prince becomes enamored of a far-away princess by seeing her picture or (b) by dreaming of her.

II. *The Princess is Carried Off.* With the help of a faithful servant, brother or foster brother, he carries her off (a) by enticing her aboard a merchant ship, (b) by stealing into her presence in women's clothes, or (c) through an underground passage, or by other means.—(d) The servant woos her as adviser of the prince.

III. *Perils on the Voyage.* (a) On the return voyage the prince and his bride are submitted to three perils, such as (a^1) poisoned food, (a^2) poisoned clothing, (a^3) meeting with robbers or a drowning person, (a^4) crossing a stream or passing through a door, etc. (a^5) The last peril is the entrance of a snake into the bedchamber of the bridal pair. (b) These perils are arranged (b^1) by the father of the princess, (b^2) by the father, or (b^3) [by] the stepmother of the prince.

IV. *The Misunderstood Servant.* (a) Through the conversation of birds (ghosts), (b) the faithful servant learns of the dangers and strives to prevent them. (c) Since he has touched the prince's sleeping wife, he is thought to be treacherous to his master and must justify himself by an explanation of the circumstances. (d) Immediately following the explanation, the servant is turned to stone.

V. *Disenchantment of the Servant.* (a) The servant can be brought to life only by the blood of a prince's child or (b) through a remedy which the prince must fetch from afar. (c) The prince kills his own child and restores the servant. The children are then resuscitated.

A comparison between these folk tales and the plot of *Ami et Amile* leads us to the following conclusions.

In the epic, the heroes' birth, the two goblets which serve as a recognition token, Ami's leprosy, and his cure have only the vaguest possible connection with Parts I, II, III(d), and V(a), respectively, of *The Twins.* These are the most general motifs and are to be found throughout world literature. The *Ami* poet could have picked them up anywhere or invented them himself. (Note the widespread occurrence of simultaneous birth and recognition tokens in medieval romances.) If he did take them from the folk tale, he transformed them almost beyond recognition. The context, the surrounding material, is entirely different in folk tale and *chanson de geste.* Only Part IV(b) and (c), the sword of chastity, could have been a possible source for the medieval *trouvère.*

In *The Dragon Slayer* only Part V(b), the tongues, bears the slightest analogy with the plot of *Ami et Amile.* It corresponds to the scene where Hardré cuts off the heads of two fallen Burgundians and ties them to his saddle as proof of valor. However, the *Ami* poet could have found this motif, as well as the sword of chastity in the Tristan romances. Other motifs—I(f), born together, VI(d), resuscitation, VII(e), recognition token— are to be found in *The Twins.* The analogy between the *Dragon Slayer* motifs and episodes in *Ami et Amile* is even less cogent than it was for the other folk type, far too vague to be of any use.

Part V of *Faithful John,* the blood cure, does bear a strong enough similarity to the epic plot to be indicated as a possible source; this is all. At the very most, one-fifth of each of two folk types and less than one-seventh of a third may have been source material for our epic. If an average of one-sixth of each tale did serve as inspiration, then the remaining five-sixths must have been left out. But we know that the folk type exists as a generic whole, not to be chopped up into fragments at a scholar's whim. What the scholars have done is to extrapolate certain motifs from each tale, and use these motifs as evidence that the tales themselves gave rise to a *chanson de geste*. And, as we have already pointed out, evidence from motifs alone is not sufficient to show a cause and effect relationship. Furthermore, not only are more than 80 per cent of the motifs of *The Twins, The Dragon Slayer,* and *Faithful John* absent from *Ami et Amile,* but, conversely, many of the folkloric motifs actually contained in the epic are not to be found in the three putative sources; hence they must have been derived from other folk tales, if they have a folk origin at all. Under scrutiny the whole argument crumbles to dust.

Until further evidence is made available no one can legitimately claim that the medieval *Ami et Amile* was derived primarily from a folk tradition based on, or whose nature can be determined from an examination of, *The Twin Brothers* and *Faithful John.* Nor should the Old French poet be condemned for having shortened, corrupted, or misunderstood the presumed source. This does not mean that all folk influence on the *chanson* can be denied. Nor do we impugn the usefulness of folkloric criticism (quite a different thing from origin-hunting) when applied with taste and discretion.[12] Quite the contrary. Certain facets of *La Chanson d'Ami,* as well as the motifs, are reminiscent of the fairy tale and partake of its aura. These facets are: a stark confrontation of absolute good with absolute evil; the persecution of innocence; the passive acceptance by the innocent of their fate; the certain, ultimate triumph of innocence and punishment of the guilty; the amoral but never to be condemned use of trickery by the hero; the sudden, decisive intervention of supernatural forces.

This granted, the hero of an epic is an epic hero, not a folk hero. An aura of romance may exist in a *chanson de geste* (or in

---

[12] See Stanley Edgar Hyman, *The Armed Vision* (New York, 1948), chap. 5.

Musset and Giraudoux) as well as in genuine oral tradition. The genius of a Jean de Meun or a Ronsard cannot be found in their sources, even when they have been determined with much greater accuracy than for our poet. Of the origin of the Ami legend we know very little; of the folkloric tone of the twelfth-century poem which has survived much can be said. The two problems, though connected, cannot shed much light on each other. The solution of one does not automatically imply the other's solution. Most important of all, undue emphasis on folkloric tradition has led scholars to forget that *La Chanson d'Ami et Amile* is what the title says—an Old French *chanson de geste* belonging to the same literary kind as *La Chanson de Roland* and *Aymeri de Narbonne*. Aspects of our poem, which scholars would like to explain in terms of folklore, can be accounted for equally well within the epic tradition.

Consider the element of friendship, the testing of which Leach considers the "only possible theme" in the Ami legend.[13] Manifestations of comradeship between Ami and Amile permeate the epic. We need not emphasize the great turning points of the narrative: Ami agreeing to fight Hardré in Amile's stead and taking Amile's punishment on his own head; Amile taking Ami's place in Blaye but respecting his wife Lubias; Amile sacrificing his sons to cure Ami's leprosy. A host of lesser examples also comes to mind. The two friends seek to find each other for seven years; one weeps upon hearing of the other's devotion (vs. 104). When Hardré offers his niece in marriage to Amile, the young man withdraws in favor of his comrade. Although Lubias twice slanders Amile to her husband, Ami will not believe her. Ami leaves home to warn his friend about Hardré's machinations and against an affair with Belissant. Ami dreams that all is not well at court; he leaves Blaye to help Amile. In Blaye Amile prays for Ami's safety. Having won the duel, Ami at first refuses Belissant's love, won't let her caress him (she thinks he is Amile). After becoming a leper, Ami desires most to see Amile before he

[13] *Amis and Amiloun*, p. xxix; also p. xxviii: "My thesis is that *Amis and Amiloun* is basically the exposition of an extraordinary friendship—a friendship stronger than any other tie, and that any other element in the story is not primitive."

dies (vss. 2673–675); if he cannot find Amile, would that he himself perish forthwith (vss. 2734–738). Amile thinks equally of his friend (vss. 2697–2702), will do anything to save him, even give up his own life. For, as he says, "Car au besoing puet li hom esprouver / Qui est amis ne qui le weult amer" (vss. 2856–857).

The exaltation of friendship is by no means rare in medieval literature. Having a friend was considered the hallmark of chivalric virtue, a necessary attribute of the hero, whether in the epic (Roland and Oliver) or the novel (Erec and Guivret). The words *amis* and *amistiet* in the *Chanson de Roland* may simply retain a primitive connotation of military alliance and do not necessarily bear overtones of personal affection.[14] Yet the warmth, devotion, and love evidenced by such pairs as Roland and Oliver, Raoul and Bernier, Girard and Fouques, Ogier and Benoît, form one of the great recurring themes of the *chanson de geste*. The breaking of *compagnonage* (or threat of breaking it) contributes nobly pathetic scenes to *Roland* and *Guillaume*, and forms perhaps the central action of *Raoul de Cambrai*. True, *Ami et Amile* is unique. Here alone the two companions are social equals and of equal personal worth, not at all hero and follower, as with Orestes and Pylades, Aeneas and Achates, Raoul and Bernier, or even Roland and Oliver. This means, however, that the *Ami* poet, using traditional material, succeeded in going beyond the tradition to arrive at a new concept of human relations. By naming one of his heroes Ami, by referring, if only occasionally, to him and his comrade as *amis* (vss. 2857, 3071, 3077) and to their relationship as *amisties* (vs. 495), by coupling the words *amors* and *amistiez* (vss. 428, 2326), he breaks away from the older meaning and moves in the direction of modern friendship.

The notion of manly love—hero and companion, uncle and nephew, friend and friend—provides an alternative to the more orthodox heterosexual passion which enters the main current of

[14] See George Fenwick Jones, "Friendship in the *Chanson de Roland*," *Modern Language Quarterly*, XXIV (1963), 88–98, and *The Ethos of the Song of Roland*, pp. 36–39; William Averill Stowell, *Old-French Titles of Respect in Direct Address* (Baltimore, 1908), and "Personal Relations in Medieval France," *PMLA*, XXVIII (1913), 388–416.

French literature with the poetry of Béroul, Thomas, Marie de France, and Chrétien de Troyes. Although courtly love gradually succeeded in ousting the older doctrine from favor, a tradition of *amicitia* had taken root in vernacular literature. It appears in *Le Roman de Troie* where love and glory are immolated (albeit with hesitation) to the notion of friendship;[15] its outstanding manifestation, at the end of the twelfth century, is, of course, *La Chanson d'Ami et Amile*.

A second theme allied with the epic tradition concerns riches and luxury. Hardré the villain is a man of wealth who uses money as a weapon. Pressed by the king, he offers to reward Ami and Amile from his own funds; in fact, Charles gives them 4 castles, but Hardré claims the credit. He offers Gondebeuf of Burgundy 1,000 pounds to ambush the companions. The assassination plot having failed, Hardré then tries to appease the victims with a bribe of 1,000 ounces of gold and his niece in marriage. With her comes the city of Blaye. Ami and Amile also live in a world of castles and sterling. Their godfather, who gave them presents worthy of the papal court (vss. 27–33), is equally generous in Ami's moment of need (vss. 2491–2500). The latter's situation in Blaye was that of the *châtelain* in full glory: food, wine, and the pleasures of the bed. After being cured of leprosy, Ami receives beautiful new clothes, described in detail (vss. 3091–97), and the two miracles are celebrated by a great feast. The poem's happy ending is exemplified in part by the luxury in which the two heroes are permitted to indulge.

In *Aymeri de Narbonne* we noticed that sheen and glitter went along with an interest in precise detail—a form of realism. Such too is the case, though to a lesser extent, in *Ami et Amile*. Scholars have been quick to notice the importance of physical detail and the poem's accuracy with respect to geography.[16] The physical and social aspects of Ami's leprosy correspond to actual

[15] Alfred Adler, "*Militia et Amor* in the *Roman de Troie*," *Romanische Forschungen*, LXXII (1960), 14–29.

[16] Hermann Modersohn, *Die Realien in den altfranzösischen Chansons de geste "Amis et Amiles" und "Jourdains de Blaivies"* (Münster, 1886); K. Körner, "Uber die Ortsangaben in Amis und Amiles," *Zeitschrift für französische Sprache*, XXXIII (1908), 195–205.

conditions in the Middle Ages. The judicial combat (highly stylized literary topic that it is) occupied an important place in real life and gave rise to manifestations of trickery and a casuistic taking of the oath as in our *chanson*.[17] Nor should it be forgotten to what extent the poem may be based on an actual historical friendship between Counts Guillaume III of Poitou (Duke Guillaume V of Aquitaine) and Guillaume Taillefer II of Angoulême.[18] We may add to these major pieces of evidence the following: details relating to the state of serfdom in medieval France; problems involving travel by sea; famine and subsequent inflation in Rome and Berry; aspects of urban politics (Lubias stirring up the bourgeoisie and commons against the bishop, to have Ami banished); the problem of sexual love (see below, pp. 81–83). Hofmann quite rightly declares that the story of *Ami et Amile* "wurde als wirkliche geglaubt, wie es denn überhaupt der wesentlichste Zug der epischen Volksdichtung ist, ihre Personen für geschichtlich zu halten und was von ihnen gesungen wird, nicht für Schöpfung der Phantasie, sondern im ganzen Ernste zu nehmen."[19] But of course the story is a *Schöpfung der Phantasie*. It is to the author's credit that he was able to maintain so great an illusion of credibility that his work appeared historical. His striving toward realism, even in so modest a way, is a salient trait of the late epic, never of folklore.

A *chanson de geste* is, as the name of the genre indicates, a "song of deeds in arms." Our poet, who in line three declares, "De tel barnaige doit on dire chanson," certainly infuses into his story elements of war and violence—*barnaige*. Whereas in Radulfus' version the companions serve King Gaifier of Gascony, in the *chanson* they repair to the court of Charlemagne. Here they help Charles in a war against the Bretons, taking two counts prisoner, and capturing two others during the Burgundian

[17] For leprosy, Rémy, "La lèpre," and Pierre Jonin, *Les personnages féminins dans les romans français de Tristan au XIIe siècle* (Aix-en-Provence, 1958), pp. 111, 115; for the judicial combat, Modersohn, *Die Realien*, Ruggero M. Ruggieri, *Il processo di Gano nella Chanson de Roland* (Florence, 1936), and Jonin, *Les personnages féminins*, pp. 59–108.

[18] See Bar, *Les épîtres latines*, pp. 65–74.

[19] *Amis et Amiles*, p. vi.

ambush. Meanwhile, Hardré cuts heads from corpses lying on the field as proof of his own valor. Whether or not this incident had a folkloric origin, it can be justified in the narrative as a bit of local color, a trait of the fierce, savage life portrayed in epic literature. And it clearly demonstrates the strange synthesis of cowardice, fraud, and vice which makes up Hardré's character. Central to this first half of the narrative is the great judicial combat, lasting two days and told (with preparations) in more than five hundred lines. Having been twice wounded, Hardré is defeated and his corpse mutilated. As a result, Ami must swear to marry Belissant. To avoid this, he defies the emperor (vss. 1694–1701), in a scene reminiscent of *Renaud de Montauban* and *La Chevalerie Ogier*. Further examples of violence may be cited from Francis Bar's essay: Lubias' refusal to permit Ami to see his own son; the cruelty Ami suffers at the hands of his brothers; Amile's savage avowal of his sons' murder; Belissant's horror on being told the deed.[20]

One of the most brutal actions, at least by modern standards, occurs when Amile strikes Lubias in the face, with Ami's permission and upon his advice, for having spoken *orgoil ne faussetez* (vss. 1068–69, 1132–134). Equally cruel are Amile's later remarks, also on the subject of woman:

> "Tant par est fox qui mainte fame croit
> Et qui li dist noient de son consoil.
> Or sai je bien, Salemons se dist voir:
> En set milliers n'en a quatre non trois
> De bien parfaitez ..."[21]   (vs. 1218)

Lubias' actions no doubt merit the diatribe. The list of her major crimes—seeking to bribe the bishop to annul her marriage, turning Ami out of house and home, wishing he were dead and to that end ordering that he be starved, beating and imprisoning their son Girard, threatening Girard with the prospect of a harsh stepfather, preventing father and son from seeing each other,

[20] *Les épîtres latines*, p. 81.

[21] "He is totally mad who trusts many a woman and tells her any of his secrets. Now I know well that Solomon told the truth: in seven thousand are not to be found three or four perfect ones. . . ."

from saying goodbye—is of a wickedness seldom matched in the *chanson de geste*. But Hardré's niece sins in other respects too. She is a sower of discord, a liar and tattletale. Does she not claim that Amile has been paying her court, seeking to cuckold his friend? She tells this story once to Ami himself (vss. 501–5) and once to Amile, thinking he is Ami (vss. 1204–215). Does she not accuse her husband twice (again once to Amile by mistake) of leaving her for Belissant (vss. 882–88, 1125–131)? She even has the effrontery to claim to Ami that Amile (Ami) defeated Hardré dishonestly in combat (vss. 2008–22).

So much for the villainess. The closest figure to a heroine in the poem, the king's daughter Belissant, is not treated with much more respect, however. A vigorous antifeminist tirade, pronounced this time by Ami, concerns her (vss. 566–74). Three times in a row the *Kurzvers* (six-syllable line concluding each strophe) repeats that the ordeal by combat, of such immense danger to Ami's life, takes place on account of her, is her fault (vss. 1505, 1534, 1562). She indeed offered herself to Amile several times in a most provocative way, stole into his bed while he was asleep, and seduced him. Although Belissant tells no lie, she will not answer when he says, "If you are the king's daughter, go away; if you are a servant girl, stay!" Thus she and Lubias are both tricksters. And sensuality acts as a further bond between them. Lubias is infuriated when sexual indulgence is denied her—either by the sword or by her husband's leprosy; at the end she offers herself to the returning hero in a manner less poetic but no less forthright than Belissant did to Amile (vss. 3433–434). *Ami et Amile* partakes wholeheartedly of the antifeminist tradition inherent in the *chanson de geste* and so much of medieval literature. Sensuality and deceit, incarnate in woman, remain a constant, almost insurmountable obstacle on the path of the male hero.

The two women differ in other respects. Belissant is shown to be weak, a slave to her passions, but, unlike Lubias, she means no harm. Once subjected to Amile's sovereignty she will reform. As wife and mother, Charlemagne's daughter diverges essentially from the pattern set by Hardré's niece. She loves her husband and sons; her devotion to them stands in absolute antithesis to

Lubias' treatment of Ami and Girard. Furthermore, whereas Lubias tries on so many occasions to blacken Amile in her husband's eyes, Belissant supports wholeheartedly the *compagnonage* (vss. 1835–839, 2758–763). She even approves of the blood sacrifice, that Ami may be cured (vss. 3228–232). This is perhaps her greatest claim to approbation in the poet's eyes, her right not to be placed in the same camp with the villains.

While Lubias and Belissant act differently in regard to husband and husband's friend, the husbands treat their own and each other's wives with utmost correctness. Amile respects Lubias when she makes advances (thinking he is Ami); Ami reacts in identical fashion to Belissant. Both men willingly sacrifice their marriages, and would sacrifice anything else, to a higher cause— friendship. Thus we perceive the interrelations and behavior pattern of the two *ménages* expressed by means of a complex fabric of correspondences and oppositions. This is the same structural development used to such great effect in *Aymeri de Narbonne*. Still other examples of parallelism or repetition contribute to the pattern: The heroes must undergo two great series of adventures, the trial and leprosy. In France they help Charlemagne first against the Bretons, then against the Burgundians, capturing two counts (presumably one per man) each time. Hardré seeks to destroy Amile; Lubias seeks to destroy Ami. But they are foiled on both occasions by the victim's comrade. Ami defeats Hardré on the second day of their trial by battle, after having twice mutilated him on the first day. He undergoes successive adventures—with the pope, with his brothers, with sailors—before arriving at Amile's castle. Finally, the comrades make several pilgrimages (see below) in the course of a narrative in which an angel appears three times: at their birth, after the trial, and before Ami's cure.

Most striking of all is the antithesis between the forces of good and evil. In a *chanson de geste* these forces are embodied not only in one or two individuals (Ami, Amile, Hardré) but form the basis for hostility between great feudal houses. Although Ami and Amile are not personally related by blood, they are the truest of comrades, companions who have sworn a pact of eternal friendship, for whom the word *amistiez* bears the medieval conno-

tation of blood relationship as well as military alliance or friendship. Their exact physical resemblance adds weight to the hypothesis of a "poetic" family bond between them. Secondly,
once Belissant is married to Amile she becomes a member of his
family and serves the companions loyally. In this respect, as we
have noticed before, she differs from Lubias, who retains ties
with her uncle's lineage. Yet from the latter's union with Ami
springs a son, Girard, who, Ami says on first mentioning his name,
will serve Amile with shield and lance (vs. 522). In the narrative
proper he serves only his father but serves him well. Girard helps
feed the stricken leper, kills a seneschal who will not obey,
argues with Lubias, offers to accompany Ami into exile, finally is
beaten and thrown in jail for his pains. Later, his welcome for
the returning hero is more than enthusiastic (vss. 3391–422). In
fact, the young man helps increase Ami's glory. At the poem's
end he inherits the city of Blaye, from which, in the epic
Jourdain de Blaye, his son will struggle against Fromont, scion
of the other family. Perhaps the greatest triumph for the heroes
(and greatest sign of their victory) is the resurrection of Amile's
sons. We all know to what extent, in medieval literature, issue
was sought after and the death of a son considered the greatest
of calamities. Ami and Amile are spared this misfortune. Their
lineage will survive to continue the good fight and to serve as an
example for all men.

In opposition to the just lineage stands Hardré's clan. The
villain provides hostages, sixty of them, all close relatives, to guarantee his accusation against Amile, whereas Belissant's lover has
difficulty in finding pledges and would have lost his case but for
the queen's intervention. On his journey to Blaye, Amile wears
armor even when sleeping:

> Car moult redoute Hardre son annemi,
> Que ne le sievent mil home de son lin
> Qui le voillent ocirre.[22]   (vs. 927)

---

[22] For he dreads very much Hardré his enemy, afraid that a thousand
men of Hardré's lineage will follow him in the hope of killing him.

After the duel Ami evokes the possibility of retaliation by Hardré's family as an excuse for not taking Belissant with him (vss. 1726–729). Nor does the hated family remain an abstraction, an undeveloped literary topic. Hardré has a godson, Aulori, who asks for and receives wicked advice at court; the number two villain of the tale is Lubias, the villain's niece. No doubt one of the strongest motivations for her wickedness is her uncle's active prodding or, at any rate, her desire to take his side and avenge his death. The various strands making up the narrative line are unified in some measure because of Hardré and Lubias. The heroes suffer not from some unaccountable piling up of obstacles but from the conscious, maliciously inspired plot of a single group of men.

This group must not be thought of as any given feudal house: Ami and Amile face the notorious race of traitors. Hardré himself is an important character in many other epics—*Gaydon, Gui de Bourgogne, Jourdain de Blaye, Doon de Nanteuil, La Chevalerie Ogier, Garin le Lorrain*, to name just a few—and always plays a villainous role. We now know that he has a historical prototype, a certain Hardradus who tried to kill Charlemagne in 785.[23] In *La Chanson d'Ami* Hardré certainly lives up to his reputation. First he counsels the emperor to dismiss Ami and Amile once the Breton war is over. When Charles reacts negatively, Hardré pretends he was testing him (vs. 260), advises giving the young men a handsome reward instead. Naturally he informs the companions he was responsible for their good fortune. He bribes Gondebeuf of Burgundy to prepare an ambush (in the meantime lying as to the reason for his absence from Paris), personally leads the heroes into the trap, and seeks to convince the emperor of his own valor by means of the severed heads. Having falsely claimed that Ami and Amile are dead, on their return he seeks to bribe them. He spies on Amile and Belissant and denounces them to Charlemagne, demanding the death penalty several times. Finally, during the trial by battle, he proves traitor to God

---

[23] René Louis, "L'épopée française est carolingienne," in *Coloquios de Roncesvalles. Agosto 1955* (Saragossa, 1956), pp. 327–460, esp. pp. 459–60.

as well as to Amile, his "friend," and Charles, his king, by praying to the devil for aid. This list of crimes (and the circumstances surrounding them) corresponds to many of the traits making up Stefan Hofer's "treason motif": the giving of bad advice; an innocent lady slandered; fanatical and unreasonable hatred for good people; a weak king, easily domineered; a hero ambushed and falsely accused but who triumphs in judicial combat.[24]

Other motifs—the banishment of an innocent person, his strangely passive acceptance of this fate—are better reflected in the scenes where Lubias holds sway. The theme concerns a young wife persecuted by a rival or stepmother and repudiated by her husband. In some cases the innocent victim's son, reacting strongly against the persecution, will set matters right. A man is substituted for the woman as martyr in our poem; it is the father, Ami, who is exiled. The persistence of the tradition, however, may well explain the docility with which Ami yields to Lubias' commands as well as Girard's much more aggressive, even violent protest. In any case, Lubias also must be considered a traitor, to her husband and lord. The theme of treason is very important to *Ami et Amile.* Much of the action hinges on the fact that innocent, guileless barons and an innocent, guileless emperor are placed in proximity to a family of traitors, who plot to corrupt the good relations between lord and vassal for the purpose of destroying both. This pattern conforms admirably to Adalbert Dessau's third classification of epics of revolt—one particularly characteristic, he says, of the late *chanson de geste,* just the period we are examining.[25]

Villainous though he may be, Hardré displays nobility, is a fascinating traitor, a man whom we are drawn to respect. His motivation for committing wicked deeds is clearly spelled out, perfectly natural in the world of the poem. Of course the

---

[24] Stefan Hofer, "Das Verratsmotiv in den chansons de geste," *Zeitschrift für romanische Philologie,* XLIV (1924), 594–609. *Ami et Amile* is not discussed in this article.

[25] "L'idée de la trahison au moyen âge et son rôle dans la motivation de quelques chansons de geste," *Cahiers de civilisation médiévale,* III (1960), 23–26.

seneschal acts in some measure from an inherent will to evil, as a Judas figure and member of the family of traitors. But equally important is a more normal, everyday human force, *invidia*. Speaking to Gondebeuf, Hardré associates the companions' popularity at court with his own decline in favor. The *invidia* he claims Ami and Amile bear him is of course a projection of his own feelings toward them:

> "Forment me het li rois et la roinne.
> Dui soudoier portent a moi envie,
> Ce est Amis et ses compains Amiles ..."[26]   (vs. 300)

Later on, Hardré again voices sensitivity to the queen's dislike, "Mais d'unne chose me vois moult merveillant, / Que la roine me vait si ramposnant" (vss. 1271–272). At the false rumor of the companions' death Hardré quite openly asks for their charges in the army and at court. He even is jealous of their unique friendship, seeks to become Amile's companion himself, and, as it turns out, only denounces him after the offer is refused.

We respect Hardré for not being a slave to brute force. The roll of his crimes has already been listed. Suffice it to say that practically everyone is a product of the intellect, carried out with intelligence. To give false counsel to Charlemagne (that the companions should be dismissed), to spread a false rumor (that they are dead), or to seek a companion relationship with Amile—such actions are natural to the stereotyped traitor of romance. However, that he should be resilient enough, when his request is denied, to pretend he never meant it in the first place; to claim credit for decisions rendered (against his will) on the heroes' behalf; to accept Amile's denial of his friendship-offer and maintain seemingly good relations between them, the better to destroy him—these are the machinations of a sophisticated temperament, a mind profound in evil but subtle in the use of techniques to bring it about. Hardré anticipates, however imperfectly, the great villains of more recent literature: Shake-

---

[26] "The king and the queen hate me terribly. Two mercenary soldiers, Ami and his friend Amile, are envious of me. . . ."

speare's Iago, Corneille's Cleopâtre, Racine's Néron, Voltaire's Mahomet. These characters all fail in the end. But their failure—a product of the author's will, structurally not psychologically inevitable—is a further tribute to their power as literary creations.

Lubias demonstrates a personality strikingly similar to her uncle's, perhaps more original (in terms of the medieval epic) because she is a woman. She too acts as a sower of discord, hoping to disrupt Ami and Amile's friendship by planting seeds of mistrust and jealousy. As an evil counselor she bears the same relationship to her husband as Hardré to Charlemagne. For this very reason, however, her efforts are doomed to failure. Whereas Hardré succeeded in gaining ascendancy over a weak and not exceptionally clever monarch, who was dependent on his services, Lubias finds herself helpless to corrupt Ami. Her husband's purity remains invulnerable to her lies. But if Lubias must fail in the act of corruption, the way is nonetheless open for her to take more active measures. Hardré, for all his insolence, would never have dared open rebellion against the emperor. Ami, a mere vassal, is subject to political power. Once he has fallen sick, Lubias will bring pressure to bear on the bishop, stir up popular sentiment against him, and with techniques as Machiavellian as her uncle's, gain a victory which never quite fell within his grasp.

Why does she persecute Ami in so furious yet cold-blooded a manner? First of all, Lubias is Hardré's niece and a member of the lineage of traitors. Like her uncle she is naturally wicked, will commit evil for the sake of evil and hate good people because they are good. Nor can we forget the factor of *luxuria*. Lubias resents Ami's leprosy (forbidding sexual intercourse) as much as she did Amile's sword, which she thought also to be her husband's doing. But most of all, she hates Ami because of Amile. Hardré had first offered her to the latter, but Amile demurred in favor of his comrade. This act of friendship appears to Lubias the grossest of insults; her rage can only increase when she is informed that the same Amile is her uncle's murderer. Thus is to be explained the feverish dislike she bears Amile, why she twice accuses him of carnal advances and another time attacks his honor as a warrior. Then, because Ami refuses to believe her, Lubias trans-

fers her wrath to him; she cannot influence him because he prefers Amile to her, in effect places a higher price on his friendship
than on his marriage. The *compagnonage* is a relationship she
can neither understand nor condone. Lubias also hates Belissant
(accusing both men of having relations with the girl) because
Amile prefers her, has chosen her, as it were, over his friend's
wife. The will to command, but also a burning need to be pre-
ferred, chosen, cherished, are the mainsprings behind a character
portrayal which exploits so deftly the theme of woman scorned.

The *Ami* poet demonstrates commensurate literary skill in the
treatment of love, e.g., Belissant's passion for Amile. First we are
told, almost in passing, of her joy over the heroes' victory against
the Bretons ("Lies en fu Karles et sa fille par non, / C'est
Belissans a la clere fason," vss. 226–27). Neither hero is singled
out for preference. If the maiden has any, we do not know it; her
name is coupled only with her father's. Almost two hundred lines
further on, we hear of her a second time. She expresses grief over
the companions' purported demise (vss. 412–20); at this point
Amile (vs. 415) obviously stands closest in her thoughts. On
their almost miraculous return, Belissant warns both of them
against Hardré's machinations (vss. 444–48). Later, Ami having
left the court, she will warn Amile alone of the menace (vss.
616–19). Only in lines 530–36 are we at last informed, directly
by the author, that the princess loves Amile. This information is
then indirectly confirmed by Ami's warnings against such a liaison
(vss. 566–74). Finally Belissant is moved to action; she mentions
that she declared her love once and was refused (vss. 612–15),
then tries again, in bolder fashion (vss. 628–30), decides she will
force her attentions on Amile (vss. 650–61), and finally triumphs
in a scene both graceful and very sensuous:

> Et elle s'est lez le conte couchie,
> Moult souavet s'est delez lui glacie. ...   (vs. 671)

> Envers le conte est plus prez approchie
> Et ne dist mot, ainz est bien acoisie.
> Li cuens la sent graislete et deloie,
> Ainz ne se mut que s'amor moult desirre.

> Les mameletes delez le piz li sieent,
> Par un petit ne sont dures com pierres,
> Si enchait li ber ...[27]   (vs. 685)

The maiden's love develops in time, becoming more and more
passionate, more and more sensual, driving her to extreme measures to satisfy it. We learn of her love and its animal nature in
an equally gradual, oblique manner. The development of Belissant's passion corresponds to our learning of it; both are reflected
by the author's mode of presentation. The *trouvère* overcomes a
rather delicate problem of storytelling with skill and *brio*.

The culminating moment of this erotic episode is, of course,
Belissant's seduction of Amile. She comes to his bed at night and,
noticing that he is asleep, employs tactics not too far removed
from the world of Crébillon *fils* and Choderlos de Laclos. It is
not unusual in the *chanson de geste* for daughters of Eve to long
passionately for the hero; nor do they hesitate to make the advances. But the hero normally will spurn them with righteous
indignation. *La Chanson d'Aiol* provides a classic example of the
topic. That the woman should employ so sophisticated a technique to gain her ends (both with caresses and the refusal to
answer Amile's query), the detail of Amile's being asleep, his
own assertion of a double standard in female comportment
(offering 100 *sols* if the girl is a chambermaid), his ultimate
yielding to her wishes, and the pervasive atmosphere of the bed—
these imply a great advance in the treatment of love from both
a social and psychological point of view. They also imply increased literary sophistication on the author's part. Fully aware
of the *Aiol* tradition, he is playing with it, gently parodying it.
He is saying, I will show you how people react to this situation
in real life, how a clever girl will conquer even the most in-
corruptible of heroes. By so doing he succeeds, if only for a

---

[27] And she lay down next to the count, slipping in very gently alongside
him. . . . She drew closer to the count and didn't say a word, but kept very
still. The count perceives her to be slender and dainty; he can't help desiring her love. Her little breasts lie next to his chest; they are nearly as firm
as stones. Thus the baron succumbs. . . .

moment, in withdrawing from his protagonist. The poet regards him (and passes on the regard to us) with an amused, tolerant detachment. Because of carnal love, hero and heroine are brought down to human dimensions and attain a charm, an aesthetic roundness they would otherwise lack.

Erich Auerbach analyzes an entirely different kind of bed realism. In his essay on fifteenth-century prose, Auerbach points out the importance of a topic new to Western literature: a husband and wife discussing domestic matters at night in the intimacy of the conjugal bed.[28] This aspect of reality is anticipated in *Ami et Amile.* On four of the five occasions when Lubias slanders Ami or his friend, she does so in bed, in the belief that she is conversing with her husband. Twice her conduct may be assimilated to Belissant's; she speaks after she and Ami have made love ("Quant gabe orent et assez delitie," vs. 499; "Quant gabe ont assez et delitie," vs. 2005), perhaps hoping that her spouse's resistance to her insinuations will be dampened by the pleasure he has enjoyed. Such is not the case on the other two occasions—when Ami wakes in the night and when Amile has specifically forbidden intercourse. Here they discuss human problems in much the same way as Antoine de la Sale's characters. Interestingly enough, Lubias' given *persona,* the ends she pursues, and the means she employs to attain them, place all four scenes in the complementary "low" tradition of the *Quinze Joies de Mariage,* also discussed by Auerbach. *La Chanson d'Ami* thus forms a bridge between the two levels of style. Such an epic may be adjudged a work of exceptional literary value, a significant form of epic in its own right; it also proves to be of no less interest as a distant but eminently legitimate ancestor of modern fiction—in the realm of ideas, psychology, and narrative technique.

*   *   *

A dominant trait in the *chanson de geste* is a theme which, for want of a better term, we shall call the point of feudal law. *Girard de Roussillon* is concerned with whether, in spite of hav-

---

[28] *Mimesis,* chap. 10.

ing been technically released from a feudal relationship to the emperor, Girard still owes him fealty. *Raoul de Cambrai* revolves around the hero's right (or lack of it) to hold King Louis to his word and seize the Vermandois, against the rights of the late Count Herbert's heirs, and whether Raoul's vassal Bernier has the right to break his bond to Raoul in retaliation for having been mistreated. Even the *Song of Roland* takes up a judicial problem: Ganelon's claim that he had the right to defy and destroy Roland in perfect legality, Roland being in Ganelon's eyes merely another particular in the feudal world. *La Chanson d'Ami et Amile* deals with such problems too, but treats them in a quite different way.

The first, perhaps most important point of law concerns whether or not Amile is guilty of the charges brought against him. Hardré, we remember, claimed that the young man had dishonored Charlemagne's daughter by having carnal relations with her. From a strictly legal point of view Hardré is in the right. The facts, as he describes them, are narrated to us directly by the poet. Hardré himself overheard their lovemaking. Amile admits he has acted as felon and enemy of God (vs. 915), though admittedly he is more concerned with having broken his pledge to Ami (not to love Belissant) than with the act itself. Later he formally pleads guilty to Ami, regretting that because of his sin their hostages will perish (vss. 983–95). And Belissant echoes this confession in the most categorical fashion:

> "Si m'ait dex, que tout ainsiz fu il,
> Com Hardrez l'a et jure et plevi,
> Que il n'i a d'un tout seul mot menti."[29]   (vs. 1436)

The case would appear, in current parlance, to be "open and shut." But it is not. The very same Belissant urges her lover to challenge Hardré if he accuses them. For, she says, Amile must surely win, given the fact that Hardré is a felon and traitor (vss. 719–22). Nor is this the only such designation of Hardré. Elsewhere in the same passage and later at the trial scene,

---

[29] "So help me God, it happened entirely just as Hardré has sworn and pledged; not one word he has said is a lie."

as throughout the poem, he is referred to as *fel, losengiers, traitres, renoiez, lerre, gloz, and cuivers*. Once, at the time of his accusation, the *trouvère* even calls him *parjure* (vs. 734). Thus, we are led to believe, a man telling the truth is a liar and vice versa!

That the poet does not condemn Amile is confirmed when his side wins the judicial combat. Although the accused finds a substitute (Ami) who is exonerated in his place, this subterfuge in no way affects the problem of Amile's personal guilt or innocence. The fact is, Amile is in no way punished anywhere in the course of the poem. He emerges unscathed from the ordeal, marries Belissant, does not suffer from leprosy, whereas Hardré, his accuser, is mutilated on the first day and perishes on the second. In the early Middle Ages, trial by battle was considered a judgment from God; by its very nature, the *judicium Dei* was a Christian act infallible in determining truth and justice. Furthermore, any sin (including Amile's) will be punished by God at once. Medieval man had great difficulty in conceiving wickedness triumphant or virtues defeated over a long period of time. Crime contains within itself, and brings about almost immediately, its own retribution. This is the principle of immanent justice.[30] God is personally responsible for the trial's proper functioning. He, who alone knows its outcome, cannot be tricked. If, in certain fabliaux, celestial beings are treated with levity, such is most definitely not the case in *Ami et Amile*. When the author says that God helped Ami (vs. 1512), he is telling us that in God's eyes, his own, and the public's, Amile and Ami are in the right and Hardré in the wrong.

How can this be when, as we have shown, Amile is so obviously guilty? First of all, a good lawyer could cite "mitigating circumstances." Technically the youth has committed an act of lust, compounded by treason to his lord and king. We know, however, that Amile did not pay court to the maiden or seek her favors in any way. She seduced him, preying upon a young man still heavy with sleep. His participation in *luxuria* must be

[30] Paul Rousset, "La croyance en la justice immanente à l'époque féodale," *Moyen Age*, LIV (1948), 225–48.

considered passive rather than active. Moreover, having been totally unaware of her identity, he can be absolved of responsibility (*in voluntate*) for dishonoring the king. Of this, by far the more important crime, Amile is for all intents and purposes innocent.

Secondly, Hardré by no means acts from altruistic motives. Twice he threatens to confound Amile as an individual (vss. 738–40, 758–64). He is using a point of law, a question of the king's honor, to further a personal vendetta. His own violence and anger, lack of charity in all senses of the word, draw attention away from the strictly legal issues involved. If Hardré himself goes beyond the law, then we too must judge the case from other than a legal point of view.

Amile is technically guilty of *luxuria*. However, in medieval as well as in modern society, committing the physical act of love, especially with a girl he is quite willing to marry, does not bring down upon a young man the wrath of public opinion. Moralists will denounce, but the literary public forgive, most actions taken in the name of love. Hardré, on the other hand, is a spy and informer. He has committed no crime as such, but is condemned as a scoundrel by the public for acts which, though in a sense useful for the preservation of society, society nevertheless considers loathsome. Contemporary slang terms for Hardré's "type"— *squealer* and *stool pigeon* in English, *mouchard* and *donneuse* in French—indicate that society's attitude has not changed appreciably in this regard. Furthermore, Hardré is a peculiarly despicable stool pigeon. He has informed against Belissant, a lady; thus he has acted unchivalrously toward ladies in general. Ami, on the contrary, claims specifically to be defending *his lady* against felonious accusations (vss. 1378–380). Whereas Ami behaves like Erec, Gawain, and Lancelot, Hardré resembles the lowest of beings in the courtly world, the *losengiers*. A courtly influence is manifest here. *Luxuria* becomes transformed and purified, may reach the level of, or lead to, *caritas*, whereas Hardré's *superbia* and *invidia* are socially and morally despicable, to be condemned at every turn.

Amile is the hero. In certain kinds of literature the hero can do no wrong. He is always right; those who oppose him are in error. The Tristan romances tell of a protagonist and his beloved who commit adultery, perjury, murder, and any number of lesser crimes. Their situation is analogous to that of Ami-Amile and Belissant in the epic. Yet Béroul cannot praise Tristan and Iseut too highly, while their enemies, even though they tell the truth and defend King Mark's honor, are excoriated in no uncertain terms. Although in both stories the heroes commit acts repugnant to society's commonly accepted standards, the very notion of ethics is transformed. Rather than that the hero be considered good because he conforms to given standards, his actions are proved good simply because it is he who commits them. In other words, right and wrong are determined not with reference to a moral code but by the hero himself, who embodies the secret desires and aspirations of society.

The poem's second moral problem resembles the first. It may be stated as follows: given the principle of immanent justice discussed above, why is Ami stricken with leprosy? Several answers have been proposed, by the various medieval poets themselves and by modern scholars. Unfortunately, Radulfus Tortarius, recounting the oldest and, in the opinion of some scholars, most primitive version of the tale, suggests no reason at all for Ami's malady: "Pluribus exactis post haec feliciter annis, / Leprae fis fedis eger, Amice, notis" (vss. 291–92).

Thus we must turn to more recent versions for an answer. One solution especially appealing to the modern reader is that God punishes the young man for having tampered with justice. Although he has perhaps conformed to the letter of the law, by taking his friend's place Ami has flaunted its spirit. Hardré was wicked and therefore had to be destroyed; Ami also sinned and was punished by leprosy. This interpretation is defended in the Middle English *Amis and Amiloun* (unfortunately a relatively late version) and may be supported by a passage in the Latin *Vita* where Amicus says to himself before the combat: "Heu michi, qui mortem huius comitis tam fraudulenter cupio! Scio enim, quod si illum interfecero, reus ero ante supernum judicem, si veru meam vitam tulerit, de me semper oprobrium narrabitur perpetuum." But has the young man actually committed a misdeed? In medieval France, as in any society which gives rise to epic, the oath is held sacred; false witness is considered a great crime. Hardré too is a false witness, however, if in a different sense; and, to preserve one's honor and that of one's lord, to avoid shame in society, are equally pressing duties for the hero, equally respected by society. The moral problem is once again more complex than it first appears. To condemn Ami, the poet must exonerate, in some measure at least, his archvillain Hardré. Together with Ami he must condemn Belissant and Amile; he must repudiate many of the virtues society holds most dear. Once again poetry triumphs over law, cuts the legal Gordian knot, as it were. The whole case rests on Amile's guilt or innocence. If Amile is guilty he must be punished, and Ami with him for trying to save a guilty man. But since he is innocent, i.e., beyond the law, Ami must not be criticized for going beyond the law to save him. Once again we invoke the Tristan analogy. Although in Béroul the protagonists are clearly guilty of adultery, the author approves of Tristan's ruse (not so different from Ami's) to deceive the court and free Iseut. Jonin has shown that such legal casuistry did exist in the Middle Ages. Significantly, it was condemned by law and canon jurists but approved of under certain circumstances, such as when employed by martyrs of the Church.[31] No medieval public would dream of condemning their hero Ami for having tricked the court into exonerating their other hero Amile.

The twelfth-century *Vita* provides a second explanation for Ami's leprosy. According to the Latin text, neither punishment nor crime is involved; God is merely testing his servant (as he had done in the case of Job): "Amicum vero cum uxore sua manentem percussit Deus morbo lepre, ita ut de lecto surgere non posset, juxta illud quod scriptum est: Omnium filium, quem Deus recipit, corripit, flagellat, et castigat." This solution is perfectly valid. It rests on the belief that both young men are innocent and that God is just. The Lord, in his infinite wisdom, chooses

---

[31] *Les personnages féminins,* pp. 99–105, 369.

to injure Ami for the greater glory of both Ami and himself. An objection can be raised against the "clerical hypothesis," however. From a literary point of view the *Vita's* structure suffers from a lack of continuity between the trial and leprosy episodes. God could just as easily test Ami or Amile anytime and the entire trial scene could be left out. And, of course, the author of the one surviving *chanson de geste* himself seems to have rejected this interpretation, and the first one, in favor of still a third.

La Chanson d'Ami et Amile declares that Ami is indeed punished by God, but for the crime of having accepted Belissant's hand in his own name (everyone thinking him to be Amile) even though he is already married to Lubias. An angel of the Lord admonishes him: Formerly you took a wife, and a very beautiful one too; today you swear to take another. God is angry. Martyrdom of the flesh awaits you for it (vss. 1813–816). This explanation for Ami's leprosy has not been accepted by the majority of scholars. Many feel that if the youth is not to be punished for a really serious crime, false witness, he can hardly be condemned for a verbal, unintentional, and non-existent bigamy.[32] Perhaps the *chanson*, in this one episode, is but a weak *rifacimento* of earlier versions. Perhaps, having rejected the two previous explanations, the poet invented his own, which is still less acceptable to a discriminating public. Perhaps indeed all three versions are more or less feeble efforts to rationalize in contemporary terms a folkloric theme whose original meaning had become lost over the years. We believe, however, that every effort should be made to discover whether the version given by the epic text itself cannot yet be justified. In our opinion it is significant that, according to the text, Ami is fully aware of the nature of his actions and the consequences which come from them. Before agreeing to marry Belissant he condemns the forthcoming bigamy in his own heart and asks for counsel from on high, at the same time deciding to plunge ahead come what may

---

[32] See Philipp August Becker, *Grundriss der altfranzösischen Literatur* (Heidelberg, 1907), pp. 99–101, and Monteverdi's refutation, "Rodolfo Tortario e la sua epistola *Ad Bernardum*," pp. 24–25.

(vss. 1768–774). When the angel reveals to Ami his judgment and
the penalty of leprosy, the young man still can withdraw. He
does not. Instead, persevering in what he believes to be the right,
he accepts condemnation in advance:

> "Je n'en puis mais, bonne chose, va t'en.
> La moie char, quant tu weuls, si la prent
> Et si en fai del tout a ton conmant."[33]   (vs. 1821)

Thus Ami is warned by his conscience and by a superior being
but twice chooses to sacrifice himself for his friend. During the
trial Ami had saved Amile's life and reputation. Though he
risked his own life (and his wife's chastity), he did not renounce
anything, nor was he harmed in any way. But the duel fulfills
only half of Ami's mission. If he leaves court directly after the
victory, once again Amile will be dishonored—for having left
without the king's permission, for having rejected his advice, for
having refused his daughter. By remaining, Ami will not only
have saved his friend's life but also have united him with the
girl he loves. He commits a sin, yes, but in a good cause; he is
punished for it, but the punishment serves to consecrate his
mission—as friend and martyr. In the public's eyes, of course, he
has not sinned at all. The second act of heroism is greater than
the first because it implies greater sacrifice, hence greater devotion. Ami's actions are depicted in terms of a progression leading
to a climax. If the *trouvère* gave a new interpretation to an old
theme, he did so with skill and with a definite artistic and
doctrinal purpose.

The same purpose justifies his resolution of the third point of
law. This problem, less developed than the other two, concerns
whether or not Amile should be condemned for having murdered
his sons in order to cure his friend's illness. Amile avows that if
he commits the act no one would blame the people for executing
him (vss. 2922–923). Later he places himself in the people's
hands, expecting, even asking for the death penalty (vss. 3166–

[33] "I can do no more, good creature; go. Take my flesh when you wish
and do with it whatever you will."

167). A double murder and infanticide were considered, then as now, the foulest of crimes. Nonetheless, one of the two victims and Belissant sanction the act; Amile's eldest son speaks so before the murder, the mother afterwards. And the children's resurrection, a miracle from heaven, clearly indicates that God approves of what Amile has done. He too commits an act of sacrifice for his friend. He too is fully conscious of the nature and consequence of his act. Amile's sacrifice is greater than Ami's, because the Lord of Rivière is willing to give up his life whereas the other had only to undergo sickness, poverty, and banishment. The progression in sacrifice is crowned by a climax worthy of the author's subtle preparations: God's double miracle, saving Ami and Amile's children, justifying both acts of sacrifice and restoring both heroes to health, happiness, and public acclaim.

In all three judicial problems the hero is judged, in the eyes of poet and public alike, to be innocent. Ami and Amile are ever in the right, given their *personae* and the literary genre in which they appear. Yet their actions, according to the law, must be condemned. In other words, the poem sets up a tension between heroic idealism and everyday life. Or we may think of the tension as between the letter and spirit of the law, between petrified custom and the living moral code of the people, both contained within the feudal world. In any case we must not consider the ethical situations propounded, or solutions given, to be somehow peculiar to medieval man. A stark contrast between medieval and modern attitudes, in this respect, cannot be maintained. In both societies tensions such as we have been describing exist. In both worlds literature differs from ethics and jurisprudence. A writer will impose "poetic justice" or "poetic injustice" as he chooses. Even though the poet proposes a solution diametrically opposed to the moralist's, his attitude is no less *true*, no less in touch with the deepest springs of human nature. The discussion of juridical problems, crucial to so many *chansons de geste*, in *Ami et Amile* is seen to be hollow. The poet cuts through them to propose a totally different attitude toward life.

From a literary point of view, the point of feudal law exists as a structural and psychological increment. It serves to create dramatic confrontations which will crystallize the narrative and reveal the heroes' fundamental character traits. We must not think of *La Chanson d'Ami*, however, as a "psychological epic." Although the villains, Hardré and Lubias, are endowed with a relatively complex psychology, the heroes are not. Ami and Amile appear no less lifelike or dramatic than their enemies, but they do not present the same complexity of motivation or natural, human reaction to empirical reality. Like Aymeri de Narbonne, they are presented in stylized fashion, as exemplary figures typifying virtues that medieval society considered important. They appear as models to be imitated by all men.

We do not refer specifically to beauty of person, seemingly eternal youth, largess, bravery, or skill in arms. These traits, by no means insignificant, are to be found in heroic poetry generally. More distinctive is a manifestation of goodness, the protagonists' ingrained sense of gentility, kindness, and princely abnegation. We shall not repeat the list of generous thoughts and actions each displays on the other's behalf. Although more than sufficient to prove our point, such actions could be ascribed to friendship, the sentiment uniting Roland and Oliver, Girard and Fouques, and Ogier and Benoît in other works.

No, the companions' goodness is most clearly apparent in their dealings with other people. Ami requests Girard not to accompany him into exile but to remain and inherit the city of Blaye. Two serfs do join their fortunes to his; when the funds necessary to support them have run out, he urges them to return home. He objects strongly to Aymon's being sold into slavery. He sheds tears on seeing Amile come to heal him with his sons' blood. The heroes even respond to evil with kindness. Twice they accept Hardré's lies in good faith (vss. 279–82, 329), although grounds for suspicion are available. Having returned from the Burgundian ambush, Amile defends Hardré against the king's censure (vss. 461–63), on his own initiative, before the villain offers him Lubias. Later the woman's husband makes every effort to reason with her, begging her to prevent him from being starved to death (vss. 2335–345). Harmed by her and by his brothers, Ami forgives them all (vss. 3457–458, 2569–571).

In the latter instance his words echo those of the Savior: "Laissiez les fols, certez ne sevent mieuz. / Dammeldex lor pardoingne."[34] With the exception of Hardré, a devil figure and sacrificial victim, neither Ami nor Amile is said to kill any man in the course of the poem. They fight in wars, they take prisoners, but we do not find them shedding blood. This, in a *chanson de geste*, is a rare, almost unique occurrence. It is a clear sign that the comrades are marked for an unusual destiny.

The protagonists embody devotion to each other and all people, temperance, integrity in worldly acts, courage in face of adversity, and humility before God. At one time or another in the poem they demonstrate the four cardinal and three theological virtues. They represent a quality of Christian perfection toward which all men should strive. Of course, the hero as a magnanimous man, an object for emulation, is not rare in the *chanson de geste*. A case can be made for the exemplariness of Roland's behavior throughout the poem bearing his name.[35] The thesis can be applied with great cogency to Vivien (in the *Chanson de Guillaume*) and the elder Girard de Roussillon, both of whom conduct themselves as true knights in the world but die martyrs of the faith. Veritable Christ figures, they are immolated for the betterment of society. Ami and Amile both stand as *vasa electionis*, chosen for great deeds, to exemplify forces and commandments. Now we understand why the author has avoided the issue of intracultural tensions, why his characters exist not to project individual behavior but as *personae*, fulfilling a specific dramatic and didactic role. In this epic, doctrine is more important than story.

La Chanson d'Ami is a poem with a message. It contains a doctrinal core of great importance, one which is not, as some scholars would maintain, limited to the exaltation of friendship. Friendship is not the legend's only possible theme, nor should the poem's clerical aspects be thought of as less important or authen-

---

[34] See Luke 23 : 34, "Pater, dimitte illis; non enim sciunt quid faciunt."
[35] Alfred Foulet, "Is Roland Guilty of *desmesure?*" *Romance Philology*, X (1956–57), 145–48; Alberto del Monte, "Apologia di Orlando," *Filologia Romanza*, IV (1957), 225–34.

tic than the romantic ones. The *trouvère* establishes a clerical
atmosphere in the first ten lines:

> Or entendez, seignor gentil baron,
> Que deus de gloire voz face vrai pardon. ...   (vs. 1)

> Ce n'est pas fable que dire voz volons,
> Ansoiz est voirs autressi com sermon;
> Car plusors gens a tesmoing en traionz,
> Clers et prevoires, gens de religion.
> Li pelerin qui a Saint Jaque vont
> Le sevent bien, se ce est voirs ou non.[36]   (vs. 5)

Ecclesiastics play an important role in the story. The protagonists' godfather is the pope of Rome; he gives them rich
presents and later befriends Ami when he is suffering from
leprosy. The Bishop of Blaye, as long as he can, opposes Lubias'
will and refuses to annul her marriage. Amile and Ami are willing
to swear on relics before participating in a *judicium Dei*. Both of
them, plus Belissant and the queen, pray to God on innumerable
occasions, for each other's safety, victory over Hardré, quick re-
union. On other occasions they invoke the Lord or thank him
for benefits received. The pilgrimage theme is also of prime
importance; we will discuss this aspect of the poem later.

Such manifestations of a Christian *Weltanschauung* are not
uncommon in *chansons de geste*, though they appear with greater
frequency in this epic than is usually the case. The sacramental
nature of *Ami et Amile* is made manifest with greatest clarity by
the role of miracles in the plot. A total of seven crucial events
can be directly ascribed to the hand of God. The heroes' coming
into the world is heralded by *sainte annuncion* (vs. 13). They
grow up identical in appearance, as if they were twins. In conformity with God's will Ami defeats Hardré instantaneously on
the second day of battle. Ami is afflicted with leprosy, either as

---

[36] Now listen, my noble lords, that the God of Glory grant you his
pardon. ... This is not fiction we wish to tell you; rather it is as true as
a sermon, for which we call several people to witness: ecclesiastics, priests,
and monks. The pilgrims who go to Santiago de Compostela know well
whether it is true or not.

punishment, a test, or part of his sacrifice. His leprosy is then cured by the blood of Amile's sons, who in turn are brought back to life. And to celebrate the miracle, church bells ring of their own volition. Three times an angel appears to the eyes of men: to announce the protagonists' births, to condemn Ami, to save Ami. These three celestial manifestations outline the poem's structure. They distinguish the heroes' promise of happiness, their sorrow through renunciation, their triumph and attainment of a new, supreme happiness.

Any work of literature so permeated with *merveilleux chrétien* and other aspects of the religious was probably written as a Christian poem and should be so interpreted. We do not wish to minimize in any way the theme of friendship in this *chanson*. Ami and Amile love each other deeply. But they love other people too: their wives, their children, their servants, their lord the king. They love and honor certain abstract concepts and devote their lives to them: public service, law and order, the defense of ladies in distress, secular justice, God's will. Although none of these loves is wrong in itself, love cannot exist in a vacuum. In confrontation with reality it must act; in confrontation with the evil of a Hardré or Lubias it must struggle to survive. It is the dialectic of goodness in relation to evil and to reality that the *Ami* poet seeks to exploit.

For Ami and Amile the answer to their problem is one of abnegation. We have shown how two of the poem's three points of feudal law are decided by means of an extrafeudal, extralegal justification of sacrifice. In fact, the theme of renunciation is interwoven with the heroes' destiny from the beginning. They waste seven years before finding each other. After Amile gives Lubias to his friend, Ami devotes seven more years, away from hearth and home, to stay with Amile at court. Ami again leaves wife and child to risk his life fighting for Amile. He accepts sickness, poverty, and banishment. Amile then sacrifices his children and risks his life to cure Ami. They both renounce family and heritage in favor of a pilgrimage to Jerusalem and die on the return voyage. Each sacrifice parallels the one that has gone before and anticipates the one to come. Seemingly easy at first, the sacrifices become more and more difficult, building up to a magnificent climax.

Great love by necessity implies, even demands, great sacrifice. How else can love be proved genuine except by demonstrating that it goes before all other considerations? Renunciation was central to the love ethos of the troubadours and *trouvères*. Some went to the extreme of rejoicing that their love would never be consummated; only thus could the poet prove himself worthy of his lady. Only thus can the two heroes in our poem exemplify to the utmost the manly love of friendship. Furthermore, reality prevents the companions from satisfying all their loves. Because of the traitors' machinations, they cannot possibly maintain home, family, friendship, and feudal service at the same time. Even if the traitors did not exist, the human condition would forbid such a utopia. The hero cannot succeed in multiple aspirations at the same time. For every idealistic gain he must undergo a corresponding loss: such is man's fate.

Ami and Amile sacrifice all worldly concerns: wife, children, material comfort, service to king, place in the hierarchy. In the end, they sacrifice the entire feudal and material world. This human, feudal world and the loves connected with it must not be considered bad in themselves. They all have a place in the universe. But other, higher values exist—humaneness, forgiveness, charity. These are at least as valid as the calls of feudal society and must enter into conflict with them. The hero is offered a choice, roughly between flesh and the spirit, prowess and charity. He is expected to make a decision, to decide what he shall love most of all. As long as he refuses to make the decision or, rather, ignores that a choice exists and must be made, he is not living up to full potentiality as a man and certainly is not living in a state of grace.

All of Adam's children are subject to original sin. The life the two friends lead in the world is by no means beyond reproach, from a medieval Christian point of view. In the Old French epics Charlemagne's court serves as a focal point for the action. It represents a standard, a norm, for the heroic life. Ami and Amile are formed at court like any other hero of *geste*. The court then perfectly embodies secular life as the poet conceives it. It provides opportunity for glory, responsibility, and happiness, yet can so easily give way to injustice if not outright betrayal. Hardré is in his element. Through flattery and deceit he readily attains most of his ends, while the heroes face blandishments, temptations, an ambush, at every turn. Although Ami and Amile are not said to kill personally, they do participate in war against other Christians. In fact, they fight side by side with Hardré, who brutally hangs the heads of fallen enemies from his saddle. To make matters worse, the companions serve Charles as mercenaries, *soudeiers*. His quarrels are not theirs; theirs are not his. And Amile is mocked for the excessive *soudees* he has purportedly taken from the emperor by having slept with his daughter. Although we know that the young man should not be severely reproached for the Belissant affair, he is to some extent guilty of *luxuria*, as he himself recognizes. His love for her differs little from Ami's attachment to Lubias, who is a far more dangerous creature, *fax Satani*, capable of bringing about unbelievable harm. The riches, the fine meals, the soft bedclothes—these represent aspects of secular life which the Christian must learn to do without. *Vanitas vanitatum*—Ami and Amile at court are not really lacking in *caritas*, but it remains for the most part latent. They possess great virtues but are, if we may say so, too happy. Neither has suffered; neither is ready for election.

Man must learn to suffer, to merit grace. Without knowledge of what is expected by God, even the best intentioned will stray from the right path. Hence the importance of the "theme of knowing" in this epic. Certain characters learn, grow, become wiser; others do not. Hardré thinks he knows how to confound the two friends. He is able to deceive an unknowing court into believing that he, Hardré, is a hero (the severed heads), that Ami and Amile have perished in battle, that Amile is a traitor deserving to be executed. Neither Hardré nor the court is aware of the real, spiritual nature of the men they are judging nor of the physical substitution in identity. Lubias, in turn, remains oblivious to her husband's inner soul, her ignorance symbolized by a parallel substitution of husbands. Later she thinks he is physically ill whereas in reality it is she, morally a leper, who will eventually be isolated from society. Even the heroes suffer from ignorance. Amile does not recognize the leper begging at his door; an angel must inform Ami of the measures necessary for his cure. But the young men finally do comprehend the realities of existence. Amile will sacrifice everything for his friend; Ami realizes that he can be cured only by God (vss. 2792-794). Having discovered the necessity of sacrifice, the goodness of suffering, they know more at the poem's end than in the beginning. They have achieved lucidity, vision, a kind of anagnorisis.

Since the heroes do not benefit from any single moment of revelation, their growth process is a long, slow one. With them, heroic and Christian virtues exist in a state of tension, not violent opposition, or rather coexist, one leading into, transformed into, the other. Ami and Amile, though human, though guilty of normal, human *cupiditas*, do not flaunt God's will. They voluntarily choose or willingly agree to abandon the old way of life. Knights at Charlemagne's court, they do not participate in any military action after the Burgundian ambush. Ami executes Hardré in almost sacrificial fashion, then leaves the court; Amile had already gone long before the trial. Neither will return. The heroes then devote themselves to their wives and children. Although they love them dearly, leprosy compels Ami to give up his family, and Amile chooses to sacrifice his that Ami might be cured. Immediately thereafter they abandon hearth and home in order to make a pilgrimage. For both protagonists war gives way to love, which in turn gives way to God. Or, in different terms, love of feudal life is transformed into love of family only to become *caritas*, love of God. As in Chrétien's *Perceval*, charity wins out over prowess. Before the end the companions have developed a sense of Christian virtue, have actualized the potential *humilitas, sapientia,* and *caritas* inherent in all men. Their final stage is one of pilgrimage and martyrdom. By renouncing the pleasures of this world (*contemptus mundi*), they demonstrate the highest manifestation of Christian perfection, to the extent of following Christ (*imitatio Dei*) in his Crucifixion. The two friends have sought for the Absolute throughout their lives. God's miracles prove their triumph. By renouncing sovereignty over wives and land, they achieve greater control of self (*ascesio*). By renouncing glory at court, they attain a place among the elect. Instead of the ephemeral renown of secular heroics, they will ever be famous among men for unique deeds of renunciation: "... tel renommee, / Que touz jors mais noz sera ramembree / Jusqu'en la fin dou monde" (vss. 3502–504).

Although the epic contains divergent spheres of value, the heroes traverse them to arrive at an absolute—the will of God. This grounding in eternal forces is exemplified in the narrative by a quality of poetic justice. Aymon and Garin, the good serfs, are rewarded with knighthood; the wicked sailors kill each other in a brawl. Girard's loyalty is rewarded (he inherits his father's land), whereas Lubias must undergo the same treatment she gave Ami. Hardré and the friends all die, but the former is tortured, executed, and his corpse vilified as befits that of a traitor,[37] whereas the latter merit a seat in heaven. For all its variety the world exists as one, *sub specie aeternitatis*. History is enacted according to God's will; all tends toward him.

If God deigns to elect Ami and Amile for salvation, he does so presumably not only for his own pleasure and for their sakes, but as an example. Other people—their sons, Belissant, her mother and brother, the two serfs—react favorably in the friends' presence, are made better because of them. The acts of the heroes as individuals affect the love borne to them by friends, relations, and neighbors; this is perhaps the greatest sign of their election. The companions help to regenerate society, to bring forth a collective response from others. Hence one reason why their names will be remembered by people "Jusqu'en la fin dou monde." This is the message of salvation embodied for men to understand.

*   *   *

In this chapter we have erected a superstructure of literary analysis which the author and his public might disavow. The

---

[37] On the first day, guilty of treason but having told the truth, Hardré is only mutilated. When, on the second day, he turns to the devil for aid, he is executed at once.

poet does not proclaim, in his own words *ex cathedra,* the "philosophy of existence" I have suggested to be inherent in his work. He does not proclaim any philosophy at all. Nor, for that matter, do Homer, Virgil, Turold, or some of their modern successors. *La Chanson d'Ami,* however, differs from the *Iliad* and *Aeneid* in that it is a medieval epic, was written in an age when men did search for deeper meaning, beyond the letter of a text. We do not presume to establish a formal, fully developed allegory for this poem. The currently fashionable school of Neo-Biblical exegetes finds Christian allegory in all medieval texts, sometimes on four levels, and maintains that serious medieval literature preaches one and only one doctrine—*caritas.* These exegetes claim that one method, Neo-Scholasticism, must be used to understand all literature written prior to 1500.[38] We believe, on the contrary, that some poems are indeed grounded in Christian belief and Christian symbolism, others not. Each literary monument must be examined as a unique entity; the poem should dictate the critical method applied to it, and not vice versa.

The interpretation we propose is based on symbolism (taken in its broadest sense), not allegory. In our opinion, *Ami et Amile* displays an unusual artistic configuration, often manifested in patterns of imagery. These images are rich in meaning and emo-

[38] See the books and articles by D. W. Robertson, Jr., esp. *A Preface to Chaucer* (Princeton, 1962); against the Robertsonians, Morton W. Bloomfield, "Symbolism in Medieval Literature," *Modern Philology,* LVI (1958–59), 73–81; Jean Misrahi, "Symbolism and Allegory in Arthurian Romance," *Romance Philology,* XVII (1963–64), 555–69; Leo Spitzer, "Les études de style et les différents pays," *Langue et Littérature. Actes du VIIIe Congrès de la Fédération Internationale des Langues et Littératures Modernes* (Paris, 1961), pp. 23–38, esp. p. 32. At the same time, we should never restrict the interpretation of every medieval vernacular poem to the *sensus litteralis.* Some will contain, and consciously strive for, a *sensus moralis* as well. Such is undoubtedly the case of many romances *and epics.* Touching on this question, Hans Robert Jauss, "Chanson de geste et roman courtois au XIIe siècle (Analyse comparative du *Fierabras* et du *Bel Inconnu*)" and the discussion which follows, in *Chanson de Geste und Höfischer Roman. Heidelberger Kolloquium, 30 Januar 1961* (Heidelberg, 1963), pp. 61–83.

tional overtones; some approach the intensity, the overriding significance, of the woman and city archetypes we found in *Aymeri de Narbonne*. Read in Christian terms, they reinforce our interpretation of the poet's message. Seen as literature, they help establish the *chanson* as a work of art of the highest quality.

Any student of *Ami et Amile* is aware that the two protagonists bear similar, almost identical names. According to the story, they are conceived, born, and baptized on the same days and resemble each other to the point of identity. Alexander Haggerty Krappe believes that in the original legend the heroes were twins, a datum obscured by the time our *trouvère* began to write. Seminal inspiration for the tale lies in twin birth, not friendship: "for it is clear that the two heroes were not conceived and born simultaneously because they resembled each other and because they suffered death on the same day, but they resembled each other and died together because they were conceived and born together, that is, because they were twins."[39] In fact, says Krappe, the Ami legend was derived from an ancient Dioscuri cult in Italy. And Krappe in turn sends us to the books of Rendel Harris (*The Dioscuri in the Christian Legends*, London, 1903; *The Cult of the Heavenly Twins*, Cambridge, 1906), a scholar who demonstrates the importance to religion and folklore of primitive taboos associated with twin births.

Although it is possible that folkloric elements dating back to pagan Dioscuri rites may have penetrated into the Ami legend, Krappe has committed the error, so to speak, of placing the cart before the horse. Rather than that the heroes, having been born together, should later come to commit great deeds and die together, we suggest that because they committed great deeds and led similar lives of heroism, they were then supposed to have been spiritual twins. Such is the lesson to be drawn from other medieval texts. Lovers, as well as heroes, are presumed to have been conceived and born on the same days and to look alike (*Floire et Blancheflor*).[40] As for the similarity in names, Krappe

---

[39] "The Legend of Amicus and Amelius," p. 153.

[40] See William Calin, "Flower Imagery in *Floire et Blancheflor*," *French Studies*, XVIII (1964), 103–11.

himself admits (p. 153) that brothers in general, not just twins, were given near-identical nomenclature. Rita Lejeune has recently demonstrated the same point (historically in the Middle Ages) for the Provençal poet Rigaud de Barbezieux.[41] In fact, the practice in literature is extended to non-related comrades (Basin and Basile, Gerin and Gerer, Ives and Ivor in *La Chanson de Roland*) or lovers (again *Floire et Blancheflor, Claris et Laris*, even *Erec et Enide*). These names often have in common only a front or back rhyme, or perhaps alliteration, but the striving toward likeness is unquestionable.

Even though we judge the twin *topos* to be merely a convention, its literary significance in the total narrative complex cannot be underestimated. Ami and Amile's spiritual likeness is the result of a miracle. Faced with so startling a manifestation of God's handiwork, the public might well feel dread. The protagonists are united by a mysterious bond, stronger even than those between Nisus and Euryalus, David and Jonathan, Roland and Oliver. Ami dreams of the dangers facing Amile; later Amile senses that Ami is in trouble. Both are destined to accomplish the greatest deeds. They already belong to a realm not accessible to ordinary mortals, a realm in which the supernatural plays a dominant role. Furthermore, Ami's name itself is symbolic and carries semantic overtones. *Ami* or *Amicus* denotes friend. He bears the name because it is his right, "secundum naturam et secundum placitum."[42] He and his comrade alone practice friendship in an ideal manner; they alone embody *compagnonage*. Ami merits his name as sign and symbol of his unique essence as a human being.

Playing an important role in the poem's symbolic texture is the concept of space. The narrative line unfolds on fields of battle,

[41] "Le Troubadour Rigaut de Barbezieux," in *Mélanges de linguistique et de littérature romanes à la mémoire d'Istvàn Frank* (*Annales Universitatis Saraviensis, VI*) (Saarbrücken, 1957), pp. 269–95, esp. n. 2, pp. 281–82: "On sait que la mode de donner à deux frères des noms presque semblables sinon identiques existait au moyen âge."

[42] From Isidore of Seville, cited by De Bruyne, *Etudes d'Esthétique médiévale*, I, 75. On the symbolism of the name, the hero's right to it, and the responsibility it entails, see Reto R. Bezzola, *Le sens de l'aventure et de l'amour* (Paris, 1947), pp. 33–61.

in or before cities or castles, on the open road, and, for a moment, aboard a transport ship on the sea. Except perhaps for the sailor incident the decor adheres to epic tradition. More significant is an emphasis, throughout the poem, on the beauty of nature in spring. Ami decides to rejoin his friend at court in May, when "li solaus luist et li oiseillon chantent" (vs. 514). Seven years later, at Easter time, the song of birds in a grove stirs in the hero memories of wife, child, and homeland. He must return to Blaye (vss. 537–51)! On the road between Paris and Blaye lies a beautiful field. Here Ami and Amile met for the first time. Here they will meet again, before the judicial combat. In fact, Amile blesses the spot for its role in the elaboration of their friendship (vss. 910–12). The poet tells us the field is beautiful, covered with flowers (vss. 170, 908, 916), with grass for the companions' horses and a brook from which to drink. It is an ideal setting for repose. We also discover, the second time the heroes meet, that nearby lie the ruins of an abandoned monastery, in a grove of pines and laurels, before an open road.

> De l'autre part ot un gaste monstier,
> Tuit sont li mur gaste et pesoie
> Et les tors fraintez et li maubre brisie.
> Nus n'i repaire, car li lieus est trop vies.
> Biaus fu il ombres des pins et des loriers ...[43] (vs. 937)

Although the grove, the flowers, the stream, the grass recall Curtius' *locus amoenus,* a topic which dates back to Homer and the Bible,[44] the poet has done more than copy a standard literary motif. The first time the heroes meet, Nature smiles with them. Later, under the menace of Hardré's treason, we are told of the ruined church and shady grove. The scene remains beautiful but in a more sombre, melancholy way. In fact, not only has a new aspect of the setting been revealed to us; the setting itself has changed. The poet's handling of decor has been characterized as an example of pathetic fallacy, Nature seeking to participate

---

[43] On the other side lay a deserted monastery, the walls all in ruins, the towers demolished, and the marble broken. No one goes there, for the place is so very old. The shade from the pines and laurels was lovely. . . .

[44] Curtius, *Europäische Literatur,* chap. 10.

in the action, its mood imitating and reflecting the protagonists' own state of mind.[45] But it should not be considered solely an aesthetic phenomenon. Scholars are aware that one reason why the *locus amoenus* appears so often in medieval literature is that it conjures up biblical images: among others, the earthly paradise. According to medieval typology, the terrestrial paradise can refer literally to the place where Adam and Eve dwelt and where perhaps the souls of the righteous await the Last Judgment (presumed still to exist somewhere on earth), and may also stand as a figure for the celestial paradise or New Jerusalem, the Virgin Mary, Holy Church (*Ecclesia*), or the individual Christian's soul. We do not insist on one interpretation to the exclusion of all others. It would nevertheless appear likely that in so forthrightly Christian a poem as *Ami et Amile* the pleasance may be interpreted as more than a common pastoral analogy. The sweetness of the landscape reflects similar qualities in the two protagonists. Nature approves of their goodness and innocence because she too is kind and pure. Yet, since men are all children of Adam, since they have undergone the Fall and are subject to original sin, our heroes must suffer. Their frailty as human beings is symbolized by the decaying, abandoned church, house of God, image of the human soul. To the extent they are still of the world, bound to the petty politics of Charlemagne's court and the erotic pleasures centered in Belissant and Lubias, the church will remain *gaste*. A wastechurch in a wasteland—lives and souls not in a state of grace. But the flower image also provides hope: some men will attain Christian perfection and return to a celestial paradise, ultimate realization of the secular *locus*. The human and vegetable worlds act in harmony, each in its own way announcing and serving God's will. Beneath the changing aspect of external things, eternal truths are to be discovered.

The *locus amoenus*, of course, exists during and stands for one time of the year—spring. Spring is the season of hope and rebirth, the eschatological season *par excellence*, when Christ himself overcame the bonds of sin and death. The over-all use of

---

[45] Asher, *Amis et Amiles*, p. 8.

time in this poem further underscores the *trouvère's* view of the universe. Indications of time are few and far between. We are informed that when the young men are knighted they have not seen each other for fifteen years (they are, therefore, fifteen years old, vss. 36–37); then they seek to be reunited for seven years (vs. 189). After certain events at court, Ami's marriage and the birth of a son (a duration of eighteen months or two years), we are told that Ami spends another seven years at court (vs. 547). Shortly thereafter Hardré's challenge occurs; Amile is granted a seven months' respite for the trial (vs. 812), even though later on it is said he has been married for only seven years *in toto* (vs. 2075). After the leprosy and banishment, Ami spends three years in Rome (vs. 2504). As to the final episodes, lasting perhaps a year or two, no details are given. This chronology, though a bit vague, is eminently plausible. The total narrative action covers roughly the period from birth to age thirty-six or thirty-seven. The heroes die relatively young men, martyrs still in their prime (though less so for a medieval than a modern public). On the other hand, the inconsistency we have noted and the almost mechanical recurrence of the number *seven* cannot but arouse our suspicion. Time in *Ami et Amile*, though rigorously chronological, has by no means been worked out with scientific precision; it is presented in stylized fashion. We have the impression of a highly fluid duration broken by moments of extreme dramatic tension. Major events, spiritual crises, appear outside of or oblivious to normal secular time. We are dealing with the life of the soul, inner and eternal states of duration—in other words, apocalyptic time. Although this notion of time is similar to that of many other *chansons de geste*, it is much more appropriate in *Ami* because of the poem's Christian theme.[46]

[46] The problem of time in medieval literature is highly complex. Even within the epic significant variations are to be found (see Calin, *The Old French Epic of Revolt*, pp. 189–96). For divergent conceptions within the *Lancelot-Grail Prose Cycle*, Paul Imbs, "La journée dans *La Queste del Saint Graal* et *La Mort le Roi Artu*," in *Mélanges Ernest Hoepffner* (Paris, 1949), pp. 279–93.

The pleasance, as we have noted, makes up part of the setting or decor. It creates space as well as time and partakes of those aspects of the poem we call spatial. A further use of space, more important in the over-all narrative, is the pilgrimage theme. Ami and Amile are baptized in the holy city of Rome. They search for each other over much of Western Europe and the Mediterranean basin, stopping at Rome and Jerusalem, two of the three prime goals for the medieval pilgrim (the third, Santiago de Compostela, is mentioned in the prologue). After having met, the friends travel to Paris, Ami marries Lubias in Blaye (to get there he must take the Santiago pilgrimage road), goes back to Paris to warn Amile, and finally returns home. Just before the trial both protagonists look for each other and finally change places. Once Hardré is defeated, Ami travels south for the third time. He turns Belissant over to Amile, who takes her to Rivière. Overcome by leprosy, Ami, riding a mule, begs his way to Rome, then to Clermont in Auvergne, through Berry to the coast, thence to Mont-Saint-Michel (still another pilgrimage center) where he takes a boat to Rivière. After the young man is rehabilitated, Amile accompanies him to Blaye whence they both enter onto a pilgrimage to the Holy Land and, on returning, are killed at Mortara in Italy.

La Chanson d'Ami et Amile contains three important trips which may be thought of as pilgrimages: the friends' seeking each other in the beginning, Ami begging his way as a leper, the friends' voyage to Jerusalem. A fourth is implied: both young men's fathers taking them to Rome to be baptized. The other examples of movement show one or both protagonists in quest of the other, often on an established pilgrimage route. Furthermore, the author chooses to mention pilgrims, to have them take part in the drama. They are invoked to guarantee the story's accuracy (vss. 9–10, 3497–498); Ami and Amile meet a palmer, without whose aid they would not have been reunited (vss. 83–143); in Berry another palmer informs Ami of the route to Mont-Saint-Michel (vss. 2609–619). At the poem's beginning and end are to be found pilgrims; movement and search pervade the work. In some sense the narrative development as a whole may be thought of in terms of a quest and is intimately tied up with that theme.

Although the sense of movement in *Ami et Amile* resembles what we found in *Aymeri de Narbonne,* space is handled in the two poems quite differently. In *Aymeri,* movement from one city to another is absolutely central to the plot: the entire narrative structure is based on the fact that the hero's responsibilities are divided, separated because of space. Such is not the case in *Ami.* The seven-year quest to meet, a voyage to give advice not accepted, wandering as a leper over much of France when a single trip to Rivière would have sufficed, the final voyage to Jerusalem—these all could have been left out. The pilgrimage theme is not necessary to the unfolding of a narrative line. It plays a symbolic role, contributes to the maintaining of a certain tone, establishes an ideal of life. In *Ami et Amile* space is moral and allegorical as well as empirical.

From the viewpoint of Christian typology, life for all men is a pilgrimage and exile. Each son of Adam walks through life a naked *peregrinus.* The true Christian does not wander idly, however, but seeks perfection and salvation. The Exodus myth serves as the prime source, as well as the finest literary example, of this theme. As Moses and Joshua wandered for years seeking the highest good, symbolized by the Promised Land, so too the Christian must seek a spiritual *terra repromissionis* prefiguring the literal Heavenly City. The voyage may be a preparation for still more difficult tasks, or the manifestation of a desire to merit grace. On the other hand, grace itself, having descended upon the Christian, may spur him to march. Hence the friends' first pilgrimage, the seven-year quest for discovery of the other. The pilgrimage may serve as an act of penance; the hero must suffer before admittance to the highest mysteries. Thus Ami must seek the pope, his brothers, etc., before going to Rivière; only in this way can he merit the saving miracle. Finally, the pilgrimage is a form of *transitus,* from this life to the next. Ami and Amile set out for the Holy Land. The terrestrial Jerusalem prefigures its heavenly analogue; and, in due course, the young men pass away to the *Civitas Dei.*

A pilgrim, by definition, is a man wandering somewhere in search of something. Many seek, in this mortal life, but not all find. Some enter on a quest without knowing what to look for; others look for the wrong things. Hardré seeks help from the Burgundians, but to hurt the companions not to help them. These enemy troops look for Ami and Amile in order to kill them, but fail. Lubias is riding to attend mass when she comes across her husband locked in his shed, whereupon she berates and humiliates him even more. She herself is participating in a kind of quest, but it is a false, distorted one. Hardré's niece obeys the letter of Christian faith but ignores the spirit. She should be seeking her husband, helping him attain his highest good. She finds him (physically) but proceeds to do the wrong things for the wrong purposes. She does not share his *sainte gloire* (vs. 2116), "Car de deu nen ot cure" (vs. 2066). In fact, it may be asked whether Lubias, though she does the persecuting, the hunting, is not really a savage prey who should be hunted. Ami, the hunted, uses a hunting metaphor (vss. 2082–94) to describe his wife's evil disposition. He knows what to hunt for and how: later he will seek it. The ultimate goals are physical and spiritual peace in this world and salvation in the next, as symbolized by Ami's restoration to health and the trip to Jerusalem. The active, external metaphor of the quest is but a representation of every man's internal struggle and growth through life.

In the tradition of the *chanson de geste* the pilgrim is also a crusader. Like the Grail hero he is seeking an ideal but must face hostile antagonists in the secular world. Most vicious of all are the Déramés, the Gormonds, the Aumonts—enemies of the faith. In our poem the key battle takes place, not between France and Brittany, or France and Burgundy, but as a ritual combat between Ami and Hardré. We have already discussed Hardré's career of treason. His *fillolaige* to Aulori, in which the latter is advised to slander good men, burn cities, and defile holy objects, is a hymn to evil, a diabolical parody of the good advice given in other poems by Charlemagne or Renaud de Montauban (vss. 1625–632). On the second day of battle, Hardré invokes the devil as his guardian defender:

"Ier fiz bataille el non dou criator,
Hui la ferai el non a cel seignor
Qui envers deu nen ot onques amor."[47] (vs. 1660)

Even more than Ganelon or Raoul de Cambrai, he exists as a Satan figure, the very embodiment of evil. An enemy of society and the Christian faith, he must be immolated.

Opposed to the Satan figure stands a *miles Christi*. Ami, because of his inherent goodness, and by the many prayers which underscore his devotion to the Almighty, proves himself worthy of the task. Like Roland and Vivien he struggles for the cause, ever maintaining those characteristics thought essential to the man of God. Christ the Savior also was a warrior who destroyed Satan's power after the Crucifixion. Just as the harrowing of hell represents an act of triumph over evil and death, so Ami's duel with Hardré stands as a ritual gesture. The trial, tournament, and execution—three class rituals here combined into one—fulfill the wishes and secret aspirations of society. A scapegoat villain is destroyed that life may go on.

For good to destroy evil, an act of violence is necessary. The traditional weapon in song and story, as in our poem, is a sword. Ami employs his friend's arm against Hardré the Satan figure. At about the same time his own sword stands as a barrier between Lubias and Amile. This blade preserves Lubias' chastity but also symbolically threatens her, a second Satan. Recognizing the threat, she interprets it in the most immediate physical sense; she is terrified for her life: "Grant paor ot ... Dex, com est effraee!" (vss. 1165–166). Then Amile uses his own sword to decapitate his children in order to cure his friend. That the poet evokes the same weapon three times, and in such crucial moments, is not a coincidence. Each time the sword upholds a cause, expresses God's will. Here, as so often in a medieval framework, it is used to defend society, the Christian faith, and God. It is a holy instrument in the Christian soldier's hands: ". . . ut dignus in gladio verbi Dei sectator Christi efficiatur miles"

---

[47] "Yesterday I gave battle in the Creator's name; today I will do so in the name of that lord who never loved God."

(Alcuin, *Epistula ad Carolum*). Heller points out, furthermore, that the sword of chastity motif (see p. 61) corresponds to recorded folk customs, that its presence in medieval narrative is an outgrowth of primitive taboos, where it served as a religious symbol and to ward off evil spirits.[48] We may add that any student of Freud will recognize, in the blade, a phallic symbol, image of the husband's authority and masculinity, terrifying his rebellious spouse. Or the weapon may be interpreted as a castration instrument, applicable to both husband and wife, used to enforce continence even in marriage. This practice, the *mariage blanc,* was by no means unusual in the Middle Ages. The sword would then serve as a willed obstacle to sensual indulgence, specifically within a Christian framework. As such, its role corresponds to that of the two other weapons. All three express and enforce God's will by exalting Christian renunciation over the pleasures and evils of the world.

If Lubias is separated from Amile by a sharp edge of steel, she is kept from her real husband by a menace no less great: the contagion of leprosy. Ami, having become a leper, is first deprived of his goods and locked in a small cabin, then exiled from the country. Alone, accompanied only by two serfs, he wanders over much of France and Italy on the back of a mule. Now as Jonin and Rémy have pointed out,[49] contemporaries believed on the one hand that the leper was undergoing a special ordeal from heaven, an act of purification, consequently, that he should be an object of love and charity. But the holy disease could also be interpreted as punishment and the leper himself a debauched criminal, deserving the moral obloquy heaped on him. These judgments stem from diametrically opposed human reactions to the misfortunes of others and are reinforced by two equally contradictory notions prevalent in the Middle Ages: Christian renunciation and charity; the concept of immanent justice *hic et nunc.* The dilemma raised by the confrontation of these notions

[48] Bernard Heller, "L'épée symbole et gardienne de chasteté," *Romania,* XXXVI (1907), 36–49.

[49] Jonin, *Les personnages féminins,* pp. 359–65; Rémy, "La lèpre," pp. 233–41.

is resolved perhaps more convincingly in *Ami et Amile* than in other works. The hero is in no sense a criminal; he is unusually free of the sin of lust (thought to be so prevalent among lepers). He has willingly accepted leprosy in order to preserve his friend's honor. But simply as a human being, a son of Adam, he partakes of original sin, inherent in even the most saintly of men; because he is a man, it must be expiated. Thus Ami's illness is the reflection of all men's suffering. Well might he invoke that other "leper," Lazarus (*saint Ladre en Bethanie*, vs. 2879), preserved from sickness and death by Christ. Ami accepts God's will in order to rise above the human condition and be saved.

Since all worldly goods come from God, it is only proper for the Christian to pay his debts joyfully: *rede quod debes.* In the Bible, Christ orders his disciples to abandon goods and family that they may follow him. The poor, meek, and persecuted will be the first to gain paradise (Matt. 5 : 3–11). These *pauperi* are specifically designated for the crusades; according to the crusade mystique, they benefit from special favor in God's eyes. The ethos of the mendicant orders, Franciscans and Dominicans, was based on the proposition that poverty and mendicancy are virtuous states, that it is the greatest honor, as the phrase goes, "Christum nudum nudus sequi." Perverted love (*cupiditas*), although a capital sin, can nonetheless be controlled by temperance. From temperance flow the virtues of continence, chastity, humility, and forgiveness. A return to the celestial paradise will be achieved only by renouncing the false, worldly values which create a simulacrum of that paradise on earth, by patience and inner discipline, e.g., mortification of the flesh. But since to renounce false values the hero must renounce the world, Ami's banishment turns out to be a blessing in disguise. He is cut off from human society, compelled to be alone. His quest for salvation is a solitary one. And in the end the two heroes, alone but for each other, perish on returning from Jerusalem. Their final abnegation is the highest manifestation of Christian virtue. *Contemptus mundi* opens the gates to the Heavenly City and eternal love. Although Lubias and Hardré appear to be healthy, rich, surrounded by relatives, friends, and underlings, in reality it is they who are sick (moral leprosy) and poor (spiritual poverty). Ami and Amile suffer physically but are rewarded spiritually. Did not Christ also undergo poverty, exile, torture, martyrdom? Did not he too ride a mule, attended by only a handful of followers? One of Ami's retainers alludes to Christ, "Qui por noz touz souffri la grant haschie" (vs. 3348). The leper then echoes him, with reference to his own tribulations: "... la grant maladie / Dont j'ai souffert tante male haschie" (vss. 3355–356). From archetypes they *become* Christ, that is, participate in the attributes of the Christ myth, whose overtones will move the literary public.

Ami's poverty, sickness, exile are cured—by the blood of children.[50] One of the most striking of Christian myths is the story of Longinus, not unknown to our poet (vss. 1305–307). According to the tradition, the blind Longinus recovered his sight by applying to his eyes Christ's blood, taken from a wound which Longinus himself inflicted. He then later shed his own blood for Christ in martyrdom. Another striking legend concerns the Holy Grail. Perhaps already in Chrétien's *Perceval* and certainly in the works of his disciples, the Grail is assimilated to the cup from which Christ drank at the Last Supper and/or the cup or basin in which His blood was collected at the Crucifixion. Now in the French *Chanson d'Ami*, Amile's children are decapitated that their blood may cure Ami's sickness; the blood is collected in a precious gold and silver basin (vss. 2962, 2969, 3158); both Ami and Amile are martyred soon after. The analogy is obvious. The blood of the Lamb (Christ) was shed for all men. He died that we may live. Ami, like Longinus, is saved through Christian sacrifice. Since the instruments of this sacrifice, innocent children, voluntarily give their lives to save others, they are assimilated to the *Agnus Dei* and figuratively give Christ's blood. Ami too, covered by this blood, represents the human aspect of Christ, becomes one with his God. Red is the color of love, human and divine (Augustine, *Quaestiones in Heptateuchum:* "Coccinum caritas, quod fervorem spiritus igne colore testatur"),

[50] On the general apotropaic powers of blood in Scripture and folklore, see Rémy, "La lèpre," pp. 210–33, and Krappe, *The Science of Folk-Lore,* pp. 217–18.

and, by analogy, of life itself. Archetype of the water of life, the blood shed here evokes the new life that companions and children attain. And as a reminder of the heroes' blood brotherhood, their spiritual twinship, it serves as a final bond between them. The blood given by Ami for his friend in the duel is returned. Both companions, by shedding their and their children's blood, will live on, reborn, in the *Civitas Dei.*

The ultimate analogy between the Longinus story and the medieval epic is the following: in both tales the sacrificial victim—provider of blood—dies (or is dead) but returns to a new life. In *La Chanson d'Ami* three miracles occur in the last five hundred lines; two of these are resurrections. After having been decapitated, Amile's sons are discovered to be alive and well. Their sacrifice ensures that Ami, a leper dead to the world, in a state of living death for which medieval society often recited the funeral office and rendered a symbolic burial, will return to the world of the living, strong and healthy, as dynamically alive as ever. Amile indeed referred to him in just these terms, as the man

> "Qui est des gens en grant vilte tenuz
> Et conme mors est il amenteuz;
> Mais or venra en vie."[51]   (vs. 2979)

The death and rebirth archetype is perhaps the most important of its kind the West has produced. In ritual, myth, and poetry, going back to the earliest texts, scholars observe a recurring pattern:

1) Man's concern with the apparent mortality of all things. The sun will set, spring give way to winter, life and beauty disappear. The hero, however brave, wise, victorious, must die.

2) Man's consciousness of renewal. Although one summer disappears, spring will come again; one day gone, the sun will rise tomorrow. And if a hero is lost to society, other men, perhaps the hero's own sons, will take his place. The individual may die but the race survives and proceeds to new heights.

---

[51] ". . . who people have held in utter contempt and who is spoken of as a dead man; but now he will come back to life."

Man conceives of an arrangement whereby continuity is impossible without death (sacrifice), whereby seed must be thrown away before a crop is gathered or a son born. The old king has to die before a new one reigns. Cyclical patterns, in nature and society, are recognized to exist; both cycles are embodied in mythical archetypes. A hero, king, or god (Saturn, Proserpina, Orpheus, Osiris) dies but is presumed to live anew, either literally himself or symbolically in the person of an heir. With the notion of a second birth, man seeks to overcome death and decay by giving expression to his deepest aspirations in a myth.

In our modern Western civilization the death and rebirth archetype has been molded into a Christian pattern and imbued with Christian symbolism. According to the Church, faith in Christ is in and of itself a victory over sin and death. Just as his Savior died on the Cross but was resurrected, the Christian will literally enjoy an afterlife in heaven. In order to live again, of course, one must first die (*Si le grain ne meurt ...*), but dying in the right way gives promise of a new life more beautiful than the old. Ami's old clothes are thrown away; he is given beautiful new ones by Amile. The old clothes are symbolic of man's corruption, the shame brought upon us by Adam and Eve, who first wore clothes as a result of sin. These are abandoned in favor of *nova vestimenta*, worn for a festive occasion just after a symbolic baptism (sacred bath and resurrection). The heroes celebrate their triumph with a banquet. The abundance and joy manifested on this occasion bear the same archetypal connotations of fruition, the same ritual consecration we saw in *Aymeri de Narbonne*. In addition the banquet symbolizes God's justice and bounty. Ami had undergone poverty, had been nourished only on spiritual sustenance. Spiritual food is proved to be the best; because of it the hero triumphs anew. To reinforce the message, when Amile's two sons are discovered alive, not dead, they are seen to be playing with a golden apple (vs. 3191). Image of bounty, of spiritual food, it corresponds to the apple from the tree of the knowledge of good and evil in the terrestrial paradise. The one had brought about man's destruction; the other consecrates his redemption. Through a rebirth, a resurrection, *veteres homines* become *homines novi,* and the old law gives way to the new. Abraham had been willing to sacrifice his beloved son Isaac; typologically, his gesture prefigures the sacrifice on the Cross of God the Son by God the Father. In retrospection Amile's sacrifice of his sons recalls and partakes of, postfigures, both previous acts. In all three cases the son's life is preserved. Death is transformed into life, and the eternal cycle fulfilled.

The notion of birth and death is central to the structure of *Ami et Amile,* as central as was space in *La Chanson d'Aymeri.* The epic begins with the two heroes' births. The central portion concerns their symbolic deaths (from leprosy, from the wrath of the populace) and rebirths. They have sons; Ami's boy is almost killed by his mother; Amile's offspring are killed by their father. But they survive to carry on the lineage. Then in the end, both heroes fall on the Lombard plains. This ending is not just an afterthought or a grafting onto the poem of a tradition found in *La Chevalerie Ogier* (where Ogier's great sin was to have murdered the companions in a fit of anger). It is essential to the narrative and doctrinal line. The heroes' symbolic deaths anticipate their real deaths at Mortara. On each earlier occasion they had been saved. Neither Ami nor Amile perishes at Hardré's hands; one escapes the living death of leprosy; the other avoids capital punishment for murder. Even the dead sons are resurrected. So, too, we have the right to expect that Ami and Amile, slain on returning from a pilgrimage, will be born anew in heaven. United physically in death, buried together at Mortara, they will sit together in the afterlife on the right hand of God.

By treating his narrative in archetypal terms, by adorning it with a profusion of symbols, a viable pattern of imagery, the poet creates a work of art which touches the alert modern reader in much the same way it must have the medieval. The overtones that reverberate from the tale of Ami and Amile, the aspects of myth it incarnates, are such as will (according to Frye's definition) "unify and integrate our literary experience, . . . fit . . . into the body of poetry as a whole."[52] Furthermore, the poet, con-

---

[52] *Anatomy of Criticism,* p. 99.

sciously working within both a tradition of semipopular art (the *chanson de geste*) and Christian letters, has been able to retain public favor while presenting a message. His images and the episodes in his narrative must be interpreted symbolically as well as empirically. He is telling a tale of adventure and of the Christian life at the same time. Each level of the narrative lends significance to the creation of a complex, artistic whole.

That *Ami et Amile* is a song of deeds in arms and a poem of moral and religious experience—a Christian epic—should not surprise us. Why should this not be the case? Religion, embodied in a clerical, Latin tradition (the *Vitae*), formed one of the currents without which epics in the vernacular would have been impossible.[53] And religion is a motivating force in two of the three earliest *chansons, Roland* and *Isembard,* and in several late ones, *Girard de Roussillon* in particular.[54] This is not the only theme in the medieval epic, but it is an important one. For all their differences, *La Chanson de Roland* and *Ami et Amile* are two epic poems which do preach Christian abnegation as opposed to more worldly considerations. They represent one aspect of the medieval mind—its striving to harmonize Christian doctrine and the secular world, to introduce a sense of the divine into human affairs, thus to justify the human by demonstrating its capacity to embrace the divine. This too is the work of individual poets. Their view of life and art is as valid and representative as the escape narrative of *Aymeri de Narbonne* or the existential anguish of *Raoul de Cambrai.* Theirs too is a world of art, a thing of beauty, revealing truth as well.

We have no proof that the Christian theme was inherent in the Ami legend from its beginning, the account in Tortarius' epistle being wholly secular. It cannot be proved, however, that Tortarius' source (a *chanson de geste*) was equally secular.

---

[53] According to Leach (p. xxviii), this particular *chanson de geste* underwent direct influence from the *Vita Amici et Amelii.*

[54] For the latter work, see Pierre Le Gentil's brilliant articles, "*Girard de Roussillon.* Sens et structure du poème," *Romania,* LXXVIII (1957), 328–89, 463–510, and "*Girard de Roussillon:* la rédemption du héros," in *La Technique littéraire des chansons de geste,* pp. 59–68.

Radulfus gives but a résumé of the story, telling it in his own words, for his own purposes. His highly stylized, rhetorical version tells us nothing about the tone of the original. Long ago it was suggested that all three major versions—Tortarius, the *Vita,* the *Chanson*—had been derived independently from an early *chanson de geste.*[55] Granting that this was the case, we must not claim any of the three to be more authentic than the others merely because of age. Yet even if Radulfus' source was different from the others, or if he reflects this source more accurately—for instance, even if the earliest *Chanson d'Ami* did not exploit the religious theme which was later to become central to the legend—our interpretation of the epic written about 1200 is not affected to any significant degree. The earliest versions of a poem or legend are not necessarily the most important historically nor the most satisfying from an artistic point of view. Several versions of *Ami et Amile* have survived the ravages of time. Each is perfectly respectable as a document; none can claim absolute authority. But of these versions the most successful as a work of art is beyond doubt the early thirteenth-century *chanson de geste.* Not only is its account of the story as authentic as any; more than the others it exists as an independent poem. It has achieved a synthesis between the ideals of war and of peace, the ethos of feudal glory and the message of Christian renunciation. The poet has succeeded in creating an exciting, moving work of art which expresses some of the most profound ideals of his age and which still has the power to move and instruct the reader of today.

[55] Carl Voretzsch, *Einführung in das Studium der altfranzösischen Literatur* (3rd ed.; Halle, 1925), p. 227.

Chapter III

THE QUEST FOR COMEDY:
Gaydon

The young Duke Gaydon (formerly Thierri d'Anjou, who had convicted Ganelon in the Song of Roland) *is Charlemagne's favorite. Ganelon's brother, Thibaut d'Aspremont, plots to murder the emperor by sending him poisoned apples in Gaydon's name. Although Charles is spared, he believes Gaydon to have instigated the crime and accuses him of treason, a denunciation in which Thibaut concurs. Gaydon defeats Thibaut in judicial combat and defies Charlemagne. Meanwhile, the Duke's baggage train which had left secretly for Angers under the command of his nephews Ferrant [some MSS read Ferraut] and Amaufroi, is ambushed by a group of traitors led by Thibaut's nephew Aulori. The Angevins (Gaydon's men) are assisted by a rustic warrior, Gautier, and by the Duke himself, who comes with a rescue party.*

Gaydon sends Ferrant to Orléans with the mission of declaring civil war on Charlemagne if the traitors are not punished. The youth undergoes a series of adventures: single combat with Charles's messenger, quarrels with a watchman at the royal palace, a dispute at court, an ambush by the traitors, stealing a horse and treasure from Charles's vassals, and betrayal by Hertaut, a member of the traitor clan whose hospitality Ferrant had accepted. Savari, Hertaut's son, defends Ferrant; Gaydon comes to the rescue.

118

Hostilities between Gaydon and his king break into the open. On the first day of battle the Angevins take Ogier the Dane prisoner; Ferrant falls into Charlemagne's hands. Ferrant and the traitor Gui d'Hautefeuille fight a judicial duel. The former is about to win when Gui's men, lying in ambush, deliver their master; then Gaydon joins the fray, and a general melee ensues.

Although Ferrant is liberated, Gautier falls into the enemy's hands. The traitors are about to execute him. Ferrant and Amaufroi free the rustic, but are captured themselves. They too would have been executed but for the Princess Claresme, who, encountered by Gautier, comes to the young men's rescue.

Claresme has fallen in love with Gaydon from afar. Using Gautier as an intermediary, she arranges a rendezvous, but at a tender moment the three of them are surprised by Gui d'Hautefeuille; only with the greatest difficulty do they avoid capture.

Charlemagne and Naimes disguise themselves as pilgrims to reconnoiter the rebel camp. They are discovered, however, and forced to accept a truce. After one last traitorous plot is foiled, Gaydon and Charles become friends again, and the Duke of Anjou weds Claresme.

* * *

Gaydon[1] is perhaps not a masterpiece. The poem's aesthetic worth was judged harshly by most of the early scholars who worked on the text. Because of a "bad press" and perhaps for intrinsic reasons, the poem has been read and discussed less than many other *chansons de geste*. In this condemnation, however,

---

[1] Composed in the first third of the thirteenth century, ed. F. Guessard and S. Luce (Paris, 1862). Not only does this edition date from before the Franco-Prussian War but Guessard and Luce chose an inferior manuscript as *texte de base*. See W. Reimann, "Die Chanson de Gaydon, ihre Quellen und die angevinische Thierry-Gaydon Sage," in *Ausgaben und Abhand-*

all scholars make at least one exception. As a literary character
and artistic conception, Gautier the *vavassor* is praised by everyone. According to Léon Gautier: "En vérité, c'est lui, c'est le
pauvre vavasseur qui est le héros chrétien, le vrai héros de tout
ce poëme."[2] Guessard and Luce refer to him as a "figure héroï-
comique, d'un caractère très original, d'un relief très-saillant et qui
fait contraste avec les types un peu usés, un peu effacés, qu'avait
trouvés notre poëte dans l'héritage de ses devanciers."[3] Reimann
writes as follows: "Die entschieden interessanteste Figur auf Seiten
der Angeviner ist jedoch die des verbauerten Ritters Gautier . . . ."[4]
And Alfred Krehl, who has written a highly intelligent critical
dissertation on the poem, declares that . . . "Die kunst des
verfassers, wirklich individuelle charaktere darzustellen, erreicht
ihren höhepunkt in der gestalt des infolge langjähriger verban-
nung völlig zum bauern gewordenen *vavassors Gautier* . . . Sie
erst gibt unserer Chanson das ihr eigentümliche gepräge."[5] But
the *vavassor* must not be taken for a genuine, authentic hero,
au sérieux. In our opinion he exists as a comic character, and
the poem's interest, tone, *genius,* is primarily comic. Gautier's
role in the narrative structure is to help create this comic
tonality.

Consider, for example, the first scene in which he makes an
appearance (vss. 2340–3014). Ferrant and his men, having been
ambushed by the traitors, are on the point of succumbing. They
seek haven in Gautier's manor; however, the place is seized by
Aulori. Gautier, seeing the traitors on his land and thinking they
have come to steal his livestock, joins forces with the heroes.

---

lungen aus dem Gebiete der romanischen Philologie, III (1881), 49–120.
So, for the material corresponding to lines 8111–10448 we shall use the
more recent, far superior, partial edition by Friedrich Bargmann, *Die
Claresme-episode des Gaydonepos, text-critische Bearbeitung* (Greifswald,
1911).

[2] *Les Epopées françaises* (2nd ed.; Paris, 1880), III, 635.

[3] *Gaydon,* p. xii.

[4] "Die Chanson de Gaydon, ihre Quellen und die angevinische Thierry-
Gaydon Sage," p. 78.

[5] *Der Dichter des Gaydonepos. Eine literarisch-ästhetische Untersuchung*
(Tübingen, 1909), p. 60.

He puts on an ancient, dilapidated suit of armor, grasps an enormous mace, and climbs onto the back of a mare. In spite of this bizarre accouterment, the newcomer wreaks havoc in the enemy ranks. Nonetheless, he is isolated from Ferrant and Amaufroi and compelled to flee. Upon encountering Gaydon's relief party, he seeks to run away again but is reassured as to their non-hostile intentions. He rejoins the battle at Gaydon's side and criticizes the hero for not slaughtering as many enemies with lance and sword as he, Gautier, does with his mace. Having changed armor, the *vavassor* duels with Ferrant, each unaware of the other's identity. Then he urges his sons, who had also fled, to return to the fray. The emperor's sudden arrival closes this scene and suspends, for the moment, Gautier's contribution to the story.

The key to understanding Gautier's adventures, the focus around which his character revolves, is the fact that he is a *vilain* (farmer, rustic, countryman). The *vilain* figure forms a distinct character type in the Old French epic, and the particular traits—of appearance, speech, and behavior—that scholars have found inherent in the type[6] are also to be seen in Gautier. What is the classic *vilain* type? A colossal figure of a man, gross, vulgar, and uncouth, who dresses in rags or absurd, dilapidated armor, is unaccustomed to orthodox methods of warfare and knightly ways in general, and who bears a particularly naïve attachment to his weapon—a club (the *tinel*), mace, or axe. On the other hand, using his weapon and riding an old nag, mare, or mule, the *vilain* slaughters the enemy with consummate ease. He is the hero's faithful ally and wise counselor, and is rewarded by a princely marriage or in some other munificent way. The *vilain's* reappearance as a more or less fixed type in so many *chansons* of this period—*Aliscans, Rainouard, Garin le Lorrain, Huon de Bordeaux, Gaydon, Macaire, Doon de Mayence, Gaufrey, Garin de Monglane, Beuve de Hamptone, Elie de Saint-Gille*—bears

---

[6] August Hünerhoff, *Über die komischen "vilain"-Figuren der altfranzösischen chansons de geste* (Marburg, 1894). See also W. W. Comfort, "The Character Types in the Old French *Chansons de Geste*," *PMLA*, XXI (1906), 279–434, esp. 384–404, and Hugo Theodor, *Die komischen Elemente der altfranzösischen Chansons de geste* (Halle, 1913), pp. 20–38.

witness to an extraordinary vogue. His antics were beloved of the literary public, whether aristocratic or proletarian; the *trouvère* sought whenever possible to cater to the fashion.

Technically, of course, our poet explains that his protagonist is not a *vilain* at all but a person of quality, banished from Angers by Gaydon's father for having killed a bourgeois. For seven years he is compelled to live off the land (vss. 2370–379). We are to assume that the forces of circumstance alone are a sufficient cause for Gautier's occupation and the superficially rustic traits he may have acquired. At heart he remains a warrior and gentleman, deserving of our highest esteem. The *trouvère's* protestations to the contrary, however, Gautier is a *vilain* and must so have been considered by the medieval public. As Guessard and Luce point out, his titles of nobility are fragile indeed: "c'est une simple précaution de forme que notre poëte a cru devoir prendre; c'est une concession qu'il a faite aux idées du temps et aux habitudes de la chanson de geste, qui ne choisissait jamais ses personnages, même secondaires, que dans les rangs des nobles hommes."[7] Or, from another point of view, the author conforms to the *bienséances,* to a particular literary convention—that his rustic must be of noble origin, worthy of marrying a princess. Rainouard himself, we discover, is related by blood to Guillaume's wife Guibourg, thus is a Saracen prince (*Aliscans, La Chanson de Rainouard*); Rigaud is similarly allied to Garin and Bègues of the Lorraine family (*Garin le Lorrain*). Since our *trouvère* has no intention of providing a fairy tale ending, he simply announces Gautier's noble birth at once and, decorum preserved, forgets it. Gautier's literary *persona* is that of a *vilain*. If no other proof were forthcoming, it would suffice to notice the number of times Gautier's social class is thrown in his face. On eleven different occasions (vss. 2427, 2475, 7028, 7055, 7411, 7658, 7942, 8101, 8309, 8968, 8985) he is insulted in this fashion. Not once does he deny the truth of the accusation.

But why should the rustic's socio-economic status be considered an insult? Why is he a comic, even satirical figure? An answer

[7] *Gaydon,* p. xiv.

will be provided, in our opinion, by consulting Henri Bergson. In *Le Rire*, the eminent philosopher defines the comic as an act of social correction. "Le rire doit être ... une espèce de *geste social*. Par la crainte qu'il inspire, il réprime les excentricités, tient constamment en éveil et en contact réciproque certaines activités d'ordre accessoire qui risqueraient de s'isoler et de s'endormir, assouplit enfin tout ce qui peut rester de raideur mécanique à la surface du corps social. Le rire ne relève donc pas de l'esthétique pure, puis'il poursuit (inconsciemment, et même immoralement dans beaucoup de cas particuliers) un but utile de perfectionnement général."[8] Thus society uses laughter to rebuke the nonconformist, to expose and reform antisocial behavior. An individual will be subject to laughter when his excess of character threatens the complacency of the group. Now the *chanson de geste* was primarily an aristocratic genre designed to please an aristocratic or proaristocratic public and reflected an aristocratic cultural matrix. Even well into the reign of Philip Augustus, when the novel had succeeded in displacing the epic as the most fashionable genre in the vernacular, the epic's fundamental social modalities remained more or less constant. Thus the feudal barons determined its social and ideological content; they established the norm, and their interests were respected. If reality was too harsh, too cruel, too opposed to the aspirations of this class to be appropriated into literature, then poets created a world of make-believe, of wish fulfillment, catering to their public's need to escape from the realities of existence.

We have discussed elsewhere the epic of revolt and the romantic epic in this context.[9] The *Gaydon* poet caters to aristocratic susceptibilities not only by flailing out at traitors and *arrivistes*, all those not of the finest stock; he also contrasts the epic heroes to a *vilain*. The member of the third estate appears ridiculous, unreasonable, unconscionably *gauche* because

---

[8] *Le Rire: Essai sur la signification du comique* (97th ed.; Paris, 1950), pp. 15–16. Bergson, of course, never refers, directly or indirectly, to the *chanson de geste*.

[9] Calin, *The Old French Epic of Revolt*, chap. 3; chap. 1 of the present volume.

his way of life (or the way of life attributed to him) is the direct opposite of the normal, accepted way of life of the nobility. It is perfectly natural that the barons should choose the *vilain* as a foil. We know the crisis the nobility underwent during this second feudal period, how, caught between a rising bourgeoisie and the Capetian sovereign, they sought to maintain status by the creation of a closed, artificial social nexus, the institution of chivalry. To demonstrate the "natural" distinctions between knight and non-knight, what better way than to ridicule the most socially inept of the third estate? The *agricola* and *miles dominans* belong to different genres and partake of different levels of style in Latin rhetoric;[10] they also stand opposed (according to the noble) in the deepest recesses of their respective ways of life. Thus the use of class differentiation appears in literature as the projection of a very real, if unconscious, class tension, literature serving as a weapon in, and an escape from, class struggle. The individual literary character is typed according to his class, and his range of action is limited to its traditional, stereotyped traits. György Lukács writes: "The division between the personal individual and the class individual, the accidental nature of the conditions of life for the individual, appears only with the emergence of class, which is itself a product of the *bourgeoisie*."[11] In his general frame of reference Lukács is eminently correct. It is possible, however, that class consciousness first appeared in vernacular literature much earlier than he imagines and that its concrete manifestation, though brought about through the emergence of a middle class, occurred within the aristocracy and was given expression in a literature reflecting the aristocracy's views.

Satire on Gautier the rustic is not the only example of class comedy in *Gaydon*. In his still useful thesis on comic elements in the *chanson de geste*, Hugo Theodor devotes a section to the *portier* or gatekeeper, who tries unsuccessfully to prevent the hero from entering or leaving a particular *locus* (castle, prison,

---

[10] De Bruyne, *Etudes d'Esthétique médiévale*, II, 42.
[11] *Studies in European Realism* (London, 1950), p. 208.

etc.).[12] Theodor fails to point out, however, the extent to which
the porter scene is comic because of the absolute contrast in way
of life between hero and porter. This contrast is due to the fact
that the hero is, by birth and breeding, a gentleman, whereas
the gatekeeper is the lowest, most vulgar of servants. In our
poem, for example, the porter greets Ferrant in the following
terms:

> "Trai toi arrier, gloutons!
> Tu n'i metras le pié, par saint Simon,
> S'aura mengié Karles tout à son bon."[13]   (vs. 3394)

Despite this inauspicious beginning, the youth asks politely to
be admitted into Charlemagne's presence:

> Ferraus li dist: "Biax frere, j'ai besoing;
> De longues terres sui tramis à Karlon:
> Messaigiers sui, ja ne t'en mentironz.
> Preu i auraz quant noz i enterronz:
> Je te donrai mon hermin pelison."[14]   (vs. 3397)

He is rebuffed again:

> "N'ai cure de sarmon;
> Quant que as dit, ne pris pas .i. bouton.
> N'i enterras, n'ai cure de ton don."   (vs. 3403)

> "... Sire musars, car voz traiez arrier,
> Et si laissiez ester votre plaidier,
> Ou, se ce non, voz le comperrez chier."[15] (vs. 3428)

---

[12] *Die komischen Elemente*, pp. 44–47.

[13] "Back, you wretch! By Saint Simon, you won't get one foot inside
until Charles has eaten his fill."

[14] Ferrant said to him: "Dear brother, this is an urgent matter; I have
been sent to Charles from distant lands: I am a messenger (we would never
lie to you). You will profit by letting us in: I will give you my ermine cloak."

[15] "I don't care for sermons; all that you've said I don't value a pin.
You shall not enter; I'm not interested in your gift." "Sir Blockhead, now
back off and drop your [legal] pleading, or, otherwise, you'll pay for it
dearly."

Yet this same functionary, so concerned that Charles dine in peace, will admit the Abbot of Cluny, once a suitable bribe has been offered. When Ferrant follows the monk inside, the porter resorts to violence, striking him with a club (the *vilain's* traditional *tinel*). Embodied in Ferrant we find the virtues of politeness, largess, and love of peace, while the proletarian gatekeeper manifests rudeness, veniality, and violence. It should be noted that in this aristocratic genre the proletarian foil (porter) is cut down immediately. His death causes neither the hero nor his public a second thought.

The Abbot of Cluny evokes another element of comedy, this time directed against the clergy. Not only is the prelate depicted as extremely wealthy ("D'esterlins blans la borse li empli," vs. 3442) and perhaps too loyal to a wicked king (vs. 3440). He is also a coward. When Ferrant decapitates the porter, his severed head flies through the air and lands on the prelate's cassock. He and his monks, fearful that Ferrant will treat them in like manner, wish they had never left the monastery. They take flight at once. More savage still is the attack on the Bishop of Mayence, member of the traitor family, who confesses Gui d'Hautefeuille before his battle with Ferrant. The "good bishop" (vs. 6437)[16] delivers much the same diabolical sermon as Hardré preached to his godson in *Ami et Amile*. And characters with the same names as in *La Chanson d'Ami*—Hardré and Aulori—approve the bishop's speech (vss. 6471–473). Even Thibaut d'Aspremont, head of the family, received a clerical education from his uncle, the Abbot of Saint-Denis. Having learned secrets of magic, he is enabled to plot Charlemagne's death by poison.

Religious comedy need not be directed only against men who themselves have taken holy orders or, as in the case of Thibaut, were brought up in the clerical life. A pilgrim remains a lay figure but takes on certain characteristics of the churchman and will be assimilated to him by the knightly class. In our poem, Charles and Naimes disguise themselves as palmers in order to

[16] Cited by Hermann Spamer, *Die Ironie im altfranzösischen Nationalepos* (Strassburg, 1914), p. 80.

reconnoiter the enemy camp. Unaware of their guests' identity, Gaydon and Gautier threaten the emperor and boast of what they would do to him if he were in their power. Charles is enraged but, since he *is* in their power and pretending to be a man of peace, must restrain himself. Hence a comic tension. In the same episode Naimes tells him they will do better to pray that they get out of this tight spot than to indulge in threats (vss. 9842–844). The situation is humorous precisely because pilgrims, unlike epic heroes, would normally resort to prayer rather than vengeance. And when the two men are finally identified, they undergo a series of insults based on their purportedly edifying vocation (vss. 10039–42). Perhaps most damaging of all is a final trait attributed to them—drunkenness. In order not to be discovered by his two sons, Naimes pretends to have imbibed too much wine (vss. 10022–25). Charles points out that he himself must have been inebriated to have thought of coming in the first place (vs. 10102). We are reminded of the pilgrim-knights in *Le Pèlerinage de Charlemagne,* who commit similar folly under similar impulses. Pilgrims then are men of strongly Christian orientation but who may eat and drink too much. The same traits, of course, are presumed of the clergy.

Ultimately we must posit an anticlerical element in *Gaydon,* just as there are antipeasant, antifunctionary, and antipilgrim elements. Not that the poet is lashing out in violent reaction against the evils of the time. Not that he is seeking reforms. But as an artist and propagandizer serving the feudal nobility (or working in a tradition which, at one time, served the nobility), he chooses to exalt the *miles.* Other professions—*vilain* and porter, abbot and pilgrim—serve as foils to the knight. In comparison to the knight's way of life, and using his way of life as the norm, theirs seem ludicrous. It is their dissimilarity, their inability to fit into his world, a world, moreover, specifically designed to keep them out, which provides the impulse to comedy.

To return to our original proposition, comedy in *Gaydon,* and in the *chanson de geste* in general, is social in nature. But if the preceding analysis seeks to explain why *Gaydon* is in part a comic poem, or rather why Gautier and some other characters display comic traits, we have in no way determined how this is so. To help reveal certain aspects of the poet's technique, once again we turn to Bergson. In the section we quoted above, one phrase is particularly significant: laughter calms down . . . "tout ce qui peut rester de raideur mécanique à la surface du corps social." Again and again Bergson returns to the notion, in harmony with the principle of *élan vital*, that life is naturally spontaneous. The antisocial person acts rigidly and mechanically; through a fixed, artificial reaction to external forces, his personality will lose its dynamism, its creative power to adapt—in other words, become dehumanized.

Bergson's conception of *raideur mécanique* can be applied to Gautier. Consider, for example, the animal humor in that first scene discussed above. When traitors intrude on the *vavassor's* land, he assumes they have come to steal his cattle. Two times he expresses this notion:

> Ses fiuls escrie: "Seignor, or i parra
> Qui no bestaille durement deffendra ..." (vs. 2382)

> "Fil à putain, mes bestes lairez sà;
> Car je sui cil qui les chalongera."[17] (vs. 2394)

A third reference occurs in vss. 2432–433, and on two other occasions Gautier's livestock is mentioned (vss. 2370, 2632). He himself rides a mare into battle (vs. 2390) instead of the traditional *destrier*. His sons are mounted in like manner; the author even points out that their horses have just been unhitched from the plow (vss. 2414–415). Although allusions to members of the animal kingdom in the midst of a life and death struggle are incongruous enough and quite sufficient to provoke a smile, the comedy here is centered on Gautier and his sons' rigidity, their inability to adapt to new conditions. A war has come their way. But as farmers they simply do not possess the equipment requisite for so foreign an undertaking nor are they conscious of

---

[17] He calls to his sons: "Lords, now we will see who will defend our livestock the best. . . ." "Sons of whores, leave my animals alone; for I have come to challenge you for them."

its absence. Gautier the *vilain* is not capable of appreciating or even divining the issues involved. Treason at court, jealousy, intrigue—these are beyond his ken. As a farmer, with the limited, specialized, professional viewpoint of a farmer, he blithely assumes the war will be fought over his cattle. For the medieval public, the *vavassor*'s livestock fixation is every bit as ridiculous as the fixations of certain characters in Molière—the hypocondriac, miser, or bluestocking—and for the same reasons. Farming is ridiculous because it leads to a fixation and because it is considered trivial. Farming, like medicine, finance, and philology, is of professional rather than universal concern. The *Gaydon* poet and the great seventeenth-century dramatist, *mutatis mutandis,* differ from many other writers in that their brand of humor springs inevitably from their protagonists' profession and social class.

Gautier's cattle and plow horses not only point up his trade in a general way; they also emphasize the physical aspect of his life work. We are reminded of Bergson's dictum: "Est comique tout incident qui appelle notre attention sur le physique d'une personne alors que le moral est en cause."[18] Even though the *vavassor* will be fighting on the hero's side, we are made aware for an instant of his ridiculous physical appearance. Nor is this external incongruity limited to the horse. As we have seen, Gautier's armor and weapons are as ridiculous as his mount:

> A ces paroles, li vavasors s'arma
> D'un gambison viez, enfummé, qu'il a.
> .I. viés chapel sor sa teste ferma;
> Mais tant fu durs que arme ne douta.
> Prent sa masue, sor .i. jument monta.[19]   (vs. 2386)

Later, when Gaydon urges his friend to put on fresh, up-to-date armor, the *vavassor* retains his mace (vss. 2814–816) for it may come in handy someday. He regrets not having used the instrument in his duel with Ferrant and does take it up against the

---

[18] *Le Rire,* p. 39.
[19] With these words the *vavassor* put on an old padded tunic, black with soot, which he owned. Onto his head he fixed a cap, old but so hard that it need fear no weapon. He took his mace and climbed onto a mare.

traitors when his spear breaks (vss. 6348–352). In a later battle the mace too is broken, making Gautier desolate (vss. 7095–98), but he will seize a similar arm, a *perche* (vs. 7896) or an axe (vs. 8197). Then in his final engagement, as a crowning indignity, his axe and his nose are broken at the same time (vss. 9420–422).

In this concern to possess his own individual weapon, Gautier resembles Rainouard and the other *vilains* of tradition. The weapon—*tinel*, mace, axe—serves as a *point de repère*, a symbol for the rustic hero and all he represents. As such it must have delighted the medieval public. Yet for us, Gautier's mace is also symptomatic of an obsession with the physical, with externals— his inability to adapt to knightly modes of fighting. In addition, a simple tally informs us that Gautier is preoccupied with his weapon seven times, just as he referred twice to the traitors as cattle rustlers. A humorous effect is created by the element of repetition, central to the notion of *raideur mécanique*. Bergson's image of the jack-in-the-box (*diable à ressort*) is appropriate in this context. Again and again Gautier is compelled to participate in proper, knightly combat; again and again he is urged, even persuaded, to equip himself in orthodox fashion. But mechanically, rigidly, comically, like a jack-in-the-box he pops back to the rustic weapon which mashes but does not slice. Repetition of the incident further increases its comic power, since each occurrence draws some of its humorous effect from the previous ones. Comedy as well as tragedy benefits from parallels and correspondences.

Gautier's horse, armor, and weapon all characterize his physical appearance in battle. As an ensemble they are his *clothing*, and as such are humorous because, in Bergsonian terms, clothing tends inevitably to the comic, given its artificiality, its eminent physicality, when brought into contact with or forced upon natural man. Clothes-weapon humor in *Gaydon* is definitely the result of a contrast between elements of the living and the mechanical ("du mécanique plaqué sur du vivant"). The *vilain* is seeking to be a knight. He commits the actions of a knight but wears the clothes of a *vilain*, or a combination of knightly and rustic garb. Attention is called to the artificiality of his dress and to the artificiality of specialized, professional uniforms in general.

The humor inherent in clothing will help explain an emphasis on battle disguise in the *chanson de geste* in general[20] and *Gaydon* in particular. Gautier himself, having changed armor, becomes unrecognizable; he engages in combat with his ally Ferrant, neither man aware of the other's identity. The scene, which might so easily give rise to tragedy, or at least pathos, remains in the comic mode. Similarly, when Charlemagne and his trusted adviser disguise themselves as palmers, the court bursts out laughing (vss. 9769–778). The two spies, the richest men in Europe, must pretend to be impoverished beggars. Once again, in incredibly sharp relief, artifice is superimposed on nature.

Charlemagne and Naimes are comic figures even before entering the rebel camp. Once seated at Gaydon's table, they are caught up in an intolerable situation where their natural instincts as warriors enter into conflict with a set of newly acquired, artificial pilgrim traits (see above). As a result Charles will react violently to insult, only to force himself to remain calm. The brusqueness, irregularity, rigidity of his actions are most appropriately compared to a drunkard's. Or as Jean-Pierre Richard points out with reference to Stendhal: "le rire, secousse corporelle, naît du spectacle d'un homme secoué."[21] Such responses are also not far removed from those of a puppet, another of Bergson's images for explaining the comic. Fittingly enough, Charles and Naimes, torn between their natural passions and artificial disguise, lose what little freedom of action they ever had. In the end, since their whole plot is foiled, they have no more control over the story than would a real puppet. Found out by Naimes's sons, the spies themselves are unmasked. They who had come to discover the identity of Gaydon's followers find their own identity revealed. As with Pathelin and Tartuffe, the trickster is tricked, the *trompeur trompé*. This quasi-mechanical inversion or reversal of a plan itself artificial makes us laugh.

Critics have traditionally divided comic effects into three categories: comedy of situation, language, and character. Gautier

---

[20] See Theodor, *Die komischen Elemente*, pp. 65–67.
[21] *Littérature et Sensation* (Paris, 1954), p. 38.

and his mace, Gautier dueling with Ferrant, Ferrant and the
porter, Charles and Naimes disguised as pilgrims—all fit under
the heading of situation comedy or under the related ones of
gesture and position. This aspect of humor would seem to be the
one most prevalent in the Middle Ages. Jules Horrent has remarked how it dominates *Le Pèlerinage de Charlemagne,* to the
relative exclusion of the other two.[22] Such is not the case in
Gaydon, however. Comedy of language is central to Ferrant's
porter scene. The ultimate contrast between the gentleman and
the boor is revealed by a contrast in their levels of speech. The
one opens a conversation with "Biaus douz amis portiers" (vs.
3406), the other with "Trai toi arrier, gloutons!" (vs. 3394). In
fact, the porter is eminently aware of the difference between his
own style and Ferrant's. He refers to the knight's elegant requests
as *sarmon* and *plaidier,* accuses him of being a *sermonniers* who
preaches well (vss. 3403, 3415, 3421–422, 3429). The porter's
insults are comic. Although he attacks Ferrant for speaking like
a cleric, not a warrior, for seeking to talk his way (in clerical
fashion) into the palace, he will admit the Abbot of Cluny, a real
cleric, who says nothing but has offered him a bribe. The Abbot's
speech is also eminently fitting for his class. Dominated by fear,
incapable of delivering an elegant, courtly speech like Ferrant's,
he can only swear in a Latin-French jargon, unique to his profession, and wish himself back in the cloister:

> "Nomini Damme, mauvais estre fait ci!
> S'estoie en cloistre, par foi le voz plevis,
> An piece mais n'en seroie partis."[23]   (vs. 3468)

Gautier also speaks appropriately to his trade and class. He is
subject to profanity: "Fil à putain," he cries (vss. 2394, 7209), and
"Par le cuer beu!" (vss. 2405, 2410, 8811). These mild expletives
should be thought of as typical of the ill-bred rustic (seen in

[22] *Le Pèlerinage de Charlemagne. Essai d'explication littéraire …* (Paris,
1961), pp. 115–16.
[23] "*Nomini Damme,* this place is terrible! In faith I swear to you, if I
were back in my cloister, it would be a long time before I ever set out
again."

courtly eyes). As such they contribute to a humorous tone.
Furthermore, since Gautier delivers both expressions on more
than one occasion, once again we come across the use of repetition to indicate rigidity, in this case the rustic's inability to
escape from his background in a courtly ambiance. The *vavassor*
will indulge in more elaborate down-to-earth expressions. He will
criticize Gaydon's method of combat: "Je les sai chastoier, / Mais
voz ne faitez fors la gent esmouschier" (vss. 2738–739); or he
will become angry when his spear breaks: "De Deu soit il
maudis / Qui fist tele arme! ne vaut pas .ii. espis" (vss. 6348–
349). Nor does Gautier hesitate to boast of the great actions he
will perform. One incident of braggadocio, directed against the
emperor himself, is humorous because of the way the *vilain*
peeps out from behind a knightly exterior. A true knight, even in
rebellion, remains conscious of his feudal obligations, avoids
menacing his suzerain personally except in moments of the
greatest duress. Hence the barons' laughter over Gautier's
threats:

> Il jure Deu, le roi de paradis,
> S'il ataint Karle, le roi de Saint Denis,
> Tel li donra sor son hiaume burniz
> Ne li vaudra vaillant .ii. parisis
> Que ne li froisse le chief desci qu'an pis.
> Li baron l'oient, durement en ont ris.[24]   (vs. 6353)

In one of the most finely wrought speeches of the *chanson*,
Gautier promises his sons that if they fight well, their mother
will serve lamb, peas, and cheese for dinner; if not they will be
obliged to fast (vss. 6986–7000). This is a direct parody, of
course, on the epic hero's traditional exhortation to his men,
promising them castles, wives, spoils, or salvation. Our rustic
warrior offers a different reward and introduces the notion of

---

[24] He swears to God, King of Paradise, that if he catches up to Charles,
King of Saint-Denis, he will wield such a blow on Charles's burnished
helmet that it won't give him two cents' worth of protection, and he will
shatter Charles's head down to his chest. The barons, hearing Gautier's
threat, burst into laughter.

punishment. Epic matter in high style (*miles*) is transposed onto a lower register, repeated in low style (*agricola*). With Gautier, as with Ferrant, the abbot, and the porter, humor is attained by manipulating diction, by creating a variety of textures. The abrupt, mechanical juxtaposition of disparate styles, or an individual's employing the inappropriate style in a given situation, creates the desired effect.

The author also provides comedy of character. Gaydon, Ferrant, Charlemagne, Naimes, are not essentially humorous personages, although they may, from time to time, accidentally participate in a comic situation. But Gautier is such a character. He is enormous, a colossus given to extremes in every way, a prisoner of his background who has difficulty in adapting to the external world. Such themes as the contrast of large and small, beautiful and ugly, poised and clumsy, are evoked. Yet at the same time he is the naïve innocent, pure and laughable in his maladroitness. In this way (if only in this way) he resembles Don Quixote. The humor of his *persona* is one of contrast and opposition. Seen either as a false knight, whose mechanical, laughable rusticity shines through, or as a peasant seeking to hide his natural self under an artificial chivalric code, it is the juxtaposition of two worlds—heroic and peasant—as yet unassimilated in his character, which provides the moment of comic truth.

That we can see Gautier either as rustic knight or pretentious peasant points up a very important fact: we cannot always be certain who is natural and who artificial, which characters and social classes are meant to be objects of our laughter at a given moment. It is quite possible, probable even, that the poet had no intention of restricting comedy to the peasant side of Gautier, or, for that matter, to Gautier at all. In other words, the knightly class is also subject to raillery. In no other way can Gautier's insult of his friend Gaydon be explained. The *jeune premier* has unhorsed several traitors (we do not know whether they are killed); he then strikes still another, but the enemy's hauberk holds good and Gaydon's spear breaks into pieces. Gautier reproaches his leader for being too chivalric, for not knowing how to kill the enemy. You boasted you could defeat them, says

Gautier, but you hesitate to kill them once they are knocked down. May he be cursed who dubbed you knight! I am sorry I ever joined your company; you're not worth a red cent! (vss. 2714-726). Gautier is made to look ridiculous by leveling such extreme criticism, which he really doesn't mean in any case. After all, the Duke of Anjou almost always wins. His failure in this episode is a minor one, created especially for the sake of comedy. Yet Gautier is at least partly right. He is the strongest, best fighter in the rebel army; his mace is without a doubt more efficient than Gaydon's lance or sword. And more than one of Gaydon's antagonists did get away. Leaving aside questions of personal heroism, honor, and sentimentality, if you wish to win battles, unhorsed adversaries must be dispatched lest they remount and charge again. From a purely military point of view, Gautier's advice is well taken. We would be going too far to suggest that this passage reveals in embryo the spirit of Du Guesclin or Dunois opposed to that of the defeated generals at Poitiers and Agincourt. But Gautier's comments on traditional epic warfare are revealing. Practicality and poetry stand opposed as ways of life. Both are valid positions; the sword of laughter cuts both ways.

Nor is this the only episode to slight the heroic ideal. Before entering into combat with Thibaut, Gaydon mounts his horse in inelegant fashion and falls to weeping, demonstrations of weakness which quite properly horrify Naimes (vss. 1374-376) and Ogier (vss. 1474-478). Later Ferrant admits being afraid of Gui d'Hautefeuille in almost identical circumstances. But Gaydon's nephew justifies his fright: "Moult seroit cil fox et desmesurez / Qui à tel home seroit en champ meslez, / S'il nel doutoit" (vss. 6514-516). Naimes agrees. An aspect of realism, of critical comment, has entered the epic.

Although Gaydon loves the princess Claresme and is destined to marry her, it is Gautier who discovers her lost on the field of battle, rescues her from the attention of potential ravishers, and brings her to Angers. Once again his deeds surpass those of his master, this time in an area encroaching on love.

Battle disguise is a traditional motif in the *chanson de geste*.

Usually a Gautier type, Maugis in *Les Quatre Fils Aymon* for instance, indulges in what is to some extent a degrading business. If an epic hero commits such practices (Guillaume in *Le Charroi de Nîmes*), he does so for the most serious of reasons—the winning of a city—and even so brings ridicule upon himself. In *Gaydon,* however, the emperor and his faithful minister descend to spying in the rebel camp. Once when Ogier had been made prisoner in Angers, Gaydon ordered his men to remain out of sight lest the fathers in Charles's army discover that their own sons are fighting for the rebels. Upon his release Ogier recounts his experience, and the commander-in-chief is as troubled as any by the mystery. It is out of curiosity and vanity, the itch to find out who Gaydon's men are, that Charles places his life and throne in danger.

In the end the emperor of Christendom loses neither life nor throne but does suffer indignities to his person. Gautier boasts that if Charles were in his power, he would pull out his moustaches (vss. 9906–911), an insult which enrages Charles to the extent that he almost gives himself away. Less than two hundred lines further on, Naimes's son then does injure the pseudo pilgrim in this extremely sensitive domain by grasping his beard and yanking out one hundred strands (with blood) (vss. 10070–74). The emperor's plan is foiled in a particularly humiliating way. Considering that earlier in the poem Naimes, Riol, and Hardré had been insulted in like manner, we realize that the author is playing with an old tradition which is to be found already in the *Song of Roland,* that the old hero or king figure placed an enormous prestige on his facial hair. If, however, the old hero reveres it in an artificial, mechanical way, he becomes subject to laughter when, for all his power and dignity, it is pulled out. His inadaptability to society is demonstrated by a corresponding inability to avoid what he most fears. The fact that the issue at stake is so irrelevant, as non-universal as Gautier's cattle, contributes to the humorous effect.

Thus, in our opinion, the author pokes fun at the knights as well as the proletariat and clergy. Imperial dignity, heroism, idealism, the stylization of an exalted, restricted mode of life—

these are the objects of his taunts. He is writing a *chanson de geste* which is a parody of the genre and a satire on certain traditional literary characters and motifs. We use the terms *parody* and *satire* advisedly. *Gaydon* was written in much the same way as *Le Pèlerinage de Charlemagne*.[25] We do not imply, of course, that it is a particularly radical or bitter work; the author is not seeking drastic reforms. Principles as such are not being undermined as much as the human beings who cannot live up to them. From another point of view the *trouvère* is mocking literature, not life. The stilted formalism, the pompous, stylized way of life portrayed in the epics—these are his meat. Yet who can say how much of life is reflected in literature and to what extent people then try to live what they have read in books? Literature and life constantly interact. The medieval public, listening to an epic recitation, blurred these distinctions no less than the average reader of today. And if people appear foolish in trying to live up to certain ideals, do we not inevitably, in the world of the poem, call the principles into question as well? Such was undoubtedly the case with Molière's public, and this helps explain the Church's opposition to *Don Juan* and *Tartuffe*. We know that medieval nobility was eminently capable of appreciating self-parody. It was done in the fabliaux;[26] it could be done in the epic.

One reason for playing one class off against another is, as in *Aymeri de Narbonne* and *Ami et Amile*, the more accurate, detailed, profound representation of reality. Literary stylization is

[25] Excellent studies have been written on *Le Pèlerinage* in recent years, specifically Ronald N. Walpole, "The *Pèlerinage de Charlemagne*: Poem, Legend, and Problem," *Romance Philology*, VIII (1954–55), 173–86; Jules Horrent, "La chanson du *Pèlerinage de Charlemagne*. Problèmes de composition," in *La Technique littéraire des chansons de geste*, pp. 409–28, and *Le Pèlerinage de Charlemagne*. *Essai d'explication littéraire*; Hans-Jörg Neuschäfer, "*Le Voyage de Charlemagne en Orient* als Parodie der Chansons de Geste," *Romanistisches Jahrbuch*, X (1959), 78–102; Bruno Panvini, "Ancora sul *Pèlerinage de Charlemagne*," *Siculorum Gymnasium*, XIII (1960), 17–80; Guido Favati, "Il *Voyage de Charlemagne en Orient*," in *Studi Mediolatini e Volgari*, XI (1963), 75–159.

[26] Per Nykrog, *Les Fabliaux* (Copenhagen, 1957).

slowly giving way, on some fronts at least, to a more modern treatment. In place of the rousing but conventional leadership portrayed in the *Song of Roland,* Gaydon's mentor, Riol, gives eminently practical, commonsensical advice. After Ferrant has been made prisoner, he says pretty much the following: It is a mistake to rebel against one's rightful lord; we are in a bad spot, let's put up a good front. Pretend that we are joyful, confident, and without strife. The men in the ranks will not lose faith nor will their morale be dampened. In any case, maybe the enemy will trade us Ferrant for Ogier, our prisoner (vss. 5555–590). A Roland, even an Aymeri, would never have admitted the difficult situation, much less have suggested hypocrisy as one means of overcoming it. Nor in their poems could we find the explicit mention of those less romantic elements which join armies—not only heroes, knights, and vassals, but also ugly lackeys, *jongleurs,* and whores who quickly drain one's purse (vss. 4812–815). Other references to the people—archers defending Gaydon's retreat, a sympathetic doctor, a peasant bringing news, the city dwellers' prosperity in Angers—are more conventional. Most of all we find the ever-present Gautier. The young hero's ally is technically a *vavassor* but a *vilain* in spirit. He is, to employ a not too anachronistic Victorian phrase, the "gentleman who has fallen onto hard times." But he also represents the new third estate laying claim to aristocratic privilege. We know from the writings of Georges Duby, among others, to what extent fluctuation in the class nexus was a reality in thirteenth-century France. Inflation, luxury, the encroachment of royal and feudal power, contributed to the decline of many houses in the lesser nobility and to the corresponding rise of affluent city dwellers and peasants.[27] These tendencies converge in the Gautier figure, a stylized, literary deformation of everyday life, but which reflects life nonetheless. His presence in the epic is indicative of the cultural patterns (and intracultural tensions) of the day and of the *trouvère's* willingness to recognize this aspect of social reality and turn it into art.

[27] *La société aux XIe et XIIe siècles dans la région mâconnaise* (Paris, 1953), pp. 494–527.

For all his ambiguous social standing and overtly comic nature, Gautier is not always a figure of reproach, an enemy of society whom we stand off from and seek to reform. He also appears as a warm, human, sympathetic figure, popular with the literary public and to some extent enjoying its approbation. It is not difficult to prove, for example, the esteem in which he is held by other characters and the good he does them. The *vilain* is a great warrior, a man successful in feats of arms. He wins battles. Even his ridiculous armor serves a purpose: the helmet may be old, "mais tant fu durs que arme ne douta" (vs. 2389). He loses four sons in defense of the ambushed contingent. The enemy themselves admit Gautier's prowess: "Will our side be beaten on account of eight peasants?" cries Aulori (vss. 2426–428). Gaydon proclaims that the *vavassor* has done more for the rebel cause that day than anyone else (vs. 2853). Even when insulted by Gautier, he only laughs and prays God to preserve the *vilain* from harm (vss. 2740–741). We are told that the latter will reap great rewards for his services. In the meantime, he, his wife, and three remaining offspring follow the duke to Angers (vss. 2997–3000). In a later battle he rescues Naimes's sons. Gaydon then chooses the *vavassor* to be his only companion for the rendezvous with Claresme (vs. 8787). His choice turns out to be most appropriate, since after the ambush Gautier will bring back the lost princess. From this point on he is referred to by the epithet *prosdon* (vss. 9593, 9616). Although he was a plowman, Gautier has acquired status and Gaydon's love. So says the poet (vss. 9173–176). So says Gautier himself, restating the medieval cliché: *Vilain* is who villainously acts ("Cil est vilains qui fait la vilonnie," vs. 7057). I am not villainous, he says, for I live on what I earn and have never plotted treason. But you, fomenters, felons, you deserve to be hanged. You are the real *vilains*.

Not only does Gautier share the glory of knightly achievement with Gaydon and Ferrant; he also avoids excessive participation in literary conventions. Although he will appear ridiculous in the eyes of a public used to these conventions, the sincerity and warmth of his gaucheness will elicit a sympathetic reaction too. Furthermore, from a different point of view, the *vavassor*'s position contains truth. One may think of him as natural and the tradition artificial. Whatever common, down-to-earth reality the poem does contain is embodied in him, not in the epic world. He is the man of the people, the natural man, free from society's restrictions, capable of infusing it with new life. A thirteenth-century Huron, like Voltaire's Ingénu, he is laughable but at the same time appears more vital and alive than the outside world which has created his laughableness. Gautier's attachment to a mace or *tinel* and his successful handling of them elicit respect for the vibrant, successful worker. Gaston Bachelard writes the following on the psychology of the smith: "Quoi de plus ridicule qu'un ouvrier qui s'essoufle? Et de quelle moquerie l'on charge l'ouvrier qui fait le matamore, qui manque précisément de l'intelligence des forces, de la connaissance des rapports dynamiques de l'outil et de la matière."[28] At times Gautier wielding his mace does resemble this clumsy, boastful, inept figure; hence comes part of his comic appeal. More often, however, he recalls Bachelard's good forger with his hammer, embodying the great natural urge to conquer with a tool. In Gautier's case it is a tool from the farm, from the lowest of professions, which is metamorphosed into a supreme military arm. For the smith also, the hammer, if need be, will serve as a weapon and will always be one archetypally. Employing the weapon is a new type of hero. Suffused with a particular combination of joy and anger, he even becomes a creator: "Par le marteau ouvrier, la violence qui détruit est transformée en puissance créatrice."[29] Do we betray Bachelard's vision by suggesting that the humble thirteenth-century *vilain*, himself radiant with life, also creates by infusing life into a stagnant tradition?

In any case, Gautier certainly equals in vital force most of the smiths of legend. He clubs the enemy into submission, in a peculiarly physical manner:

> Le hiaume fraint et le test li quassa,
> Jusques en piz touz les os li froa ...   (vs. 2400)

---

[28] *La Terre et les Rêveries de la Volonté* (Paris, 1948), p. 52.

[29] *Ibid.*, p. 134; also p. 135: "Avec le marteau naît *un art du choc*, toute *une adresse des forces rapides*, une conscience de la volonté exacte."

Et froisse hiaumes et espiés noelez,
Bras, et espaules, et visaiges, et nés:
Plus de .xiiii. en a escervelez.   (vs. 2487)

Et va ferir Girart de Montrevel
Parmi son elme qui fu fais à noel;
Ausiz le fent com féist .i. gastel.
La coiffe blanche ne li vault .i. rosel;
Les os li froisse ausiz com .i. aignel ...   (vs. 7968)

"Ne t'esmaier! Venuz est li prevoz
Qui as genz Challe fera merrer les os."
Fiert Anquetin qui fu nez de Monfors,
Que par l'eschine saillent li boël hors.[30]   (vs. 9179)

The recital of Gautier's victories is, of course, more than a trifle
sadistic and anticipates the techniques employed by Hollywood
to stem a diminishing box office in our day. Did the Old French
trouvère face a similar problem? His use of violence, nonetheless,
differs from that of the contemporary cinema. Violence in the
medieval spectacular is consciously humorous, whereas the
modern version, alas! is meant to be taken seriously. The crushing of bones and marrow by Gautier is humorous for the same
reasons that Aulori is joyful (*liés*, vs. 217) upon observing how
successfully Thibaut's poison works on one of his own men
("... li volerent andui li oil dou chief; / Li cuers dou ventre li
part en .ii. moitiés," vss. 214–15); that Ogier tortures a prisoner
without being reproved for it (vss. 1297–1300); that Ferrant cuts
the porter's head off and bloodies the abbot's cassock for a trifle;
that the traitor Hertaut slaps his wife; that a treasonous mes-

---

[30] He smashed the man's helmet, his head, and all his bones down to the
chest. . . . He shatters helmets and nielloed spears, arms, shoulders, faces,
and noses: he has brained more than fourteen. . . . He goes to strike Girard
de Montrevel on his nielloed helmet, cutting through it the way he would a
cake. Girard's white coif is of no avail; Gautier breaks his bones as he
would a lamb's. . . . "Don't be frightened! The provost has come who will
mash the bones of Charles's men." He strikes Anquetin de Monfort with
such a blow that Anquetin's intestines spurt out through his backbone.

senger, having asked for a reward, is slaughtered by his masters
(vss. 9028–38). For the same reasons again we laugh at "mous-
tache humor": the spectacle of an emperor and his prime minister, having their beards pulled out by the roots. Exultation in
violence may also help to explain the presence in *Gaydon* (and
so many other epics) of what Theodor calls "Hohn- und Spott-
reden der Gegner im Kampfe."[31] When Ferrant, defending a
castle, casts the assailants into a moat, he invites them to bathe
or drink, while his friend Savari pretends concern over whether
they will be left to drown (vss. 4442–445). Under the same heading may be placed Gautier's famous insult of Gaydon (Who ever
made you a knight!) discussed above. On another occasion the
hero even mocks himself. Severely wounded by Thibaut, Gaydon
pretends to be glad he is losing blood; it is "bad blood," he says—
"C'est mauvais sans qui de mon cors s'en va; /Mestier en ai, ne
fui saigniez piesa" (vss. 1567–568).

Bergsonian analysis may fruitfully be applied to the humor
of violence and insult. Gautier crushing heads with his stick acts
more like a machine than a man; when Charles's moustaches are
pulled out we are conscious of his fixation on their preservation,
the vanity inherent in his person; and the traitors' frantic efforts
to get out of the moat undoubtedly contribute to Ferrant's and
Savari's taunts. Although in each case our attention is centered
on the physical, we laugh for other reasons too. We are dealing
with a literary genre and a century in which high spirits,
bravado, and lust for life predominate. The comic stock figure
of *miles gloriosus* becomes a second hero—and fulfills his boasts.
An entire battle is fought over whether Amaufroi can succeed in
seizing Gui's horse—and the public exults. The beatings, dis-
guises, insults, cases of mistaken identity, flow from one source:
a comic tradition popular and non-literary in essence, which
nonetheless has been enshrined by such literary masters as
Rabelais, Molière, Diderot, and Dickens. This so-called popular
spirit screams out against sentiment and sham. It is often cruel
by nature, appeals to instincts which many of us today ignore

---

[31] *Die komischen Elemente,* pp. 97–99.

or wish to ignore.[32] Cruelty, violence, lust, are indulged in for
their own sakes; they create within us a burst of life and joy.
We laugh.

We also laugh at Gautier. We laugh at him but draw him
close. A warm heart beats underneath the tarnished old breast-
plate; from behind the comic mask shines sympathy, life, and
strength. Bergson would have us believe that comedy requires
distance, a lack of emotional involvement on the part of the
public. Often this is so. But equally often the public, while
recognizing the comic hero's foibles and laughing at them, will also
sympathize with him in his ridiculous situation. I suggest that
the medieval public did sympathize with Gautier, even identified
with him, in the way that a more modern public may at times
have identified with Pathelin, Panurge, and the narrator of
Cyrano's *L'Autre Monde*.

The public admired Gautier above all for reasons of character.
We are impressed more by his "literary stature" than mere
physical height. While other warriors—Gaydon, Ferrant,
Amaufroi—remain two-dimensional figures on the printed page,
the humble *vavassor* gives the illusion of reality. In fact, as we
have noticed before, Léon Gautier considers his namesake
Gautier the rustic to be *the* hero. It is indeed Gautier's force,
the genius the author has endowed him with, which explains his
popularity with the scholars. Yet, as we have tried to indicate,
Gautier is an immensely complex character. He does incarnate
the vital force of nature—as he incarnates the ineptness in military
and social matters presumed by the noble classes to be the lot of
inferiors. It is this mixture of weakness and strength, of rigidity
and resilience—a fundamental *ambiguity*—which determines his
literary essence. One may be for or against Gautier, exactly as
undergraduates tend to laud or blame Don Juan and Alceste.
We can expect a divided reaction to the comic hero. "Du
mécanique plaqué sur du vivant," artificial and natural at the

---

[32] With reference to Molière, see Will G. Moore, *Molière. A New
Criticism* (Oxford, 1949), chap. 7, and "The French Notion of the Comic,"
Yale French Studies, No. 23, pp. 47–53.

same time, the comic hero merits rebuke and praise. In the last analysis, what is more human than that? Is not the role of art to imitate and re-create the human condition?

*   *   *

Although Hugo Theodor recognizes the existence of a comedy of love in the French epic ("Die Frauen und die Liebe," pp. 76–80), neither in that part of his book nor at any other time does he refer to love comedy in *Gaydon*. This was a most important lapse on Theodor's part. How can one ignore the humor inherent in the Claresme episode? A beautiful princess arrives, as by magic, to save Ferrant, Amaufroi, and Gautier from execution. She declares her love for Gaydon on the spot and empowers Gautier to act as go-between. The *vilain* declines on the grounds of moral scruples, only yielding under duress. Gaydon too hesitates to accept Claresme's love; when he finally does agree to court her, Gautier must accompany him. Although once again our rustic misogynist seeks to avoid participating in a love adventure, Gaydon and Claresme invite one of her *suivantes* to pay him court. He brutally spurns the proffered love. Meanwhile, the traitors, having been informed of Gaydon's presence, attack in force. The Angevins seek to escape with Claresme. Although lost during the fray, she is found and returned to Angers—by the *vilain* Gautier! Squires and valets try to seize her but are clubbed into submission, and she is restored to her true love. As we shall attempt to demonstrate, many of the comic motifs which function with reference to war are put to even greater use with the introduction of this new theme, the comedy of love.

Love traditionally occupies a small place in the epic. La Belle Aude appears only briefly in the *Song of Roland*, to lament the hero's death and to expire herself shortly thereafter. No women at all are mentioned in *Gormond et Isembard*. Even in those poems where a female character plays a larger role (*La Chanson de Guillaume, Renaud de Montauban,* etc.) she remains subservient to the men. Her adoration—as lover, wife, mother—contributes to the hero's glory; she exists for him. But her own personality, individual desires and aversions, count for nothing.

Her role in the epic corresponds to a very real feudal social
inferiority, historically speaking, and to a stylized literary topic:
the hero's superiority and invulnerability to anything as meek,
common, and effeminate as love.

Some scholars claim to have noticed a moral divergence between the earliest poems, which supposedly reveal a spirit of
chastity and equality, "breathe a purer air, where woman as a
rule occupies a worthy place," and later works populated by
lustful Saracen princesses who "are not attractive morally and
could not have existed as a standard in any conceivable state of
society."[33] Such a view of the epic is nonsense.[34] Passion, desire,
a woman making the advances—these are to be found already in
La Chanson de Roland. Aude differs little from Heluis of *Raoul
de Cambrai* and Esclarmonde of *Huon de Bordeaux*. Throughout
the history of the epic, woman remains subservient to man, loving
him, adoring him, serving as witness to his glory. The scholars
are correct in noticing a shift in emphasis and tone, however. In
the later poems, even though the hero retains a measure of stoic
indifference, love does play a larger role in his life. But this love
does not manifest a return to a masculine dreamworld of pulp
magazine standards. On the contrary, in the best late epics it
reveals a way of coming to grips with the modes of courtly love.
At the end of the twelfth and beginning of the thirteenth centuries the *chanson de geste* is influenced by the newly fashionable, dominant genre, the *roman*.[35] One of the most important
areas of borrowing from *roman* to epic is in the domain of love.
Even if Hofer is correct in stating that the *jongleurs* adopt external details of the courtly world (for purposes of *Reklam*) but
not the courtly ideal itself, nonetheless a new force has come into
being and must be taken into account.

[33] Comfort, "The Character Types in the Old French *Chansons de Geste*"
pp. 381, 379; H. A. Smith, "La Femme dans les Chansons de Geste,"
Colorado College Studies, IX (1901), 6–24; X (1903), 24–40.

[34] Calin, *The Old French Epic of Revolt*, pp. 166–71; Pierre Jonin,
Pages Epiques du Moyen-Age Français (Aix-en-Provence, 1963), p. 2.

[35] Stefan Hofer, "Der Einfluss des höfischen Epos auf das Volksepos,"
Zeitschrift für französische Sprache, XLVI (1920–23), 169–82.

The increased emphasis on love in the late epic, however much it diverges from the ideals of Andreas Capellanus or Chrétien de Troyes, can be traced to the literature of *courtoisie*. The erotic elements are, to some extent, imitations or parodies of similar elements in the novel. It is our opinion that the Claresme episode cannot be understood if it is viewed uniquely in the tradition of the early *chanson de geste*. On the contrary, Gaydon's and Gautier's loves may be considered from a courtly vantage point, as *amour courtois* in a *chanson de geste*, imposed upon a heroic pattern. Since juxtaposing two world views often appears incongruous, the extent to which this juxtaposition is shown to be mechanical or artificial will determine whether or not comedy is born.

By suggesting the foregoing hypothesis we do not conflict with earlier scholars who have worked on the text. The editor of the Claresme episode declares in the strongest possible terms that the poem has undergone a courtly influence.[36] Reimann, followed by Krehl, suggests that Claresme herself was patterned after the historical Eleanor of Aquitaine.[37] Her love for Gaydon, Duke of Anjou, in preference to Charlemagne's favorite, Gui d'Hautefeuille, would parallel Eleanor's marriage to Henry II, Duke of Anjou and later King of England, after her divorce from the Capetian Louis VII. We also know that Eleanor was one of the leading exponents of the Provençal courtly ideal in Europe. She and her family propagated the new doctrine, introducing (or popularizing) it in northern France and England. It is only natural that writers should use her as a model, given the romantic hue of her personal life and the spiritual and material sustenance they received in her entourage. Krehl further points out the analogy between the *chanson*'s narrative structure and that of Chrétien de Troyes's *roman*.[38] In the epic, as in Chrétien, says Krehl, the action may be divided into three main sections (the *Haupthandlungen*), separated by two *Zwischenhandlungen* which

[36] Bargmann, *Die Claresme-episode des Gaydonepos*, pp. 5–6.

[37] Reimann, "Die Chanson de Gaydon," pp. 89–94; Krehl, *Der Dichter des Gaydonepos*, p. 4.

[38] Krehl, *Der Dichter des Gaydonepos*, pp. 15–25.

contain retarding elements or digressions. Ferrant's exploits as messenger supposedly constitute part of one of these digressions and were patterned after the adventures of the knight errant in *Erec* or *Yvain*. Even Gautier the *vilain* could have been an imitation of the grotesque rustic in the forest of Brocéliande from whom Yvain seeks directions before undergoing the ordeal of the fountain.

These hypotheses may be correct. It is by no means impossible that the *Gaydon* poet introduced into his work contemporary historical personages and events of courtly flavor, or that he was influenced directly by Chrétien de Troyes. But for us the crux of the problem lies elsewhere—in the over-all tone of the poem and the particular way in which love is treated. *La Chanson de Gaydon* recounts three reciprocated loves: between Claresme and Gaydon, Esmeree and Ferrant, Blonde and Amaufroi. Claresme's *suivantes* (Esmeree and Blonde) fall in love with Gaydon's knights on first sight, and their love is returned (vss. 8249–259, 8284–288). Both couples part from the first meeting with sighs and downcast eyes (vss. 8338–338b). The tradition of a heroine's companions playing a role in the narrative, capable of knowing love, comes from the Tristan poems and Chrétien's *Yvain*. Meanwhile, Claresme herself has become enamored of Gaydon strictly on the basis of his reputation. The woman's loving the man before having seen him, before he is aware of her existence, is an old tradition in the epic. We find it in *Aymeri de Narbonne*, among other works. But this form of love does not necessarily conflict with the conventions of romance. Although love generally occurs in the courtly world on visual contact, Jaufré Rudel pined for his *amor de lonh* without ever having seen her, a tradition of Arabic provenance which was to become of the greatest importance in Provençal letters.[39] According to Andreas Capellanus' *De Amore*,[40] love is grounded in a limited

[39] René Nelli, *L'Erotique des Troubadours* (Toulouse, 1963), pp. 57–58, 139–45.

[40] Ed. Salvatore Battaglia (Rome, 1947). We recognize Andreas Capellanus to be one of many sources for information on courtly love. By citing him we do not presume him to be the chief authority nor do we take sides

number of factors, one of which we may call good reputation: *morum probitate* (p. 18) in the woman, *probitas* (p. 358) in the man. As Jean Frappier has pointed out, the troubadours preached that love was neither inevitable nor capricious but determined by free choice based on good qualities observed in the loved one.[41] One loves because one admires. Thus the courtly tradition joins that of the epic; the two merge in *Gaydon.*

The further we enter into the love relationship, the more courtly traits are to be found. The poet tells us that Claresme's maidens are not only beautiful but *sanble chascune d'eles fee* (vs. 8138). The allusion to a non-Carolingian world, to the realm of Marie de France and the *Lancelot-Grail Cycle,* is apparent.

Love tokens are given in the most orthodox chivalric fashion. Amaufroi will receive Blonde's *manche* (vs. 8253) and wear it in battle as Lancelot wears the Maiden of Escalot's sleeve in *La Mort Artu.* Claresme sends a messenger to Gaydon bearing her ring (vss. 8668, 8733–735). In fact, it is the sight of this band which ignites a spark of love in the duke's breast. So too the ring plays a crucial role in Béroul's *Tristan,* Chrétien's *Yvain,* and Jean Renart's *Lai de l'Ombre.*

Traditional romantic love symptoms make an appearance. Love is a flame which sets Claresme's heart on fire (vs. 8380). Blonde changes color for love (vs. 8251). Claresme cannot sleep (vs. 8731); she falls sick: "Sofle et sopire et gemist en recoi; / L'amor Gaydon l'a mise en grant effroi" (vss. 8652–653). Although touched on lightly, these details recall the amplified, classic treatments of lovesickness in *Le Roman d'Enéas* and *Cligès.*

Certain technical words are derived from the courtly tradition. Upon receiving Claresme's ring, Gaydon *de fine amor*

---

in the current scholarly controversy as to whether or not the *De Amore* was written as parody. Although there is no one doctrine of courtly love, no one courtly world view, a consensus of some kind can be reached, as in Pierre Jonin, *Les personnages féminins.*

[41] "Vues sur les conceptions courtoises dans les littératures d'oc et d'oïl au XIIe siècle," *Cahiers de civilisation médiévale,* II (1959), 135–56, esp. 139–40.

esprent (vs. 8735); later, upon embracing, both he and Claresme tremble *de fine amor* (vs. 8907). Their love is termed *amistez* (vss. 8379, 8901, 8911). When Ferrant and Amaufroi woo Claresme's *suivantes,* she uses the term *donoier* to describe their courting (vs. 8285). The same verb is emphasized for Gaydon's visit to her tent (vss. 8386, 8431, 9040, 9069, 9117) and the proposal that Gautier pay court too (vss. 8790, 8971).

Gaydon finally consents to *donoier.* He salutes his lady *molt ... bel* (vs. 8883), and she replies in an equally gracious manner. The splendor of her accouterments, the munificence with which she lives, also belong to the purest Arthurian tradition. Then Gautier discovers the traitors coming, in a scene worthy of Chrétien de Troyes:

> Gautiers regarde delez une garance
> Et vit de hiaumes flanboier la luance
> Contre la lune qui de corre s'avance.
> Oit des destriers la noise et la bruiance. ...[42]
>
> (vs. 9062)

Does not this brief touch recall the famous moonlight ride of Erec and Enide?

> Par nuit s'an vont grant aleüre,
> Et ce lor fet grant soatume
> Que la nuit luisoit cler la lune.[43]   (vs. 4898)

Gaydon decides to take only one confidant on his courting venture. Thus he obeys Andreas Capellanus' sixth commandment of love: "Amoris tui secretarios noli plures habere" (p. 124). The reason for this stricture is easy to divine. One of the most sacred principles of courtly love, in the south as in the north, was that love affairs must be kept secret. The lover is required to act with discretion, lest his passion be discovered and the lady dishonored.

---

[42] Gautier looks in the direction of a madder plant and sees, coming at a gallop, the bright flashing of helmets against the moon. He hears the din and clamor of war horses.

[43] They speed away through the night and are very happy that the moon shines brightly in the night.

Once again, to quote Andreas: "Sapiens igitur, si sapientem suo connectit amori, suum amorem in perpetuum facillime poterit occultare . . ." (p. 20). In such manner did Lancelot, Tristan, le Châtelain de Coucy, and other knights act (or try to act) for their ladies' sakes. Gaydon merely follows the tradition. But who could wish to dishonor the lady? According to the troubadours, she is surrounded by *lauzengier* who seek to break through the lover's discretion, discover his secret, and inform the lady's husband or family. These are the poet's greatest enemies. In the Claresme episode we find one such *lauzengiers*. He is the Gascon princess's servant, who rides to the imperial camp and informs on Gaydon. Gui d'Hautefeuille is the man to whom the spy appeals since he had asked for Claresme's hand and expects to marry her. Thus, although Claresme has not yet married anybody, Gui plays the role of a deceived husband. In the troubadour songs the *gilos* was a standard literary type, often coupled with the *lauzengiers*. He also appeared in the *romans*, e.g., King Mark and King Arthur, or Fénice's husband in *Cligès*. Since the unmarried courtly heroine was as prevalent as the married one north of the Loire, however, we find the traditional *marits* replaced by a husband surrogate, that is, a jealous boor who hopes to marry the lady but is discomfited by the hero. Erec, Perceval, Ille (in Gautier d'Arras's *Ille et Galeron*), and several of Marie de France's protagonists, as well as Gaydon, must cope with the husband surrogate. Gui d'Hautefeuille also resembles many a villain of romance in that he appears ridiculous to the other characters and the public. He had already made a fool of himself, displaying anger upon hearing of Claresme's love for the Duke of Angers, then immediately seeking excuses for her conduct (vss. 9014–27). Later Ogier laughs (vs. 9725) on hearing that Gaydon has made off with the girl. The unfortunate traitor receives all the blame due a tyrannous husband and the mockery due a cuckolded one without ever having received those benefits commonly attributed to the marital state.

Gui's discomfiture must be ascribed, first and foremost, to the personal exertions of his fiancée. Claresme is an active, intelligent heroine in the finest tradition of romance. Described by the

author as *senee* (vss. 8121, 8124), she uses her head to outwit
Gui. Compelled to marry the traitor, she realizes that protesting
will do no good. Instead, she agrees to the match, asking only
that Gui prove his valor first (vss. 8606–609), and thus gains time
to warn Gaydon and escape. The princess even explains away
her earlier declaration of repugnance for Gui, a statement obviously in contradiction with the more recent one of feigned ap-
proval. She claims that her first position was just a ruse to test
his love. Thus Claresme says one thing, means another. In a two-
fold distortion of reality, she pretends she was pretending and
hoodwinks her enemies in a coup worthy of Hardré (*Ami et
Amile*) or Ganelon (*La Chanson de Roland*). Later in the narrative, having fallen off Gaydon's horse into a ditch, the young
woman not only is not the least afraid ("ne fu mie esbaïe," vs.
9370); she jumps out, runs toward Angers, and hides in a vineyard. Wisdom, cleverness, intelligence, are praised by Andreas
(p. 20) as essential to the successful prosecution of love. And in
practice, such heroines as Fénice, Iseut, and Guenevere carry
through their affairs by means of stratagems similar to Claresme's.
One may retort, of course, that it is Gaydon's strong right arm
and his army of rebels—in other words, force of arms—which
ensure the victory. True enough. Yet at least three times (vss.
8437–440, 8666–667, 9272–273) it is said Gaydon will join battle
for Claresme, inspired by her. We will discuss later the numerous
occasions on which Gautier proclaims his bravery comes from a
feminine attachment. Suffice it to say, as Frappier has remarked
(pp. 155–56), the tie between love and valor, the one a source
for the other, is a unique characteristic of the *roman courtois* in
the north. In the *chanson de geste* the two are usually distinct.
Their union in *Gaydon,* and the all-important role Claresme plays
throughout this section, indicate to what extent the poet is drawing upon a courtly as well as heroic tradition.

In many respects the love modalities of the Claresme episode
give rise to a courtly flavor, help create a courtly world. In other
respects, however, the poem stands diametrically opposed to
what we should find in Chrétien de Troyes or the *Lancelot-Grail
Cycle.* For instance, Claresme shows herself to be crafty and

brave, dominating the action like Iseut or Guenevere. But she should also maintain dignity in each and every act, stand out by graciousness of bearing, establish a feudal relationship with her lover (herself playing the role of suzerain), and be a paragon of *mezura* at all times. How does the princess bear up to this ideal? First of all, she cannot restrain displays of anger. Incensed over the traitors' having wounded Gautier in her presence and spattered blood on her garments, she cries *come fame aïree* (vs. 8156) that he must be avenged. Later she becomes *enragie* (vs. 8574) and *correcie* (vs. 8575) at the thought of marrying Gui, indeed weakens her case by a violent denunciation of the match. And when attacked by ravishers in the vineyard, she defends herself with a rock, severely wounding one of them (vss. 9605–609). Thus Claresme does not live up to the austerity of her calling. She reacts in a warm, all too human fashion to the environment, her humanity forming a striking contrast to the dignity we expect her to maintain. The juxtaposition of these two attitudes—the natural and the literary—is cause for laughter.

Even more, Claresme does not participate in the love relationship as a courtly heroine ought. The courtly knight worships his lady from a distance, serves her over a long period of time in order to merit her love. She, meanwhile, remains aloof, reserving an avowal of love for the proper moment. In *La Chanson de Gaydon* the classic situation is reversed. It is the lady, Claresme, who falls in love first. Andreas Capellanus found it natural for the lover to send an intermediary (an *internuntium*, p. 8) to prepare the groundwork; but in our poem it is the lady who employs Gautier for this purpose. She makes the advances by sending Gaydon her ring and proposing a rendezvous. When the two meet, once again Claresme declares her love first: "Car tant vos aing en bone loiauté, / Tot i ai mis et cuer et volanté" (vss. 8899–8900). We hear nothing of Gaydon's lovesickness. Instead it is the lady who pines for her beloved. By reversing roles the poet in a sense makes his hero behave like a woman, his heroine like a man. His characters are wearing, or rather living, a disguise. By refusing to behave in a conventional way, they appear to be funny, and by reversing the usual courtly roles, they demonstrate how artificial are the very conventions being flaunted.

Less amusing, perhaps, but by no means insignificant is the role of eroticism, allusions, as in *Ami et Amile*, to the physical details of love. Claresme tells Gautier that if Gaydon comes to the rendezvous, he will be rewarded by kissing and embracing (vss. 8289–291). The scene indeed takes place, lovingly described by our poet, who perhaps ironically characterizes the protagonists as having been moved by *fine amor:*

> Li dus la baise, ne l'en sot nul mal gré
> Cele qui l'a dolcement anduré,
> Que molt li sont li baisier savoré.
> En baisant sont si fort enamoré;
> Car an .II. ont de fine amor tranblé.[44]   (vs. 8903)

As everyone knows, the physical as such was never entirely banned from the courtly love domain. Andreas Capellanus defines love as a passion whose goal is physical consummation: "Amor est passio quaedam innata procedens ex visione et immoderata cogitatione formae alterius sexus, ob quam aliquis super omnia cupit alterius potiri amplexibus et omnia de utriusque voluntate in ipsius amplexu amoris praecepta compleri" (p. 4). In Chrétien's *Lancelot*, the *Lancelot-Grail Prose Cycle*, Béroul's *Tristan*, and *Le Châtelain de Coucy*, the young lover succeeds in going to bed with his mistress. But with a difference. The courtly hero generally receives the *don de merci amoureux*, if he receives it at all, only after a long wait, after having proved himself by exploits of valor. His patience and *mezura* are tested by a period of coldness on the lady's part. Furthermore, Andreas himself, while admitting the physical, denies love to those goaded by an excess of desire (rule twenty-nine: "Non solet amare, quem nimia voluptatis abuntantia vexat"). He defines the various stages of love-making and estab-

---

[44] The duke kisses her, and she, having gently endured it, is not at all angry at him, for she delights in his kisses. In kissing they have fallen very much in love; both of them trembled from true love.

lishes them in a hierarchy: "Ab antiquo quatuor sunt gradus in amore constituti distincti. Primus in spei datione consistit, secundus in osculi exhibitione, tertius in amplexus fruitione, quartus in totius personae concessione finitur" (p. 38). The lady must slowly, carefully, permit the lover to advance from grade to grade, according to his merits and services rendered. Above all she must never grant him the ultimate favor too quickly. Although Claresme will not go to this extreme, she does indulge in the first three grades on her very first encounter with the hero. The suddenness and violence of their passion is certainly meant to contrast with the more chaste, reserved comportment of a Guenevere or, for that matter, Ermengarde in *Aymeri de Narbonne*. We are dealing with a parody of *fin'amor* and all it represents.

To complete the parody the hero also acts in an improper manner; his role too is reversed. Normally, the lover conforms absolutely to the courtly discipline: he serves the lady with enthusiasm, obeys her humblest wish, is ever a perfect example of gallantry and chivalry. Only by impeccable conduct can he hope to win her love. As Frappier says, "Savoir bien courtiser les dames est assurément une règle capitale de la *fin'amor*."[45] Needless to say, Gaydon hardly measures up to this ideal. When Gautier reports Claresme's love, the Duke of Anjou at first refuses to listen. We are fighting a war, he says; don't poke fun at me (vss. 8389–396). Although reassured by Gautier and encouraged by Ferrant and Amaufroi, he seeks still further advice before accepting the invitation to a rendezvous. Riol sees through his master's punctiliousness and rebukes him in no uncertain terms, pointing out that a true lover never hesitates at the prospect of seeing his lady (vss. 8743–749). Once the war is over and a reconciliation possible, Charlemagne suggests that the lovers be married. The difference in tone of their responses indicates where lies the strongest, bravest love:

[45] "Vues sur les conceptions courtoises," p. 139; Nelli, *L'Erotique des Troubadours*, pp. 183–96.

"Sire," dist elle, "Jhesus voz benéie!
Soie serai, s'il le weult et otrie."
Et dist li dus: "Il ne me desplaist mie." (vs. 10851)

"Sire," dist Gaydes, "je nel contredi mie."[46]
(vs. 10842)

More significant is Gaydon's personal comportment toward
the princess. A knight is supposed to keep his temper and never
reproach his lady. He should be a symbol of honor and bear
witness to her honor, ever the image of *mezura*. We are reminded
of three of Andreas' commandments: number seven, "Dominarum
praeceptis in omnibus obediens semper studeas amoris aggregari
militiae;" number nine, "Maledicus esse non debes;" and number
eleven, "In omnibus urbanum te constituas et curialem." Gaydon,
on the contrary, remains urbane only while things are going
smoothly. As soon as the band of traitors appears, he bursts forth
with reproaches against Claresme. Twice he says that it was she,
in league with the traitors, who plotted his downfall (vss. 9121–
123, 9211–217), and each time closes his diatribe with a brief
remark directed against women in general:

"Molt par est fox qui en fame se fie;
Tout son pansé ne descuevre ele mie." (vs. 9124)

"Qui fame croit, s'arme soit tormentee!"[47] (vs. 9218)

Misogyny is not the sole property of the hero. Other characters, and the author himself, indulge in remarks uncompli-
mentary to the fair sex. When Claresme beseeches Gautier to act
as go-between, the *vavassor* berates her for making known her
passion instead of waiting to be asked, as a lady should. Women

---

[46] "Sire," she said, "May Jesus bless you! I will be his, if he wishes and
agrees to it." And the duke said: "It doesn't displease me at all." "Sire,"
said Gaydon, "I don't say no."

[47] "He who trusts a woman is completely mad; she will not reveal her
whole mind one bit." "He who trusts a woman, may his soul be damned!"

often begin things foolishly and in haste, for which they are dishonored later, he says (vss. 8267–271). Gautier and Claresme herself admit the sex's tendency to fickleness and infidelity (vss. 8300–304, 8637–643). She cites the case of women, loving and loved by good husbands, who nonetheless enrage their men, as evidence that a man runs great risks in marrying a girl against her will. In addition, women must be adept at trickery and are presumed to have a natural talent for deceiving the male sex. This point is emphasized three times: by the author, by Gautier, and by Gui d'Hautefeuille (vss. 8588, 8824–825, 9020–21).

Finally, we observe declarations against love in the abstract. Even in his most tender moments the Lord of Angers cannot resist a quip that man is blinded by love (vs. 8442). The author on two occasions, and Claresme's servant once, point to the folly of love (vss. 8325–329, 9041–44, 9262–262a). Because of love, men commit foolish acts. Furthermore, the best soldiers are concerned with war, not sex. It is said that Gaydon's knights "Plus aiment guerre et estor comunal, / Que il ne font ne querole ne bal" (vss. 10161–162; see also vss. 8703–704, 9426–427). These are epic scenes, epic reactions, epic values, a trifle incongruous when we remember that the two armies are slaughtering each other because of an erotic rendezvous. The Lord of Anjou, when he condescends to *donoier*, will pay lip service to the courtly ideal, in a sense will live and act in a courtly, love-grounded framework. But at heart he is a soldier, not a lover. He reacts in the traditional epic fashion. It is once again this contrast, this superimposition of one world view on the other, which creates the comedy of love in our *chanson*.

The love scenes in *Gaydon* are courtly and epic, courtly and non-courtly, at the same time. They are intentionally comic and should not be taken to represent love in the "high serious" mode. Léon Gautier was outraged by Claresme's aggressiveness in love; Guessard and Luce criticize Gaydon for not being amorous enough.[48] These scholars perceive neither the humor which evolves from the reversal of roles in the Gaydon-Claresme rela-

---

[48] Gautier, *Les Epopées françaises,* III, 635; *Gaydon,* p. xviii.

tionship nor the fact that heroism and romance both give way to comedy. Gaydon has obeyed courtly doctrine by wooing his lady in seclusion. As a result he is overwhelmed by an army of traitors and must flee for his life. Resembling an Erec or Lancelot, he takes the lady in his arms and they ride off together. As a result the horse stumbles; all three fall into a ditch. Gaydon would like to appear the free man, the rebel voluntarily choosing to defend a just cause against Charlemagne; but, once Claresme enters upon the scene, his actions are directed from without—by love, courtly convention, sundry external forces (the ambush, the ditch). Like his rival, Gui d'Hautefeuille, Gaydon becomes a puppet. He is drawn hither and yon, against his will. A living example of the artificial and natural coexisting in the same person, he becomes, for a time, a comic figure, and his love affair is a comic relationship.

The erotic situation we have been discussing is by no means unique to *La Chanson de Gaydon*. We know that the idea of Claresme, as a character, and the general role she plays in the story were taken from the epic *Gui de Nanteuil*.[49] The *Gaydon* poet shows originality, however, in the brilliant way he develops the comic or satiric potentialities latent in his source. He modifies the earlier work's tonality, even while conforming roughly to the basic plot outline. Furthermore, he completely departs from *Gui de Nanteuil* by plunging his brilliant creation Gautier into the world of love. Just as in war, the presence of the *vilain* enriches the possibilities for comedy and the complexity of comic treatment beyond measure.

The *vavassor*'s attitude toward love is largely hostile. Of the various misogynistic remarks we have noted above, three were made by Gautier. He accuses women of fickleness, infidelity, trickery, and rashness. None of the characters, not even Gui himself, appears so antifeminist. Twice (vss. 8267–274, 8296–304) he refuses to act as Claresme's go-between. Later he reacts in similar fashion when asked by Gaydon to accompany him on the first rendezvous. Gautier is afraid that he, too, will be dragged

[49] *Gaydon*, pp. xvii–xviii.

into a compromising relationship. When Gaydon suggests that one of Claresme's maidens has fallen in love with him, his reaction is violent. Nevertheless, a girl does come forward, pretending to enact the courtly ritual with him. She speaks *cortoisement*, for she is *gente* and *bele* (vss. 8941–942) and delivers her message in polite, graceful tones, the exact parallel of Claresme's welcome to Gaydon. But Gautier answers, "tel parole qui ne fu mie bele" (vs. 8950). In a most uncourtly, unchivalrous way, he advises the girl to cool her ardor by jumping into a nearby fountain—just as he said he would!

Why does the *vavassor* object so strongly to his master's loving Claresme? Why does he refuse so adamantly to conform to the ways of the court? One reason, by no means a negligible one, is his age. We know early in the poem that Gautier has seven grown sons, four of whom are slain by the traitors. In the Claresme episode the theme is introduced again. How old is your companion, Claresme asks her lover: "Est il vielz homs ou est de jone aé?" (vs. 8924a). He is over fifty, replies Gaydon. The lady's reaction: "Il n'a cure d'amer" (vs. 8933). Later in the narrative, when Gautier rides in from the battlefield with Claresme, the squires and stable boys, hoping to enjoy the maiden's favors themselves, pretend that he has no right to the girl. To emphasize the point, they allude to his being an old man (vs. 9637). Gautier does the same, ironically, in his speech to Gaydon. I have conquered the lady, not you, he says. If she believes an old codger like me, she will never make love with you (vss. 9659–665).

The problem of age, the conflict of young and old, of fathers and sons, exists as a regular thematic component of this epic. The graybeards stand on the side of Charlemagne; their offspring support the rebels. An open conflict breaks out between Naimes and his two sons. In *La Chanson d'Ami* this increment, appearing in a Christian context, contributes to an aura of Christian symbolism. We propose that the courtly world plays a similar role in *Gaydon*, at least where Gautier is concerned. Andreas Capellanus absolutely denies love to men over sixty and women over fifty years of age (p. 14). The *vavassor* Gautier is all too close to the borderline. Whereas Andreas' strictures are based on purely physical criteria (that love is grounded in physical desire, which must at least bear the potentiality of consummation), we know that the troubadours exalted youth or *jovens* as one of the qualities most important in a lover.[50] True, Moshé Lazar has striven to minimize the term's concreteness. He writes: "*Jovens* ne signifie guère (sauf dans quelques rares passages ...) jeunesse d'âge, jeune homme, esprit particulier à la jeunesse. Il semble plutôt représenter un ensemble de vertus et de devoirs exigé par le code de la *cortezia*, une somme de qualités morales qui font qu'un homme est courtois."[51] Nonetheless, however general or abstract the virtues associated with *jovens* may have been, youth still means youth. The medieval public, when confronted with the word and/or the virtues it evokes, could not remain oblivious to its more concrete, direct meaning. Furthermore, are not many of the virtues associated with *jovens* and *cortezia*— enthusiasm, good nature, a warm heart, exaltation of love and the love discipline—often ascribed, even if mistakenly, to youth? In the courtly world, as throughout world literature, love is a game for the young. Sons triumph over fathers, young girls over their guardians, young women over doddering or blind husbands. Gautier's age, rendering him unfit for love in the context of a courtly erotic, helps explain his attitude toward love and the peculiarly comic role which he, as a potential lover, must play.

At the center of the amatory problem, however, just as at the center of the problem of war, lies not Gautier's age but his status in society. He is a *vilain*. The notion of a rustic or peasant as courtly lover was almost unthinkable. The courtly discipline was a way of life reserved for an aristocratic, initiated elite. Love is based on physical desire, but also on admiration for the good qualities, including birth and breeding, inherent in the beloved.

---

[50] See Alexander J. Denomy, "*Jovens:* the Notion of Youth among the Troubadours, its Meaning and Source," *Mediaeval Studies,* XI (1949), 1–22; cf. with Nelli, *L'Erotique des Troubadours,* pp. 85, 111–14.

[51] Moshé Lazar, "Les éléments constitutifs de la 'cortezia' dans la lyrique des troubadours," *Studi Mediolatini e Volgari,* VI–VII (1959), 67–96, esp. 81.

According to commandment four and rule eleven in the *De Amore* you must not love any one whom shame would forbid you to marry. True, Andreas sympathetically discusses courtship problems of the third estate. But these *plebeii* and *plebeiae* are rich burghers. With what a different tone he treats the *rusticus*, whose love is equated to that of a mule (p. 272). The possibility of such a one loving a noble lady is not even considered. Andreas merely points out that if one is taken by "love of their women" (*illarum ... feminarum amor*), the use of force is not to be disdained. Those *vilains* who appear in narrative poetry—in *Yvain* and *Aucassin et Nicolette,* for example—are rude, almost sadistic caricatures. Their incapacity to understand love, much less participate in it, is brought out clearly.

That a *vilain* cannot participate in the courtly erotic is further made manifest by the semantic overtones of terms basic to the courtly ethos. All good qualities are included under the heading, or are necessary for the attainment, of *cortezia*. These virtues and the good love itself are, according to the troubadours, opposed to *vilania* (*vilanatge, vilan, vilaneiar,* etc.). In fact, the first moral distinction in the vernacular between *cortes* and *vilan* is made by the first troubadour, William of Aquitaine. The *vilain* is depicted as coarse, gross, vulgar in speech and manner, lacking in *mezura,* one who disdains the love discipline and the poetry of its practitioners. As with *jovens, vilania* or *vilonnie* does not entirely lose its primitive, concrete denotation even when referring to a moral state. The word may refer to the social condition of being a rustic or may represent the more abstract qualities of inaptitude for love or downright wickedness (cf. modern French and English *villain*).[52] The same is true, at the opposite end of the scale, for the *courtois* hero—to be considered an aristocrat and/or perfect lover. Confusion is possible, a certain sliding in semantic values inevitable. Thus it is unnecessary to ask whether the *vilonnie* attributed to Gautier refers to his being

[52] In the *Chanson de Gaydon* the following words are used in a pejorative sense (and seldom refer specifically to Gautier): *vilonnie,* vss. 3073, 3412, 3939, 6089; *vilain,* vss. 3437, 8985, 10322; *vilainnement,* vss. 6808, 7165, 7172, 7272, 7301, 7622.

a peasant or to his being a non-courtly lover. He is both. Each reinforces the other, in his own mind, and in the opinions of others.

Gautier himself insists he is unfit for the service of love. He cannot act as go-between, confidant, or courtly lover because he is ignorant of such matters and has specialized in another domain, that of the horse and plow (vss. 8272, 8296, 8299). In reply Claresme accuses the *vavassor* of speaking *vilainement* (vs. 8309), that is, not in a courtly manner and against courtly conventions. The maiden whose advances he rejects echoes the theme with vigor:

> "Mes sires Gaydes ...
> Fait molt forment certes a blastengier
> Qu'il a vilain se fist aconpaignier.
> Cil seïst mielz a estre charretier
> Et la charrue tenir et paumoier,
> Qu'a bele dame parler ne donoier."[53] (vs. 8967)

Thus a physical occupation impinges directly on Gautier's spiritual nature. He is not and cannot be a lover because of his calling. And his maladroitness as a lover in turn impinges on his abilities in war. The maiden reproaches him for being a *vilain chevalier* (v. 8985). Obviously the adjective is to be interpreted in its double meaning and in both senses reflects pejoratively upon the *vavassor*'s military as well as social capacities. She also maintains that no nobleman who cares for glory in arms (Gaydon) should be accompanied by such a person.

On several occasions, however, Gautier defends his anticourtly stand. He declines to enter into a love affair, or even help Gaydon in his, out of regard for his wife Lorance (Aelis). He loves her and would not for all the world be unfaithful. Referred to as *ma dame* and *courtoise et bele*, she inspires him. He will fight for her, so that through her he may triumph. It can be maintained that Gautier, by loving and remaining true to his

[53] "My lord Gaydon ... most definitely deserves censure for having a peasant as companion. It is more fitting for the latter to be a plowman and guide a plow than to converse with and to court a fine lady."

beloved, enters into the courtly world and thus sheds some of his rusticity. But such is not the case. He remains a comic figure and his love for Lorance a comic parody of *service d'amour*. First of all, she is his wife. As we have noted, the troubadours and Andreas Capellanus considered love between husband and wife impossible. Andreas has the Countess of Champagne pass judgment on the question. She declares: "Dicimus enim et stabilito tenore firmamus, amorem non posse suas inter duos iugales extendere vires" (pp. 178–80). Even in the northern romances, where youth and maiden are permitted to marry, the author is usually interested only in their prenuptial adventures. Chrétien de Troyes (*Erec, Yvain*) and Gautier d'Arras (*Eracle, Ille et Galeron*) do concern themselves with the problem of love in marriage, with what happens *after* the happy ending. In this they remain almost unique.

Like her husband, Lorance is a rustic, thus as unfit as he for courtly love. Note the parody of the love regret, a courtly motif transposed into *sermo humilis*:

> "Ahi, Lorance dame bien coneüe,
> Gentil moillier toz jorz vos ai eüe;
> Se me perdez, ce est chose seüe,
> Tote joie est de vostre cors issue.
> Vos solïez venir a la charrue
> Aporter moi la grant crote cornue,
> En la toaille la grant tarte fessue.
> Quant vos veoie, s'iert ma joie creüe,
> Puis vos tenoie au vespre tote nue;
> La vostre paie n'estoit pas acreüe."[54]   (vs. 9089)

In these lines courtly conventions are reversed or completely destroyed. The relationship is avowedly sensual, and it is the woman, the *dame*, who will suffer most from separation. Gautier

[54] "Ah! Lorance, lady of great renown, wife of gentle birth, I have always had you in my possession; it's a known fact, if you lose me, all joy well be gone from your person [body]. You used to come to the plow, bringing me a large horned wine flask and a big round loaf under a napkin. When I saw you, my joy increased; then in the evening I enjoyed you nude; your reward was [in cash,] not on credit."

is presumably more taken by the *grant crote cornue* and *grant tarte fessue* than by his wife's no doubt ample charms. The very notion of *joie* is held in contempt. But as we know from Andreas, desire for a person such as Lorance, at the plow or in the evening, cannot be thought of as love at all. She is neither of great renown nor of gentle birth; and lovers of romance do not employ monetary imagery to describe the moment of consummation. By parodying courtly love and the concept of courtly fidelity (à la Tristan or Lancelot), Gautier only places himself in a still more ridiculous situation.

Our peasant hero reacts against chivalric love in much the same way he reacted against chivalric heroism. From the viewpoint of the medieval public, certain highly stylized conventions are accepted as the normal order of things. It is possible for an outsider, representing a different world, not to conform, but because conformity to the norms of society is the "natural" thing to do, Gautier's obstinacy appears laughable rather than heroic or tragic. On at least three occasions the other characters bait him intentionally or laugh at him (vss. 8797–798, 8814, 8829). They have good reason to do so. Referring to anything as prosaic, as physical as the horse and plow, while others speak of love, is in itself humorous. Furthermore, Gautier's three refusals—to deliver Claresme's message, to accompany Gaydon, to accept the *suivante*'s love—are each delivered twice. And he refers seven times to his wife, the beautiful and courtly peasant woman (vss. 8296–298, 8791–796, 8821–822, 8959–960, 9074–78, 9089–102, 9291–294). The Bergsonian element of repetition is employed brilliantly to emphasize the unnatural, artificial side of Gautier's behavior. He reacts mechanically, as if dominated by an *idée fixe*, whether it be fidelity to his wife or his rustic calling. His mechanical reaction, in the face of supposedly natural, human situations, provides comic *détente*.

Yet, like Arnolphe and Harpagon, in the long run Gautier yields to the flow of life. He does deliver Claresme's message, he does escort Gaydon, and only the traitors' ambush cuts short what might have been an equally humiliating defeat in his *vie sentimentale*. The *vavassor* participates in a sort of courtly relationship, a parody of courtly love, with his peasant wife; he also quite properly refuses to commit adultery with the confidante, to be a *marits drutz*. On one occasion, in reaction to Gaydon's own heretical attitude toward love, he praises Claresme's beauty, comparing bliss in her arms to the celestial paradise, and claims that a knight who refuses her love is dishonored (vss. 8397–408). Even his attack on Claresme for making the first advances may be assimilated to the courtly tradition since in this respect Gautier is more orthodox than the Gascon princess. It is she who acts in a non-courtly, sensual manner. And in the end she is saved from the traitors' clutches by Gautier, not her lover.

Thus Gautier often conforms, in spite of himself, to the conventions of love. Even when repudiating the courtly world, he cannot help being a part of it. The false repudiation and very real conformity contribute to, and may well be at the center of, his comic spirit. He acts in a flagrantly contradictory manner, saying one thing and doing another. The eternal conflict of words and deeds, of theory and practice, of intellectual construct and empirical reality, is set into relief. We are made aware of a fundamental ambivalence in Gautier's personality. Once again, *du mécanique plaqué sur du vivant*—the world of laughter.

We must be ever careful not to oversimplify the analysis of a highly complex literary personage, however. To the extent that Gautier does conform to the courtly discipline, he becomes a courtly knight and attains greater sympathy in the public's eye. The man who denounces Gaydon's own cowardice, upholds the notion of chastity in love (*De Amore*, commandment two, rules three and twelve), defends Gaydon in battle, rescues Claresme and returns her to her lover, cannot always be thought of in a disparaging way. His exemplary traits reflect on the total personality, ennobling the more obviously rustic ones; or, seen from the opposite vantage point, if Gautier remains a figure of ridicule, his espousal of love and love itself are laughed at along with his peasant intransigence.

On occasion, we come across a scene where the *vilain*, attacking love, is shown to be right and the representative of the traditional view clearly in the wrong. (By "right" and "wrong" we

mean, of course, benefiting from the author's and public's approbation.) Such is the case when Claresme's maidservant pays
court to Gautier, who advises her to cool her ardor in a nearby
fountain:

> "Alez vos ent aval cele praele
> Anmi cel pré a une fontenele!
> Clere en est l'eve et blanche la gravele.
> S'avez trop chaut, si i alez, pucele!"[55] (vs. 8953)

We laugh at Gautier for refusing the love of a beautiful girl out
of abstract principle (faithfulness to his old, peasant wife). But
we laugh far more at the girl who offers herself, believing her
advances to be irresistible, and discovers, to her outrage, that
they are not. It is the girl, trying to live up to a literary tradition,
who is naïve and artificial, while Gautier acts in a far more
natural manner. Several images in this scene further reflect and
parody the imagery of the troubadours and *trouvères*. The flame
of love, exalted in so many courtly lyrics, is reduced to the
physical heat of passion, the same drive which possesses a dog
or cat in heat. The cool, flowing water of a fountain, a *locus
amoenus* symbolic of springtime and young love, the only proper
décor for love, is transformed into a very non-metaphoric cold
stream, where one may bathe (!) to cool the sexual drives gen-
erated by the aforementioned flame (cf. Doctor Rondibilis's
recommendations to Panurge, *Tiers Livre*, chap. 34). Gautier,
cutting through the sham of courtly doctrine and imagery, brings
intellectual constructs down to a physical level. We do not mean
to say that his parody necessarily excludes poetic overtones. A
Freudian interpretation can be made for the above passage, the
burning human body (male) thrust into the cool, placid fountain
(female). But once again the roles are reversed. A woman in
heat enacts the man's role, and a man, cool and immobile, suggests the fountain as a substitute for himself. The reversal of
roles gives forth laughter; love in general, and the erotic conventions of the time in particular, are made sport of.

---

[55] "Go away down to that fountain in the meadow! The water is clear
and the gravel white. Go there if you feel too hot, my girl!"

To return to the problem of doctrinal emphasis; are we to assume that the poet is mocking an old peasant, the outsider, who has intruded into a domain where he does not belong? If so, the *vilain* and all he represents would be attacked, the ideal of courtly love exalted. Or is the poet not indulging in a parody of courtly artifice? In this case Gautier would represent a source of strength and natural common sense in comparison to the conventional, literary posing of Claresme, her lover, and her confidante. The epic or courtly hero would be exposed through contact with the new, more vital world of the third estate.

The answer to both questions must be affirmative. Gautier is a foil to Gaydon and Claresme just as they serve as foils to him— in the same way that Gaydon and Claresme are foils to each other. In *Gaydon* several ways of life are held up to scrutiny. The courtly world is seen through the eyes of a *vilain,* and the *vilain's* reactions are perceived through the eyes of courtly knights and ladies. Both world views are also refracted through a heroic prism, and vice versa. The fact that our poet is dealing with three disparate attitudes toward life gives rise to tensions and ambiguities. He is continually playing one off against the others, distorting all three for the sake of laughter. All three doctrines are right and wrong at the same time. They are right in that they embody the aspirations of large segments of society, that they contain a grain of truth, of *élan vital.* But they are wrong to the extent to which they have been erected in an artificial, mechanical, literary system impinging on the free flow of men in society. Whenever man hides behind ideas, as behind a mask, it is the role of the comic writer to dispel the illusion and lift the mask.

In the final analysis the *Gaydon* poet is not concerned with attacking heroic love, courtly love, or rustic lack of love. He is dealing with love and mankind in general. Gaydon and Gautier form an ideal pair of human beings involved in the predicament of love. One is a master, the other a form of servant; the one an aristocrat and idealist, the other a pragmatic man of the soil. They naturally hold divergent attitudes toward any and all subjects. Each, doctrinally as well as psychologically, parallels and pastiches the other. They fit into the great tradition of master-servant dialogues, exemplified by *La Celestina, Don Quixote,* and the French theater from Molière to Beaumarchais. The author does not take the side of master or servant nor does he seek to destroy either point of view. For his purpose both men serve a useful function in the narrative, exemplifying fundamental attitudes toward life and the human condition.

When an author employs literary creations largely for purposes of doctrine or satire, other considerations (psychological depth, unity of character, realism) are often neglected. In our poem, the three characters actively involved in sexual intrigue—Gaydon, Gautier, Claresme—appear more than a little ambivalent, not to say incoherent. Each one acts at times in agreement with a particular doctrine, at times against it. Each proclaims his adherence to, or reserve in face of, love service, only to repudiate his own position a few pages further on. The *trouvère*'s main concern is not in the perfect roundness and individuality of these characters as would be the case in a nineteenth-century novel. They are *personae,* existing as structural entities, playing a functional role in the narrative. On one occasion Gautier will act ridiculously, that a particular attitude he represents be held up to mockery; another time he will adopt a much wiser position, for he now is serving as a foil to someone else (Gaydon, Claresme) whose world view has become subject to laughter. So too, in more recent times, the heroes of *Gargantua et Pantagruel, L'Autre Monde,* and *Le Neveu de Rameau* will in turn appear foolish and sensible, logical and absurd.

Comedy of love, comedy of war—neither exists in a vacuum. The two interact, reinforcing each other to a far greater extent than traditional conceits (the lover besieging his lady's heart, etc.) would lead us to believe. For example, when Gaydon's rendezvous with Claresme is interrupted by traitors, a general melee ensues. A supposedly idyllic interlude is suddenly transformed into a scene of carnage. We may judge in similar fashion the scene where Claresme first meets Gautier and blood is spattered on her garment. Not only is a courtly lady forced into a martial role, but the episode once again marks a brusque transition in the narrative—this time from war to love. The Gascon princess's anger, demonstrated here and on other occasions, is more appropriate to a song of war than of love. A *lauzengiers* with Provençal overtones, Gui's spy, is killed, not rewarded, for his treason. This act of violence and the mocking insults he endures (vss. 9028–38) are also representative of epic spirit, as are the battle insults proffered by all the characters during the Claresme episode.

Certain motifs are peculiar to both domains, to love and war. An incident will deal with both worlds, be introduced in one context then repeated in another. (1) The love spy's murder closely parallels the assassination of Thibaut's messenger in a war context. The former is killed for his pains; the latter, also a *pautonniers*, is given to eat a poisoned apple resembling those he had borne to Charlemagne. (2) The blood on Claresme's garment recalls the soiling of the Abbot of Cluny's cassock (also in ermine) when Ferrant kills the watchman (see p. 126). The princess's anger is as comic a reaction to violence as the monk's fear. (3) When Gautier invites Claresme's maidservant to cool her lust in the fountain, we are reminded how Ferrant and Savari insulted the traitors by asking them to bathe or drink in a castle moat (see p. 142). Both times an ironic fear is expressed as to whether the interested parties (the traitors, the girl) will drown (vss. 4442–445, 8978).

Although the worlds of love and war do interact, they are never completely fused in a structural framework, do not provide the consciously harmonious pattern we found in *Aymeri de Narbonne*. Motifs, themes, whole episodes, partake of both registers, but the divergent modes of love and war remain separate in time and distinct in tone. Before line 8121 the poem contains, for all intents and purposes, no mention of love whatsoever. At this point Claresme appears, and the serious conduct of war is forgotten. Then, fifteen hundred lines further on (vs. 9678), the love intrigue is abandoned with equal suddenness, and our heroes return to the business of heroism. Except for a brief announcement of her marriage (happy ending), we hear no more of Claresme, even though she is now safely behind the walls of Angers. The narrative itself provides neither inspiration nor preparation for these sudden shifts in matter and tone. Indeed, the Claresme episode plays no indispensable role in the development of the plot. It appears structurally as nothing more than a digression, a gratuitous retarding element setting off the more important epic scenes. The *Gaydon* poet may quite justly be criticized for having failed to integrate the various blocks of his narrative structure. Nevertheless, as Horrent pointed out with reference to *Le Pèlerinage de Charlemagne*, a poet may choose to develop one aspect of his work, an artistic level which, though not of importance thematically or structurally, intrigues him and offers scope to his creative powers.[56] The same can be said for *La Chanson de Gaydon*. We should also like to suggest that such an irregular, seemingly irrational pattern is especially appropriate for the representation of comedy. We are shown the use which a comic writer makes of interference and disproportion. A character seeks a particular goal, but the result will be far different, perhaps the opposite of what he intended. Great efforts give rise to ridiculously small results, or the least significant deeds bring about staggering consequences. The structure of the *chanson de geste* itself is being consciously or unconsciously parodied. A gratuitous, irrelevant love story develops in the midst of a cruel, violent, but equally gratuitous and irrelevant civil war (caused by the eating of a gratuitous poisoned apple). Then the erotic increment disappears in an equally irrelevant manner. The poet imposes his will on the poem, demonstrating the artificiality of love and war (in books) and his own mastery over both. His work is a series of contiguous narrative blocks, some serious, some comic. Comic scenes exist in their own right, not just as relief from the more serious ones. Levels of style are mixed; the

[56] "La chanson du *Pèlerinage de Charlemagne*. Problèmes de composition." On some other aspects of medieval humor, see Ronald N. Walpole, "Humor and People in Twelfth-Century France," *Romance Philology*, XI (1957–58), 210–25.

result is a series of patterned contrasts and an artistic whole of some ambiguity and perhaps uneven value, but a whole which bears striking witness to how the medieval poet comes to grips with and to some extent surmounts an old, time-tested tradition.

*   *   *

La Chanson de Gaydon is an example of the epic as comedy. The work stands as a sincere, genuine manifestation of the comic mode, of the author's intention to unmask through laughter much of the world about him. He pokes fun at different classes of society (the knights, the peasants, the clergy) and different literary figures (the epic hero, the courtly lady, the hero's rustic ally) who typify the epic and courtly worlds. A fundamental ambiguity characterizes the *trouvère's* attitude toward his characters. He mocks each in turn, and the doctrines they represent, using the others as foils. Thus he does not choose between epic, courtly, and rustic world views. All three are subject to laughter; all three contain enough of the reality of human nature to merit approbation as well as disapproval. The ambiguity is resolved only when we realize that the *trouvère* is not defending one doctrine at the expense of others but showing how any doctrine, mechanically applied, will enter into conflict with human nature. The conflict in *Gaydon*—on both the martial and sentimental registers—exists less between heroic, romantic, and rustic philosophies than between philosophy (dogma, doctrine) and empirical reality. Men uphold an ideal but must live in a real world. By too vigorous an allegiance to particular ideals they would become fanatics, incapable of leading normal lives in society, and could exist only as heroes of romance. However, being natural human beings, they are unable to live up to their doctrines. Torn between a world of words and one of deeds, these characters vacillate from one to the other. They are comic because of their vacillation, because of the very humanity which prevents them from either actualizing the ideal or adhering to the real. The *Gaydon* poet treats the same fundamental aspects of life as Bertrand de Bar-sur-Aube in *La Chanson d'Aymeri*. But whereas the latter creates a romantic, stylized view of the universe and permits the hero to attain his ideals, triumphing in both love and war, the singer of Gautier and Claresme chooses to play off love and war, one against the other. He will demonstrate their incompatibility, their absurdity even, when taken too seriously by his characters, or when taken in strictly literary archetypal terms (the very terms essential to a sympathetic reading of *Aymeri*). Thus the comic world of *Gaydon* differs from the romantic world of *Aymeri de Narbonne,* as it differs from the religious world of *Ami et Amile.* It is by the success or failure of the *Gaydon* poet's attempt to make his ambiguous, satiric, ridiculous world live that he must be judged.

Chapter IV

THE QUEST
FOR ADVENTURE:
Huon de Bordeaux

Huon and Gérard, sons of the late Duke Seguin de Bordeaux, are ambushed by the emperor's son Charlot, in league with a traitor, Amauri. Charlot wounds Gérard; Huon kills Charlot. Amauri then accuses Huon of the murder before the court. A judicial combat ensues; although Huon is victorious, Charlemagne will not forgive him for having killed Charlot unless he fulfills the following conditions: he must travel to the court of the pagan emir Gaudisse of Babylon, kill the first knight he lays eyes upon at the king's table, kiss the king's daughter, and bring back 1,000 falcons, 1,000 bears, 1,000 hunting dogs, 1,000 youths, 1,000 maidens, Gaudisse's moustaches, and his four molar teeth. Furthermore, Huon must not touch foot on his own land before having reported to Charlemagne and received his permission first.

Accompanied by a small troop of supporters, Huon travels to Rome and Jerusalem, then is aided by an old hermit, Gériaume, who advises against traversing a forest inhabited by Auberon, King of the Fairies. Contrary to expectations, Auberon befriends Huon and gives him a magic horn and goblet. Although forbidden to do so by Auberon, Huon visits the French renegade Oede at Tormont and the giant Orgueilleux at Dunostre. He defeats both monsters and at

172

Dunostre liberates a beautiful girl, Sebille, who had been Orgueilleux's slave. Upon arrival at Babylon, however, he is disarmed and thrown into prison. Fortunately, Gaudisse's daughter Esclarmonde has fallen in love with the youth and comes to his aid. Huon defeats Orgueilleux's brother Agrapart on Gaudisse's behalf. Then, with the help of Auberon's army, he takes command in Babylon. Huon is enabled to fulfill his pledge to Charlemagne and in addition brings home Esclarmonde to be his bride.

Auberon orders him not to consummate his passion before he and the girl are married by the pope. Upon Huon's disobedience a storm casts the lovers onto a desert island. Esclarmonde, captured by pirates, falls into the hands of the emir Galafre at Aufalerne. Huon eventually becomes the servant of a minstrel, Estrument, and finds his way to the court of Gaudisse's brother, Yvorin, at Monbranc. War having broken out between Yvorin and Galafre, Huon supports the former, Gériaume the latter. The two Frenchmen join forces, seize Aufalerne, and escape to France with a treasure and Esclarmonde.

Meanwhile, Gérard, having married into the family of traitors, has no intention of giving up control over Bordeaux. He seizes Huon's treasure, kills his friends (except for Gériaume and Esclarmonde), and casts the survivors into prison. Since Huon appears to have come back without Gaudisse's teeth and hair and to have visited his lands without the emperor's permission, Charlemagne condemns him to death. Only Auberon's miraculous apparition saves the day. The traitors are punished. Huon's fief is restored to him; he marries Esclarmonde and will one day inherit Auberon's kingdom as well.

* * *

Huon de Bordeaux[1] has given rise to a long and varied tradition which produced Shakespeare's *Midsummer Night's Dream,* Wieland's *Oberon,* Weber's *Oberon,* etc. Unlike most *chansons de geste,* it has also benefited from an excellent modern scholarly edition (Ruelle's) and has been analyzed with taste and sensitivity from the viewpoint of criticism. In a volume containing the most outlandish historical theories, Carl Voretzsch wrote an extraordinarily perceptive short chapter discussing *Huon* as literature. About thirty years ago Lawrence Levin examined the theme of *folie* or *desmesure* and its functional role in the narrative. Just recently Alfred Adler has devoted a chapter to *Huon* in his brilliant book on the *chanson de geste:* he delivers a running commentary on the action, with emphasis on such problems as divided loyalties, guilt and innocence, the quest for sovereignty and identity.[2] The interpretations of Voretzsch, Levin, and Adler contribute to our understanding of the whole work. Without in any sense rejecting them, however, we should like to try a different approach. We believe that the poem belongs first and foremost in the domain of romance.[3] Although certain themes—*folie,* divided loyalties, etc.—which form the doctrinal core of the revolt epics are also to be found in *Huon de Bordeaux,* they serve an entirely different purpose and create a different tone. Whereas *Raoul de Cambrai* or *Renaud de Montauban* plunges directly into the most anguishing juridical problems of the day (i.e., wrestles with reality as it is), this epic reacts

---

[1] Ed. Pierre Ruelle (Brussels-Paris, 1960); subsequent references to the poem will be from this edition. According to Ruelle, pp. 90–93, the poem was written between 1216 and 1229; against this view, Jacques Monfrin, "Sur la date de *Huon de Bordeaux,*" *Romania,* LXXXIII (1962), 90–101. Most recently, Richard O'Gorman has convincingly posited the year 1212 as *terminus a quo:* "The Legend of Joseph of Arimathea and the Old French Epic *Huon de Bordeaux,*" *Zeitschrift für romanische Philologie,* LXXX (1964), 35–42.

[2] Voretzsch, *Epische Studien I: Die Composition des Huon von Bordeaux* (Halle, 1900), pp. 60–81; Lawrence Levin, "The *Folie* of Huon de Bordeaux: Its Dramatic Function," *Studies in Philology,* XXX (1933), 445–54; Adler, *Rückzug in epischer Parade,* pp. 257–90.

[3] See chap. 1, n. 44.

to contemporary problems by escaping from them, establishing an ideal world where such problems are resolved through wish fulfillment, where we judge things by how they ought to be rather than how they really are.

Huon de Bordeaux illustrates, perhaps more than any other French epic, the archetypes of romance. Maud Bodkin defined archetypes as "themes having a particular form or pattern which persists amid variation from age to age, and which corresponds to a pattern or configuration of emotional tendencies in the minds of those who are stirred by the theme."[4] The archetypal structure of romance often resembles that of the folk tale, the fairy story, or popular ballad. An epic such as *Huon de Bordeaux* will give the impression of having been patterned after a fairy tale. Such is to be expected, given the role of *persistence* or *resemblance* inherent in the notion of archetype. Above all, the general outline of the protagonist's life will adhere to that pattern established by Raglan, Campbell, and De Vries, traditional to heroic-romantic literature everywhere.[5] True, Huon de Bordeaux does not partake of each and every characteristic of the popular hero: he is not endowed with supernatural parents; he is not born in striking fashion; he is not separated from family during infancy or given an unusual upbringing. Adhering to the tradition of the *chanson de geste,* the poet says nothing of his protagonist's life before early manhood. But from this point on, from the moment the great adventure begins, his career corresponds to that of the typical hero of romance. Joseph Campbell has summarized it in the following terms: "A hero ventures forth from the world of common day into a region of supernatural wonder: fabulous forces are there encountered and a decisive victory is won; the hero comes back from this mysterious adventure with the power to bestow boons on his fellow man."[6]

In most such literature the protagonist must first be separated

[4] *Archetypal Patterns in Poetry,* p. 4.

[5] Raglan, *The Hero;* Joseph Campbell, *The Hero with a Thousand Faces* (New York, 1956 [1st ed., 1949]); Jan de Vries, *Heroic Song and Heroic Legend* (London, 1963).

[6] Campbell, *The Hero with a Thousand Faces,* p. 30.

from his environment, compelled to lead a life of adventure. Our poet provides a structural catalyst to this effect in the hero's disinheritance. In the very first section Charlemagne is worried over the imperial succession. He wishes to crown an heir, but the logical choice, his son Charlot, is found to be inadequate. The emperor realizes that Charlot is a bad heir: "Si engerrai un malvais iretier" (vs. 93). To prove the point, he tells the story of Ogier the Dane (roughly as it appears in *La Chevalerie Ogier*). This tale, recounted as history, as "real" events having occurred in the recent past, is intimately concerned with the problem of family succession. Charlot had killed Ogier's son, leaving Ogier without an heir. Ogier then sought to kill Charlot; but if he had succeeded, France herself would have lacked a legitimate sovereign. This problem of inheritance, the same crisis of family-feudal relations—between father and son, king and vassal—is echoed in *Huon de Bordeaux*. The Ogier story exemplifies in actual fact Charlot's past history of incompetence, thus his inaptitude for the crown; characters in *Huon* will act in much the same way as those of the earlier epic. The *Huon* poet, by incorporating the story of Ogier into his own work, provides a striking counterpoint, a built-in series of structured parallels.

The inheritance problem is complicated by the fact that if France remains without an heir, other claimants will step forward, no better than Charlot and far less legitimate. The family of traitors, in the person of Amauri, seeks to assume the crown, either by election (being chosen instead of Charlot) or by force (deposing Charles and/or his son). Amauri is looking for a pretext to stir up trouble; he finds it in the person of Huon de Bordeaux. Huon too is an heir, his father, Duke Seguin of Bordeaux, having died. Amauri accuses Huon and his brother Gérard of being bad sons and unworthy inheritors (*malvais iretier,* vs. 237), of being no better than Charlot. Such is not at all the case. Gérard becomes an unworthy heir, largely because he marries into the family of traitors. Huon's goodness persists throughout; in marked contrast to Charlot and Gérard, only he is worthy of the honor bestowed upon him. For this very reason, perhaps, he poses a threat to the other two. Amauri insinuates that Huon's sovereignty threatens Charlot's (vs. 474–79). And when Huon returns from the Holy Land to claim his duchy, Gérard, who had acted as regent, finds himself without land. He will be disinherited by his brother, he says (vss. 8922–924).

Although the problem of succession is rendered complex, certain guidelines for conduct can be drawn. In spite of juridical wrangling we recognize that Huon is the legitimate heir to the duchy of Bordeaux. He is the eldest son but has been disinherited—first by Charlemagne, later by his brother. These others have no claim to our sympathies. Conversely, Charlot is Charlemagne's eldest son and rightful heir to the kingdom of France. The legitimate heir, good or bad, Huon or Charlot, must be respected. If he is repudiated because of absence (Huon) or for weakness or incompetence (Charlot), an even more dangerous figure (Gérard or Amauri) will take over. Gérard remains a legitimate successor to Huon only so long as the latter is involved in a foreign escapade. But once the elder brother returns, Gérard must give up sovereignty at once or else be considered a usurper as illegitimate as the traitor Amauri. Naimes of Bavaria proclaims, undoubtedly with the poet's approbation, that disinheritance merits damnation (vss. 2214–218).

To accept the call to adventure, the hero severs ties with the old world; he must participate in a new one. Thus Huon is driven into exile. Charlemagne declares the conditions under which the young man will be permitted to regain his favor. To fulfill them he must leave the territories of Christendom and proceed to Babylon (Cairo). Woe unto him if he returns without having succeeded! Nor is this the only example of exile. Banishment, like disinheritance, appears often in the poem, worked into a subtle thematic pattern. Huon is threatened with exile before ever having seen Charlemagne's court (vss. 240–46). One of his followers, the Prince of Nivele, has undergone a similar fate. He killed a man, was banished for the crime but later recalled. Although Huon's great friend Gériaume also commits murder, also is banished, he is not recalled. Huon himself saves the old hermit and restores him to society. Gériaume's brother Guirré, also banished, is restored by Huon. Sebille and her father, having undertaken a pilgrimage to the Holy Land, are captured by the giant Orgueilleux, who kills the father and imprisons the daughter. Until Huon arrives, she is prevented from returning home. Even Auberon, King of the Fairies, has been driven by the same Orgueilleux from his castle at Dunostre. The villainous characters undergo a similar fate. Amauri is ordered to leave Charles's court (vs. 447); the renegade Oede had originally been exiled from France because of a plot against the king's life. All of these figures, good and bad, heroes and villains, face banishment; most have been disinherited. Reduced to nothing, they must stand on their own two feet. They are offered an opportunity to lead the heroic life, to participate in adventure. Their acceptance or refusal of the call depends upon their capacity for greatness; this in turn helps determine where they belong in the epic hierarchy.

Unlike most of the others, Huon is not guilty of any serious crime. True, he has killed Charlemagne's son: the literary and juridical conventions of the age did not permit the emperor to banish him on whim. But our poet does everything in his power to mitigate Huon's responsibility. He describes with loving care how the orphans set out from Bordeaux to Paris like lambs to the slaughter. He warns us that they will never see their mother again. Although Gérard has had a nightmare, a prophecy of doom, the brothers persist. At the moment of crisis, Huon cannot understand why he is being ambushed since he is hated by no one. He begs help from some monks whom he has befriended, but they refuse. Charlot severely wounds Gérard, who is unarmed. Huon, believing his brother to be dead, grieves terribly. He seeks Charlot's identity and receives a false answer. Only after Charlot strikes first does Huon (also unarmed but for a sword) retaliate and dispatch his assailant. Ignorant of Charlot's identity, he fights only to avenge his brother and defend his own life; his every action conforms to the knightly code. Huon's innocence is then confirmed by three incidents later in the narrative: (1) his winning a judicial combat against Amauri, a combat sanctioned by miracles (cf. the concept of immanent justice discussed above, p. 85); (2) an interview with the pope in Rome, in which he is formally absolved of guilt and no penance of any kind is imposed, provided he forgives Charlemagne; (3) a triumphal voyage to Jerusalem, where he beholds the holy lance and prays in the Temple of Solomon. These form a three-fold, graded ordeal; Huon is absolved in battle (secular justice), by the pope (clerical justice), and by taking mass in the very spot where Christ served mass, by partaking of his body and blood, he who was the greatest of martyrs (divine justice).

Given the goodness, innocence, and exceptional strength inherent in the young duke, how is it possible for him to be undone in the world's eyes? The force of circumstance alone will not suffice; he can only be defeated through treachery. As Christ was betrayed by Judas, so Huon undergoes treason at the hands of felons. He is betrayed by Amauri before Paris, by his host Oede in the Orient, and by his brother Gérard on the return to Bordeaux. Amauri and Oede act thusly because they are members of the family of traitors, Gérard because he has married into the clan and is under the influence of his father-in-law Gibouard. The clan of traitors plays an important role in this *chanson de geste*, as in *Ami et Amile* and *Gaydon*. It provides an element of gratuitous evil, of outrageous circumstance necessary to force the hero into a life of adventure and to awaken the reader's sympathy for an otherwise too perfect being. It provides that *structural* increment without which romance is impossible.

These traitor figures, though not perhaps as striking as in *La Chanson d'Ami*, are nonetheless endowed with sufficient vitality to play their role effectively. Amauri's ambitions do not lack scope. His plan is to depose Charlemagne and seize the Christian empire for himself. He is driven by greed, envy, and sheer innate wickedness. So too for Oede, infuriated by Huon's generosity in Tormont and eager to seize his magic goblet, and for Gérard, who lusts after the treasure Huon has brought back from the Orient. Even worse, the traitors are avowed enemies of God and his Church. Amauri is said to be an unbeliever, as bad as a Saracen (vs. 1759); Oede is a renegade who kills or imprisons any Christian visiting his city; and Gérard, at Gibouard's instigation, sacks the Abbey of Saint-Maurice, kills the abbot, and replaces him with a member of the traitor's own family. All three prove to be as wicked in their relation to God as to other men.

Although the traitors plot the most heinous crimes, they often lack the physical might, or courage, to execute them. Instead they resort to sneak attack. Huon is ambushed at the beginning of the story by Amauri, at the poem's end by Gérard; in the middle he is invited to Oede's castle where the latter also plans to attack him by surprise. Even worse, the traitors plot to discomfit good people through subterfuge, thus avoiding violence altogether. By setting Charlot against Huon, Amauri knows that the latter will either perish himself or, if he is victorious, be punished for *lèse-majesté*. The traitor is well aware of Charles's weakness, his tendency to make decisions on the basis of personal emotive reactions. He can predict that Huon will be exiled. Later on, Gérard and Gibouard play on Charlemagne's greed: they send him rich gifts, seeking to influence him favorably in their cause. Charles not only accepts the gifts but drinks with them in Bordeaux. In fact, the traitors' influence extends so deeply into the feudal hierarchy that one of their family, a certain Gautier, is peer of France, equal to Naimes and Huon himself. Given this family's nefariousness, power, and ubiquity, we can understand why they are so feared by good men; we can comprehend the damage they are capable of doing even to so great a warrior as the Duke of Bordeaux.

In what manner will Huon come to grips with the family of traitors and participate in the heroic life? One possibility, of course, is a series of ordeals leading to acceptance in the community, which we might call the initiation to society. This theme, we noticed, is central to *Aymeri de Narbonne*. The author of *Huon de Bordeaux* probably had a similar idea in mind. His protagonist rides to court in order to obtain recognition by the king and fulfill his duties as peer of France. Before leaving he receives useful advice from his mother. He is slandered but succeeds in justifying himself before the court. The author describes every detail of the stylized ritual preparations for the *judicium Dei* with Amauri: how the two men appeal to Charles, present divergent testimony, defy each other, offer hostages, attend mass (Huon giving money to the poor), pray before the altar, make an offering, arm, swear on relics, ride to the field of battle, and hear the emperor's final instructions. The peripeteias of the combat itself are evoked in no less minute detail. The sword which killed Charlot, a felon through weakness, now dispatches Amauri, a true felon, the incarnation of wickedness (vss. 1851–852). And the youth who had befriended monks on the road to Paris is now aided by them in turn. The Abbot of Cluny gives Huon a kiss of peace before the duel, and prays for its successful outcome. His prayers give the young man strength. Even God protects Huon in battle and creates a miracle whereby his horse defeats Amauri's just as the one master will defeat the other. Huon's triumph is given religious sanction. He succeeds in a rite of initiation—the trial-tournament—and merits the place in society won by his purity and valor.

Huon is banished from court. Our *trouvère* does not consider this first initiation sufficient to establish his hero's prestige. Perhaps he wished to prolong the story by adding more adventures; perhaps he was imitating the two-part structure which defines so many courtly *romans*.[7] If so, however, the *Huon* poet departs from his sources. In the novels of Chrétien de Troyes the protagonist first achieves status as an individual through deeds in arms but must undergo a second initiation, with far greater trials, before being accepted as a full-fledged member of the community. In *Huon de Bordeaux*, on the contrary, the first initiation is intimately concerned with social, feudal problems. When the hero then departs for further adventures, he leaves the court behind, acting almost in open defiance of it. His is the individual adventure, heroism for its own sake. If in the course of his adventures Huon does penetrate into different societies—the courts of Oede, Gaudisse, Yvorin—he himself decides whether he will be initiated into these communities or whether he will destroy them.

---

[7] See Bezzola, *Le sens de l'aventure et de l'amour*, pp. 87–91.

Huon's second, far more serious task embodies the theme of the quest. Charlemagne orders him to proceed to the court of Emir Gaudisse in Babylon (Cairo). There he must kiss the emir's daughter and bring back a horde of treasure including 1,000 falcons, 1,000 bears, 1,000 hunting dogs, 1,000 youths, 1,000 maidens, the white hairs of the emir's beard, and four molar teeth from his jaw. Once these tasks have been accomplished, Huon must report directly to Charles in Paris. If for any reason he sets foot on his own land first, the entire victory will be nullified. Alfred Adler has demonstrated that this facet of *Huon de Bordeaux* corresponds closely to the quest and interdiction framework of the Arthurian *roman.*[8] So often the Arthurian hero receives a *don:* he leaves the court to destroy a wicked *coutume* established by an enemy of society. The hero succeeds in replacing the innovation by a good *coutume* and thus restores a properly functioning, balanced feudal community. However, as Adler points out, *Huon* differs from the *romans* in one important point: since Charlemagne himself had introduced the wicked *coutume* (Huon's exile), he acts as King Arthur figure and villain figure at the same time.

It is certainly possible that the quest theme, and even the particular objects Huon seeks, were derived immediately from French courtly narrative, ultimately from Celtic legend. On the other hand, the quest, found throughout world literature, is one of the most vital of literary achetypes. The adventure which most often gives form to romance and provides a climax to the hero's career is the quest. We may assume that the *Huon* poet was capable of finding material in both literary and popular tales or of inventing the story himself, drawing from his own experience and creative imagination.

Huon must kill a man and kiss a woman. This double ordeal reminds us of how Aymeri de Narbonne conquers a city and wins a bride, or of Malraux's character in *La Condition Humaine*

---

[8] *Rückzug in epischer Parade,* pp. 266–68; see also Erich Köhler, "Le rôle de la 'coutume' dans les romans de Chrétien de Troyes," *Romania,* LXXXI (1960), 386–97.

who declares that one must kill a man and possess a woman to arrive at adulthood. Throughout the ages, conquest in love and war is considered a necessary attribute of the heroic life. In our *chanson*, interaction of the two motifs is emphasized since Huon's victim turns out to be Esclarmonde's fiancé, and the girl the emir's daughter. Thus by killing the man he runs greater risks in love, and by kissing the girl he will face far greater dangers in war. Huon, like Aymeri, participates in a *Brautfahrt*. Unlike Aymeri, he seeks renown in war and a bride at the same time and in the same place.

Discovering or capturing a treasure is a standard motif of the folk tale. Gold, silver, youths and maidens, exotic birds and beasts—these are traditional tokens of victory. One of the greatest of medieval epics, the *Nibelungenlied*, makes conquered treasure a prime symbol of the hero's glory. Not only do great men possess treasure but he who is master of this particular horde becomes a powerful, feared leader.

Are the teeth and hair motifs Occidental, of Celtic provenance? Or do they recall folk tales from the Orient, where supernatural tasks are set by a hostile king?[9] Whatever the answer, we can agree with Scheludko that Charles's ordering Huon to seize Gaudisse's hair and teeth force him to kill the emir, since we cannot imagine Huon's obtaining these tokens without having slain the man first. We also noticed in *Gaydon* what a price the old hero places on his beard, how it represents the innermost reaches of his honor and virile force. Thus by seizing the emir's hair and teeth, Huon proves his own force and honor to be superior to the other's. Once again, traditional motifs evoke in symbolic fashion the young man's victory in combat and his newly won sovereignty.

In the last analysis, Charles's conditions serve above all as an excuse for adventure. On several occasions Huon rejects the suggestion that he adhere strictly to his mission. Rather, he says,

[9] Dmitri Scheludko, "Neues über Huon de Bordeaux," *Zeitschrift für romanische Philologie*, XLVIII (1928), 361–97, esp. 368–71; Alexander Haggerty Krappe, "Über die Quellen des Huon de Bordeaux," *ibid.*, LIV (1934), 68–88, esp. 71–4.

he has come to the Orient for the sake of *adventure,* and adventure will have priority.

> "Sire," dist Hues, ...
> "Jou ne lairoie por vo grant disnité
> Que jou ne voise le gaiant visiter;
> Car por çou vin ge de France le rené,
> Por aventures et enquerre et trover."   (vs. 4617)

> "Sire Gériaumes," dist Huelins li frans,
> "Por l'amor Dieu, c'alés vous dementant?
> Tres puis cele eure de France fui tornant,
> Si m'aït Dix, n'aloie el querant
> Fors aventures, ce saciés vraiement."[10]   (vs. 4716)

(See also vss. 2633–634, 3827, 8513, and 9025). Huon certainly lives up to his claim. His meeting Auberon in the forest is a gesture of bravado which places the entire mission in jeopardy. Later he indulges in side trips to Tormont and Dunostre, escapades which not only again appear to be of no help to the quest but are carried out in defiance of Auberon's orders. Then, having captured the quest tokens in Babylon, Huon further defies Auberon by making love to Esclarmonde, thus inviting another round of adventures. A storm at sea, pirates, a desert island, separation of the lovers, a war between Saracen armies— these are some of the increments which make up the second half of the narrative. The fact that Huon's escapades are not as irrelevant to the accomplishment of his quest as they first appear does not affect the theme of adventure. Huon participates in them as if they were gratuitous; to the best of his knowledge they are gratuitous. He enjoys life for the sake of living, enjoys each moment for itself, leaps from one crisis to another, truly a picaresque hero *avant la lettre*.

According to Frye, "the essential element of plot in romance

---

[10] "Sire," said Huon, ". . . for all your great power, I will not fail to go visit the giant; that is why I came from the kingdom of France, to seek and find adventures." "Sir Gériaume," said the noble Huelin, "for the love of God, what are you bewailing? Know the truth: since that hour I left France, so help me God, I have sought nothing but adventures."

is adventure. . . ."[11] Alphandéry and Dupront have pointed out how search for adventure became more and more a conscious, accepted reason for, and justification of, the later crusades.[12] Even more, it occupied a serious position in the ethos of the *roman courtois*. Love and adventure were considered the necessary, indispensable forces which spur a knight to the attainment of honor and sovereignty. He sets forth as an individual, voluntarily assuming risks and covenants, seeking the fatal moment, the stroke of destiny which will come to him (*advenire*) and which he must accept without faltering. Unlike Erec, Lancelot, and Gawain, Huon leaves the court with a definite goal in mind. But he resembles the great heroes of romance in that he is *disponible*. He will depart from his path without hesitation, for the pleasure of the risk and the test of his manhood.

In archetypal terms, quest and adventure imply a departure. The hero leaves home, family, friends, the world of ordinary mortals behind. He is exalted by the concept of travel and movement, a search for the unknown. Through the voyage he penetrates to the very limits of his world and himself. Jason and the Argonauts, Ulysses, the Israelites seeking the Promised Land—these are the most famous embodiments of the archetype. The critic would perhaps be wiser to assimilate Huon's journey by sea (and, for that matter, Perceval's adventures in the *gaste terre*) to this tradition than to posit hypothetical Celtic sources. Northrop Frye has pointed out three stages in the action of romance—journey, struggle, and exaltation—which correspond to the three stages of classical tragedy: agon, pathos, anagnorisis.[13] Of these, the journey is without a doubt the most distinctive for medieval man.

The other phases are also important, however. For all the hero's greatness, for all our faith in his capacities and in a successful resolution of his problems, he must work hard for victory. Struggle against opposition forms one of the principal aspects of romantic narrative, indispensable to keep the public's

[11] *Anatomy of Criticism*, p. 186.
[12] *La Chrétienté et l'idée de Croisade*, II.
[13] *Anatomy of Criticism*, p. 187.

interest aroused and to create sympathy for the protagonist. Huon de Bordeaux will encounter obstacles on the path to the objects he seeks; he too will struggle to accomplish his quest.

His most immediate adversaries are Saracens. Charlemagne specifically refrained from ordaining a task in the Western world; Huon must proceed to the Orient, outside the realm of Christianity. The potentates he encounters and in whose domains he travels—the renegade Oede, the emirs Gaudisse, Yvorin, and Galafre, the giants Orgueilleux and Agrapart—are all pagans. Indeed, Gériaume, one good Frenchman whom Huon enlists in his service, admits that he has not seen another Christian for thirty years: "En ce boscaige ai més plus de trente ans; / Puis ne vi homme qui fust en Dieu creans" (vss. 2972–973). Huon, who in the long run travels as much as Gériaume, fares little better. After a plethora of adventures, he too meets very few Christians: Gériaume, the prisoners he rescues, Hondré (provost of Tormont), and the merchants who will transport him back to Europe.

The presence of Moslems is foreboding only if they are irrevocably hostile to Frenchmen. Such is not the case in all medieval narrative. Certain late works—*La Chevalerie Ogier, Les Enfances Ogier, Aucassin et Nicolette*—demonstrate a conciliation or comprehension in matters of faith quite modern in tone. We find a similar attitude implicit in the oldest of all *chansons, Gormond et Isembard*.[14] But the *Huon* poet partakes of another tradition, one which posits the implacable, fanatical confrontation of East and West exemplified in so many poems of the Guillaume cycle and the *Song of Roland*.

Oede is a monster of fanaticism; he imprisons or kills every Christian found in his city. Upon Huon's arrival a good sevenscore are languishing in his dungeons. Hondré aids the young duke but must keep his faith secret, terrified lest someone find him out. In fact, Huon survives Oede's dastardly plot through the reconversion of Joffroi, one of Oede's vassals, a renegade like himself.

[14] Calin, *The Old French Epic of Revolt*, pp. 101, 104, 166.

Orgueilleux had seized Dunostre by expelling Auberon, friend of God. He then killed Sebille's father, a pilgrim, while retaining the daughter as his slave. He indulges in cannibalism, scours the countryside for prey, and presumably dispatches any one daring to confront him, Christian and Moslem alike.

The *coutume* of Babylon declares that all those wishing to enter the city must traverse four bridges, each defended by two guards. If the visitor admits to being French (Christian), he will have a hand severed at the first bridge, another at the second, a foot at the third, and his remaining member at the fourth. The guards will then carry him before the emir to be decapitated.

Yvorin and Galafre treat their guests in not dissimilar fashion. Christian sailors are terrified by the prospect of landing at Aufalerne, and Huon pretends to be a Saracen so that his life may be spared.

Given this atmosphere of hatred and violence, we understand why the Frenchmen, once they attain the upper hand, react in kind. Twice Huon and Auberon indulge in a forced, mass conversion of their enemies—at Tormont and at Babylon. Those who accept baptism will be spared; all others pass by the sword. As a result some five hundred men in Tormont and two thousand in Babylon survive (vss. 4546, 6700) out of the total populations of those cities. Even the poet breathes hatred when recounting the battle of Saracens (Yvorin versus Galafre) before the walls of Aufalerne: "What difference does it make that they were all killed? They were Saracens, may God wipe them out!" (vss. 8230–231).

Huon de Bordeaux, for all its romantic aspects, is also an epic of the crusades. The hero, a pious young man, friend and protégé of clerics (the Abbots of Cluny and Saint-Maurice), visits Rome and Jerusalem before proceeding with the quest. He is a crusader and wears crosses on his armor (vss. 4792–794); he speaks to Auberon because the latter invokes God's name (vss. 3436–439); he respects Orgueilleux's slumber because of God (vss. 4997–5002); he honestly seeks to convert Gaudisse; he is married to Esclarmonde by the pope; his patron, Auberon, although a supernatural being of faintly pagan pedigree, invokes God's name at every turn, proclaiming that he is not a deity, only a man serving God, and in the afterlife will sit at God's right hand (vss. 10429–433, 10510–514). *La Chanson de Huon* recounts a religious war, pagan versus Christian, East versus West. Although the crusade theme is not central to the action, as in the *Song of Roland*, it does exist and provides an important functional increment in the narrative.

Opposition to the hero must be seen as more than the hostility of two empires or two religions. Once the protagonist leaves Jerusalem he enters into an exotic, magic realm which, despite a few realistic details added for the sake of verisimilitude, bears little resemblance to the real world of the thirteenth century or the conventional world of *chansons de geste*. Great cities, vast armies, uncountable riches, wonders of all kinds, fall upon Huon's route. Of the five cities or fortresses he visits—Tormont, Dunostre, Babylon, Monbranc, Aufalerne—four have never existed anywhere else than in the poet's imagination.[15] The one real community, Babylon, is described in a way hardly conducive to our dissociating it from the fictional ones. Its magic features include a fountain, guarded by a hideous serpent, which will restore a man's youth and a woman's virginity, and the *coutume* of the four bridges. Furthermore, the city itself, patterned after Constantinople in *Le Pèlerinage de Charlemagne*, radiates splendor: it contains a pine tree, planted near fifty pillars of fine gold, under which the emir administers justice, and a population of happy pagans participating in their happy tasks:

> Mil paiens trove qui vienent d'oiseler
> Et autres mil qui i doivent aler.
>
> Mil en trova qui ferent les cevaus
> Et autres mil qui traient es travaus.
> Mil en trova qui juent as escas
> Et autres mil qui del ju furent mas.

---

[15] Except that he took the name Dunostre from a literary source; the ultimate prototype is the Scottish castle of Dunnottar at Stonehaven, near Aberdeen. See E. Brugger, "'Huon de Bordeaux' and 'Fergus,'" *Modern Language Review*, XX (1925), 158–73.

Mil en trova, saciés a ensiant,
Qui as puceles juent a lor talant
Et autres mil qui del vin sont bevant.

Mil en trouva qui el palais s'en vont
Et autres mil qui repairié en sont.[16]   (vs. 5433)

The pagan world is flooded with aspects of the supernatural. It has been said that in *Huon de Bordeaux* the *merveilleux* is so important that, if it were suppressed, the narrative as a whole would have to be conceived in radically different terms. It is the author's great innovation, his finest contribution to the *chanson de geste* as a genre, and a determining reason for the poem's success with the medieval public and modern reader.[17] In fact, the way in which *Huon* is bathed in the supernatural, the supernatural becoming natural, appearing to be the only possible way of life, places the poem in direct association not with other epics but with the *roman courtois.* According to Alfred Adler, among others, the fabulous Orient in *Huon de Bordeaux* has been derived from Arthurian romance and reflects the Celtic other world, that famous mythological realm containing supernatural beings who enter into our world, which is from time to time open to select members of the human race. D. D. R. Owen, however, suggests that the *trouvère's* immediate source is a lost version of *La Chanson de Huon d'Auvergne,* and that the protagonist's quest in the Orient is patterned after Huon d'Auvergne's ordeal—a voyage to hell.[18] Thus would be explained Charlemagne's insistence on the Emir of Babylon's moustaches (the "three hairs from the devil's beard" motif in folklore), Huon's

---

[16] He found 1,000 pagans just returned from hunting birds and another 1,000 about to go. He found 1,000 shoeing horses, and another 1,000 driving them at work. He found 1,000 playing chess and another 1,000 checkmated at the game. He found 1,000—this is the truth—enjoying young women at their pleasure, and another 1,000 drinking wine. He found 1,000 repairing to the palace and another 1,000 who have returned.

[17] Dickman, *Le rôle du surnaturel,* pp. 55–57.

[18] Adler, *Rückzug in epischer Parade,* pp. 270–71; Owen, "The Principal Source of *Huon de Bordeaux,*" *French Studies,* VII (1953), 129–39.

statement he would gladly travel to hell to satisfy the emperor, and Charles's reply that his task will be even more difficult:

> "Voire en infer, se j'i pooie aler,
> Iroie jou por a vous acorder."
> "Certes," dist Karles, "en pïeur lieu irés
> Que en infer as diasbles parler,
> Car en tel lieu vous convenra aler
> Se vous volés envers moi acorder."[19]   (vs. 2330)

In our opinion, either Adler or Owen may be correct. Professor Adler has the weight of scholarly tradition on his side and presents his case, as always, with great skill. An Arthurian influence on *Huon de Bordeaux* cannot be denied. Yet, as Howard Rollin Patch has demonstrated, the other world motif is to be found with the Greeks, Romans, and Hebrews, in Germanic mythology, in medieval vision literature, journeys to Paradise, and strictly allegorical works, as well as in a Celtic-oriented tradition.[20] It was the most universal of topics in the Middle Ages, a literary commonplace. The *Huon* poet could have drawn his material from a wide variety of sources and may have invented a few elements himself. To quote Patch: "The possibility that an author has added a completely new element out of sheer inventiveness must be especially great in the field of medieval romance, and the chances that this will happen to duplicate something already familiar are considerable" (p. 319).

From the vantage point of literary criticism, the other world appears throughout world literature, transcending spatial and temporal boundaries. It is an archetype, an essential constitutive element in romance: a foreign, perhaps supernatural, realm into which the hero must penetrate to commit great deeds. The other world may indeed be an inferno, as was the case with Theseus, Hercules, Odysseus, Aeneas, and Christ. Certainly the notion of hell provides sufficient opposition to inspire the hero's

---

[19] "If I could, I would go even to hell in order to make my peace with you." "Indeed," said Charles, "you will go to a worse place than to talk to the devils in hell, for you must go to such a place if you wish to make your peace with me."

[20] *The Other World* (Cambridge, Massachusetts, 1950).

greatest efforts. It also implies a struggle with, and triumph over, the forces of sin and death, and is, therefore, bound to the theme of death and rebirth inherent in so much of romance. Representation of the other world will often inspire a pattern of demonic imagery (wicked gods, wolves, dragons, serpents, a wasteland or forest, tower, maze, fire, blood) and suggest an inferno, even if, in principle, hell does not belong in the narrative or enter into conflict with specific religious tenets of the poet or his age.

What leads us to suspect the other world in *Huon de Bordeaux?* First of all, since this realm is denied to the vast majority of humans, insurmountable barriers, physical and spiritual, separate it from our own. Only a chosen elite are permitted to cross the threshold. Now, in *Huon,* the fabulous Orient is separated from the West by a series of most unusual, exotic, and quite fictional lands. Voyaging from Jerusalem to Babylon, Huon must traverse Femenie, a country of great poverty where the sun never shines, women do not bear children, dogs do not bark nor cocks crow; the territory of the Kumans, a savage tribe who eat raw meat, live like the beasts, and are covered by their own long ears; Foi, land of milk and honey, where grain is free and all men kind and good; a terrible desert where nothing can grow. In three of the four regions, demonic imagery abounds; the fourth is a *locus amoenus,* symbolic of paradise, an idyllic spot anticipating the end of Huon's journey. In fact, the land of faith, sandwiched between savage, desert-like areas and protected by them, symbolizes and prefigures the other world in its entirety (also surrounded by an impenetrable frontier). Huon's successful voyage through the infernal-celestial frontier prefigures his equally successful conquest of the other world as a whole. He is enabled to succeed in part by having confessed and been absolved of sin by the pope and by having visited the holy places in Jerusalem. A first crisis has been met and successfully overcome.

Having traversed the desert, Huon now stands in enemy territory, Babylon lying directly before him. Gériaume informs the hero that two distinct routes lie at his disposition. He may choose a route comporting the greatest dangers from which no man can escape, a route, however, which will bring him to his goal in only fifteen days; or he may take an easy road through populous cities, but the trip will last a year. The motif of the two roads is not uncommon in folklore and romance. Among the most famous examples in medieval literature are the two bridges to the land of Gorre in Chrétien's *Lancelot* and the *Lancelot-Grail Prose Cycle*. Like Lancelot, Huon chooses the more dangerous route. To pick the difficult road is a test of the hero's courage; the dangers he actually overcomes test his strength and manhood. They stand as a supernatural obstacle (to crawl on a naked sword, to affront the notorious fairy king) which the hero must overcome. Only by passing the obstacle can he hope to succeed in the quest. The hero's success depends not only on inherent spiritual and physical resources but also on his actual presence in the other world. The two roads are a test and a physical presence, the only way of acceding to the inner sanctum.

In *La Chanson de Huon* the short road leads through Auberon's forest. The trip, as Gériaume describes it, is a redoubtable one: "Un bos i a, certes, a trespaser /Qui moult est grans et moult fait a douter" (vss. 3171–172). It is Auberon's realm, a region from which no man who has answered the fairy's greeting escapes. Between Tormont and Dunostre lie other wooded areas (vs. 4656) containing wild beasts. And we know that Amauri and Charlot launched their ambush from a *bruellet* (vs. 685) or *bos* (vs. 828). In medieval literature the forest stood traditionally as a place of mystery, a locus apart from society where the hero participating in adventures is liable to undergo supernatural ordeals.[21] The forest may be idealized as a refuge for lovers (Tristan and Iseut), prophets (Merlin), or good outlaws (Girard de Roussillon, the four Aymon brothers). It may equally well be deemed a setting for evil. We are aware of the great struggle between man and the forest which took place historically in the Middle Ages, the great period of *déchiffrement*, which reached its peak in the twelfth and thirteenth centuries.[22] To

[21] Marianne Stauffer, *Der Wald: Zur Darstellung und Deutung der Natur im Mittelalter* (Bern, 1959), chap. 2, esp. pp. 40–5.

[22] The definitive studies on this subject are Marc Bloch, *Les caractères originaux de l'histoire rurale française* (2nd ed.; Paris, 1952), and Georges

medieval man it appeared an enemy, an implacable opponent to be withstood at every turn. In addition, the wood retains demonic overtones of a more poetic nature. Owen is quite right to mention that in Germanic mythology hell was often imagined to be surrounded by dense forests.[23] Throughout world literature the *selva oscura,* dark, impenetrable, unknown, evokes connotations of mystery and is conceived as an ante-region to the inferno or an extension of hell.

More ways of proceeding to the other world are to be found than by an exclusively land route. The barrier will often be conceived in terms of a river or sea.

Huon travels by ship to Jerusalem and the exotic lands. The Mediterranean provides an outer barrier to be overcome before all others. Huon himself thinks in these terms, admitting his inability to proceed further (to "find" Babylon, vs. 2788). Without the timely intervention of Garin de Saint-Omer at Brindisi he would not have continued.

Auberon creates a body of water in front of Huon to block his path. Later, in an incident reminiscent of the Moses story, he helps the Frenchmen cross still another unfordable river.

Dunostre lies by the sea. Its master, the giant Orgueilleux, may be assimilated to those watchmen, guardians of a bridge or ford, in Arthurian tradition.[24] Even with the giant out of the way, Huon requires supernatural aid to cross over to Babylon.

Gaudisse's castle is surrounded by water. Huon must undergo the *coutume* of the four bridges; the narrow bridge is a typical other world motif.

Returning to France, Huon discovers the sea to be ever hostile. It gives rise to a storm which destroys his boat and casts him on a desert isle, *l'Ile Moysant,* only three leagues from hell; it contains pirates, Saracen emirs, and other malignant forces unleashed against him.

Duby, *L'économie rurale et la vie des campagnes dans l'occident médiéval* (2 vols.; Paris, 1962).

[23] "The Principal Source of *Huon de Bordeaux,*" p. 137.

[24] Adler, *Rückzug in epischer Parade,* pp. 274–75.

But the sea may also be a force for good. The young duke's followers travel by boat to Aufalerne where they enlist in Galafre's army. Guirré and the French sailors also come by water; succored by their timely arrival, Huon escapes.

Similar to the forest, the sea evokes an aura of mystery. It stands for primeval nature, those elements of the universe untamed by man, hence ever a potential threat. Like the forest, it remains a physical barrier to man's enterprises. Such is the role the English Channel plays in Thomas' *Tristan*. A storm, plus subsequent calm, prevents Tristan and Iseut from being reunited; then a willed misinterpretation of naval signals, the white and black sails, results in the hero's death. A tempest at sea also provides obstacles to Huon's union with Esclarmonde. Huon consummates his love and, as if in immediate response, a tempest brings him to the edge of death. The difference between these two poems lies in the fact that Huon comes upon a desert island; though naked and unhappy, and despite his certainty of perishing like Tristan (vss. 6848–850), he will live and recast his existence.

The Duke of Bordeaux succeeds in traversing strange lands and difficult routes, in conquering forest, river, and sea. He arrives at the ends set for him by the emperor or by his own will or caprice. These goals generally take the form of a castle or tower. One after the other he conquers Auberon's castle in the forest, Oede's city of Tormont, the tower of Dunostre, and the emir's palace in Babylon. Each of these structures bears an aura of mystery, gives the impression of being reserved for a chosen, proven elite. Auberon erects his castle in magic fashion and provides a banquet as an inducement (and threat) directed solely at the hero. Oede invites Huon to spend the night with him; ordinarily the Frenchman would never have been allowed to penetrate into Oede's retreat since all other strangers enter only as prisoners. Christian typology has traditionally associated Babylon with hell and the antichrist, an impression furthered by the *coutume* of the four bridges. Dunostre too is intimately connected with the number *four*. Sebille explains to Huon how he must proceed to confront Orgueilleux: he is to traverse four chambers, the first containing provisions, the second treasure, the third four idols, the fourth the redoubtable master of the keep himself, whose bedstead is adorned with magic birds (singing automatons) at the four corners. Once again we find progressive initiation to an inner sanctum, fraught with danger and consecrated by the number *four* (see *Roland*, vs. 2690). We also find Orgueilleux's fortress designated a tower. The tower has always been conceived as a particularly romantic structure, in Northrop Frye's terms a "point of epiphany" joining heaven and earth, symbolically a place of confrontation between the human and the supernatural.[25] A conventional demonic motif ("Childe Roland to the dark tower came," "Le Prince d'Aquitaine à la Tour abolie"), it has had great vogue in modern as well as medieval romance.

If no other evidence were forthcoming, we should be convinced of the tower's demonic overtones by the fact that for the hero it becomes a trap: he is imprisoned as in a cage. The prison image is introduced in the first Auberon scene, where the king of the fairies immobilizes Huon and his suite against their will. Oede keeps one hundred and forty Christian prisoners in Tormont, and Orgueilleux keeps Sebille prisoner in Dunostre; both seek to capture Huon but fail. Nevertheless, once the Duke of Bordeaux enters Dunostre, he cannot escape without first killing Orgueilleux; the automatons flailing before the entrance symbolize Huon's captive state, provide still another barrier. Within, the place is depicted as a labyrinth: "Tant i ot canbres et soliers et degré / Que l'enfes Hues ne sot en quel torner" (vss. 4819–820); in one hall are to be found the corpses of fourteen men, beheaded. At Babylon the hero literally is made prisoner and cast into a dungeon. He escapes but is again captured by pirates and left on a desert island, blindfolded with his hands tied. Esclarmonde is captured by the same pirates and, though rescued by Galafre, forcibly detained in his castle. He has made her his wife—an unusually refined variation of imprisonment. Three castles (Tormont, Dunostre, Babylon) serve as jails; all three

25 *Anatomy of Criticism*, p. 203.

contain dank, dark dungeons where good people languish. With the desert island and Galafre's harem, they embody concretely the infernal aspects of Huon's quest.

The other world does not always present a frightening façade, however. The tower serves as a fortress as well as a prison and often defends or is contiguous to a *locus amoenus*. We remember that on the frontier various desert regions enclosed the *terre de Foi*, a version of terrestrial paradise. A second garden spot is to be found fifteen leagues from where the heroes left Auberon, perhaps still within the confines of his *bos;* there Huon sounds the magic horn for the first time. Still another pleasance lies within the city of Babylon, just outside the palace. Each and every tree created by God can be seen there, as well as a magic fountain of youth and virginity. Since we are told the fountain flows from Paradise (vss. 5575, 5583) and is guarded by a serpent (an allusion, no doubt, to Satan in the Garden of Eden), there can be no doubt as to its apocalyptic significance in Christian typological, as well as strictly literary, terms.

For each *locus amoenus* a guardian serpent of one kind or another is provided. Danger to the hero lies less in physical topography (forest, desert, prison) than in the actual living monsters who block his path. Oede the renegade, though personally a coward, presents a menace due to the following he commands. His demonic nature is apparent from the fact that he has renounced Christ to become a Moslem. For the *Huon* poet, apostasy is symptomatic of the most fiendish cruelty, a monstrous disregard of basic human values (the laws of hospitality, blood ties, etc.). More frightening, from a purely physical point of view, are the guardians of Dunostre: the giant Orgueilleux and his two metallic automatons. The former is a cannibal and brags that he is related by blood to all the devils of hell (vss. 5142–143); the latter wield enormous steel flails with such precision that even the swiftest bird will be cut down trying to enter. All three evoke a supernatural horror reserved in our day for the prose of science fiction. In much the same category are to be placed the serpent guarding the Babylonian fountain of youth and the *coutume* of the four bridges and eight watchmen. Alfred

Adler is quite correct in drawing our attention to the analogy between Orgueilleux's keeping Sebille prisoner or Gaudisse's guarding his daughter and the monster who imprisons a lovely *pucele* in Arthurian romance.[26] Later, when Orgueilleux's brother Agrapart defies Gaudisse, only Huon accepts the challenge. Once again he resembles Erec or Yvain, killer of giants. The *Huon* poet emphasizes the monster's frightful, disgusting, personal traits:

> Dis et set piés ot de grant li maufés;
> Les ex ot rouges com carbons embrasés;
> Demi piet ot entre l'uel et le nés;
> Entre sorciex, un grant pié mesuré.[27]   (vs. 6322)

Huon is tiny in comparison; their duel recalls the David-Goliath theme. A little man triumphs over a gigantic, wicked antagonist. He does so through superior intelligence but above all because his heart is pure.

Our hero will triumph over the monster. In spite of insurmountable obstacles—desert, forest, water, prison, storm, serpent—Huon penetrates to the very heart of his symbolic other world and succeeds in the quest. Success is due in part to the young man's personal qualities, the mark of a hero. First of all, he is strong and brave and, as a warrior, stands without peer. Although some of his exploits may border on folly (*desmesure*) and would be condemned in a more serious work, the recklessness of youth can never be anything but a virtue in romance. Riding unarmed against Charlot, he succeeds in avenging his brother and killing the *felon*. He defeats in single combat four adversaries: Amauri, Orgueilleux, Agrapart, and Sorbrin. The latter was Galafre's champion, and the two giants are supernatural creatures invincible to the great run of mortals. The Duke of Bordeaux shows similar capacities in open battle. Standing alone against Gaudisse's court, he kills fourteen knights before being taken prisoner, then almost single-handedly routs Galafre's army be-

[26] *Rückzug in epischer Parade*, p. 280.

[27] The devil was seventeen feet tall; his eyes were red like burning coals; there were six inches from either eye to his nose, a whole foot between his eyebrows.

fore the walls of Aufalerne. Finally, he is able to rescue Estrument the minstrel, accompanying this deed with further slaughter
of the enemy. We note a progression in the rhythm and importance of Huon's victories. His early triumphs, or at any rate
some of them—over Amauri, Oede, Gaudisse—are either normal
heroic exploits, of almost pedestrian variety, or are due to supernatural help. But as time goes on, Huon flings himself directly
into the action. Voluntarily or involuntarily he commits great
deeds himself, arriving at mastery over immense pagan hosts
without need of help. Thus he proves his valor and merits the
confidence entrusted in him by Auberon, Gériaume, and the
others.

Huon does not win battles because of sheer force alone. Our
poem was written in the early thirteenth century, at least a
hundred years after *Roland* and *Guillaume*. Its protagonist stands
much closer to Aymeri de Narbonne than to the rough, unsubtle
heroes of the early *chanson de geste*. For instance, Huon's victory
over Sorbrin is due specifically to his fencing ability (vs. 7774).
The feat accomplished, he will seize Sorbrin's horse and give a
lesson in equitation to the assembled hosts (vss. 7781–787). A
more striking example of *escremie* takes place during the combat
with Amauri in which Huon severs the traitor's left hand, leaving
him shieldless (vss. 2089–94). And on two occasions the Duke
of Bordeaux deftly sidesteps mortal blows—from Orgueilleux
(vss. 5211–213) and Agrapart (vss. 6580–581).

Striking agility, mental this time, characterizes Huon's pleading
at Charles's court. He is in a difficult situation, guilty of having
shed royal blood; only an intelligent presentation of his case
stands the slightest chance of success. Acting consciously or unconsciously on the theory that the best defense is a good offense,
Huon begins by accusing Charles himself of having plotted the
ambush. He exhibits Gérard's wounds, that the courtiers be
moved on his behalf. Only after Charles publicly disavows the
murder and promises to punish the assailant does Huon in fact
admit that he has slain him himself. All would have gone well
had this murdered man been someone other than the king's son.
Nonetheless Huon persists in his defense, citing feudal law, urg-

ing Charles to act according to reason rather than emotion. He even points out quite sensibly that he could not have known his adversary's identity—for had he so known, he would never have come to Charlot's father's court (vss. 1345–353). Once he has defeated Amauri in a judicial combat, Charles still refuses to forgive him (on the grounds he cannot stand to behold his son's murderer at court); Huon offers to remain in Bordeaux and have his brother Gérard render feudal service in his stead (vss. 2268–272). Although Huon loses his case, he has done his best, mentally as well as physically. If reason and intelligence could have prevailed, they would have done so. Only the king's fanaticism was capable of defeating him.

Intelligence stands as an outward manifestation of the hero's noble, upright character. On several occasions Huon demonstrates eminent fairness, a sense of justice even when against his own best interests, unusual in the *chanson de geste*.

A raw youth in Bordeaux, he rebukes his mother for not having advised him to render feudal service. We ought to have served the king and are in the wrong for not having done so, he says; we have lost fiefs by just decision (vss. 366–73).

At court he asks to be tried according to the law of France as it will be decided by the Bavarians and Germans: "Au jugement de France je me rant / Com jugeront Baivier et Alemant" (vss. 1203–204). The court's international character was certainly not invented by our poet. Nevertheless, it may not be pressing the case to notice that, at this point in the narrative, Huon still believes the man he slew to be German. Such was the lie Charlot told him. Huon's request to be tried before Germans would reflect an exquisite sense of decorum on his part. He realizes that his case is just; by leaning backwards to preserve the dead man's rights, by appealing to his compatriots, will he be most surely vindicated.

Twice the outcast refuses to strike a sleeping enemy. At Dunostre he wakes Orgueilleux before attacking him; in Babylon he turns down Esclarmonde's suggestion that he slay her father in his slumber. He forgives Charles for the latter's unjust decision (vss. 2561–570) and even wishes to forgive Gérard (vss.

10403–410). He remains loyal to Esclarmonde, not yielding in the least to the seductions of Yvorin's daughter. He stands, throughout, a pillar of the Church, befriending and befriended by the Abbots of Cluny and Saint-Maurice.

Most of all, Huon is the very archetype of innocence. We have already discussed how he is absolved of Charlot's murder. This theme recurs later in the narrative. He is formally cleansed of sin by the pope—before setting out, and on returning from his quest; in the Orient his purity is demonstrated on six distinct occasions: by drinking from the magic goblet at Auberon's table and at Tormont; by wearing the magic hauberk at Dunostre; by resisting the serpent in Babylon; by wearing the hauberk again in his duel with Agrapart; by drinking triumphantly from the goblet in Bordeaux. Passing these tests proves Huon's good character, his right to sovereignty in the feudal world. In capacity and performance he adheres to Frye's characterization of the romantic hero: one "superior in *degree* to other men and to his environment . . . whose actions are marvellous but who is himself identified as a human being."[28]

Even when Huon does receive aid (without which he would not have been able to fulfill the quest), he is to some extent responsible for it himself. Not the least of his powers is the ability to inspire loyalty in others. This most certainly is the case with regard to women. Seduced no doubt by the young man's skill in arms, even more by physical beauty (vss. 5822, 5827, 5829, 6534, 7493, 7518, 7557, 8035) and his kiss (vss. 5728–730, 5881–888), they deliver him from more than one crisis, a fact which the following examples illustrate.

Although the intruder has killed her fiancé, Esclarmonde falls passionately in love with him. She sustains his life in prison, sacrificing religious and blood ties for his sake. Later she offers herself to marauding pirates on condition that they spare Huon's life, and pretends to have made a temporary vow of chastity lest she be forced to make love with Galafre. If Huon has died, she

[28] *Anatomy of Criticism*, p. 33.

says, she will take the veil to pray for his soul (vss. 7987–8000).

Yvorin's daughter also falls in love with the handsome stranger. She too saves him from certain death by losing a fatal game of chess. (If Huon had lost, he would have been executed.) This situation parallels exactly the earlier one in Babylon.

Even Sebille is of use to Huon. She admits him to the tower of Dunostre; without her he could not have passed the automatons. Then, when Orgueilleux turns to run, she trips him, enabling Huon to deliver the *coup de grâce*. She resembles the Ariadne figure in romance, a young girl helping the hero defeat the Minotaur, and the damsel in distress rescued by a gallant knight in Arthurian legend. Although the knight often loves or marries the grateful damsel, no forthrightly amorous relationship is hinted at between Huon and Sebille. Our *trouvère* is prevented from so doing for reasons of *bienséance:* because Huon is to be saved for Esclarmonde and because, having been the slave of a monster for seven years, it is perhaps not fitting for Sebille to marry the greatest of heroes. Nonetheless, Huon's relationship with her is substantially the same as with Esclarmonde and Yvorin's daughter; in all three cases a young man accepts favors from a girl subjugated by his youth and beauty. The meeting with Sebille anticipates his adventures with the other two. In fact, the poet touches on this motif still a fourth time, when Gériaume recounts that in his youth a Saracen maiden helped him escape prison and that he was twice married in the country (vss. 3093–95, 3098).

Similarly, though obviously not for the same motives, Huon is rendered aid by other men. Although he sets out in life an orphan, alone in the world (his father was the great Duke Seguin of Bordeaux), Huon is his father's son, the descendant of a distinguished line; it can almost be said that Duke Seguin, though dead, plays a significant role in the narrative. Huon commits his first great deeds, killing Charlot and Amauri, with the sword and hauberk Seguin had given him (vss. 873, 1603). Furthermore, since the old duke had been Charles's most faithful and valuable counselor and had warned against the family of traitors, his memory is beneficial to Huon. Naimes cites the "precedent" on the young man's behalf. It might have saved him but for Charles's inherent instability and lack of a sense of justice.

Seguin's influence extends further than the imperial court. Because of him, people will rush to Huon's side. Duke Naimes, the Abbot of Cluny, the pope in Rome, Garin de Saint-Omer, Gériaume, Joffroi, Sebille, Guirré—all mention Seguin when greeting Huon, love and honor Huon because of his father. Significantly, most of these are also blood relations of the Bordeaux clan. This patently artificial literary device led Gaston Paris to remark, "Ces parentés finissent par ne plus surprendre; il semble que tout ce qui est chrétien en Asie soit de la famille de Huon."[29] Yet non-relatives will aid Huon: Gériaume, Guirré, Joffroi, Hondré, Estrument the poet, and the ten knights who, with Guischard, Garin, and Guirré, follow the young duke to the ends of the earth. Abandoning everything for him, they all perish in the Orient or at Bordeaux. We are made especially cognizant of sacrifice in the case of Garin de Saint-Omer, who leaves wife, children, and heritage for the protagonist's sake; the latter can only return a dead body to his cousin's family. Garin's destiny is the most moving of those who make up Huon's band.

We refer to the hero's followers as a band intentionally. Like Bertrand de Bar-sur-Aube, the *Huon* poet demonstrates concern for numerical precision. Often he refers to these men by number, whether twelve (vss. 2424, 6098, 9280, 10345), thirteen (vss. 5984, 6816, 7330, 8285, 9815), or fourteen (vss. 3272, 3281, 3287, 3374, 3403, 3775, 3856, 8190, 8210, 8365, 8434, 8638, 8657, 9156). Our author is affirming the integrity of the group. Huon's band remains a self-sufficient, purposeful social unit. Although its identity, unlike that of Aymeri's messengers, does not depend on

---

[29] *Poèmes et Légendes du Moyen-Age* (Paris, 1900), p. 50; Voretzsch, *Die Composition des Huon von Bordeaux*, pp. 72–73: "Die art und weise, wie jeder, der Huon begegnet, ihn sofort am gesicht als einen sohn Sewins von Bordeaux erkennt, wirkt auf die dauer eintönig, und die sucht jede neu auftretende person womöglich durch verwantschaftliche bande mit dem helden zu verknüpfen ist hier ebenso stark als in irgend einem epos der schlimmsten dekadenz entwickelt."

retaining a given, fixed number of men, it appears that the poet probably did not wish to increase the band's size indefinitely; fourteen, including Huon, most likely provided the ideal number. Such it will remain, except for one moment when Esclarmonde herself, firmly installed in her husband's good graces, is admitted as number fifteen (vss. 9156). In this exaltation of the homogeneous, autonomous group, we observe once again a trend in certain late epics away from the ideal of the individual to a concept of man as a member of society. Roland had Oliver, Ami and Amile each other, Renaud de Montauban was served by his three brothers, but Huon de Bordeaux has behind him a team of men. The hero as captain replaces the hero as individual; leadership of a group replaces the more strictly individual concerns of the early *chanson de geste*.

For all his personal virtues and help from other men, Huon would have failed but for supernatural aid, e.g., other-worldly beings and things. Auberon gives his protégé magic presents: a wine goblet, which can never be drained and which will pour only for those pure in heart; a horn, which, when blown, will cause listeners to sing and dance and/or cure their ills, and which can summon a banquet and/or Auberon himself with a 100,000-man army. The goblet serves to denounce Oede, Gaudisse, and Charles as sinners (they cannot drink from it), while proving Huon's own goodness of character; the horn extricates the youth from untenable military positions in Tormont and Babylon. Scholars have pointed out analogues for these objects in Celtic folklore (the Grail) and the *chanson de geste* (Roland's oliphant).[30] Joshua's trumpet at the Battle of Jericho could also be cited. Whatever the *trouvère's* source, in our opinion it is most significant that, although one of the objects serves largely to provide a spiritual and moral test, the other to summon reinforcements, both may be considered, at least symbolically, sources of abundance. They supply the hero with riches in the guise of food, wine, or men. Wine from the goblet is said to resemble a

---

[30] Voretzsch, *Die Composition des Huon von Bordeaux*, pp. 125–30; Scheludko, "Neues über Huon de Bordeaux," p. 378.

fountain (vs. 4172); both goblet and horn are recognized by Freudian analysis to be feminine images. In our text they indicate that the hero has successfully taken command of Nature and has at his fingertips the bounty, grace, and energy which Nature, depicted as the eternal feminine, bestows on men.[31]

Huon receives horn and goblet from his benefactor Auberon; from his enemy Orgueilleux he takes a hauberk and a ring. The hauberk, of incredible lightness, provides its wearer with immunity against fire, water, and the sword. Huon uses it to great advantage against Orgueilleux himself and his brother Agrapart. Like the goblet, it can only be worn by a mortal free from sin; with both horn and goblet it symbolizes the protection Huon receives and serves as a further image of his own innocence—an internal, spiritual force which protects him from temptation, granting him, as it were, the strength of ten. The ring, on the other hand, bears no overt supernatural connotations. Since it had been bestowed upon Orgueilleux by Gaudisse as a gage of their friendship and of the emir's dependence on him, it will provide safe conduct for anyone in Gaudisse's realm. Huon uses the ring to cross three of the four bridges into Babylon. The tradition of the signet ring in the Orient is an old one; no less important is the ring as love token in courtly narrative. But in our poem the ring takes on additional overtones. Representing the giant's power and sovereignty, in Huon's hands it confirms victory over Orgueilleux and the bearer's own right to command. Yet, in that it permits him to traverse the four bridges, the ring assumes quasi-magical traits. It becomes, symbolically, a talisman without which passage to the other world is impossible and as such it guarantees once again the regard with which our protagonist is held by the supernatural.

---

[31] See Campbell, *The Hero with a Thousand Faces,* interpreting an Irish legend, p. 173: "The motif (derived from an infantile fantasy) of the inexhaustible dish, symbolizing the perpetual life-giving, form-building powers of the universal source, is a fairy-tale counterpart of the mythological image of the cornucopian banquet of the gods." For the structural role of the horn in *La Chanson de Roland* see Stephen G. Nichols, Jr., "Roland's Echoing Horn," *Romance Notes,* V (1963), 78–84.

Participating in both the human and animal world stands Malabron. A fairy knight and vassal of Auberon, he has been transformed into a sea creature (*luiton*) for having offended his master. Twice he intercedes with Auberon on Huon's behalf, then comes to the youth's aid; in each case travel by water is involved. Malabron carries Huon on his back across the Red Sea from Dunostre to a place near Babylon, later from the desert isle to dry land near Yvorin's capital. Malabron renders these services at great personal sacrifice. Although he had been condemned to remain thirty years a sea monster, for the privilege of aiding Huon he is sentenced to an additional thirty-eight and twenty-eight years. This water sprite's aid to man emphasizes again the devotion which the hero inspires. But with Malabron the spirit of nature itself takes part in his adventures; even the water barrier can be rendered amicable. Huon needs supernatural help and, more than help, sympathy, intercession, expiation. Malabron provides the superhuman atonement essential to the completion of the quest.

Little indeed, however, is his contribution compared to Auberon's. The King of the Fairies is without doubt the chief factor in Huon's success and, aesthetically speaking, the most striking character in the epic, destined to acquire greater fame than the young duke himself.[32] In the first two *laisses* we are told his father was Julius Caesar, his mother Morgain la Fay; thus he partakes of the classical and Arthurian worlds, inheriting the power and wisdom of both (vss. 8–18, 3513–517). Auberon is a great sorcerer, his powers legion. First of all, he bestows magic gifts (horn and goblet) on his protégé; even the hauberk is derived originally from him since he lost it to Orgueilleux who in turn loses it to Huon. Secondly, the good magician possesses a bow and arrow capable of bringing down the fastest game, and a throne which will not burn and renders the man sitting on it immune to poison. He also has the ability to tame animals, build

---

[32] Martin de Riquer writes in *Los cantares de gesta franceses* (Madrid, 1952), p. 326: "La creación más personal y de mayor interés del poeta que escribió este cantar es la figura del mágico enano Auberón...."

a castle, provide food, unleash a tempest, or create a river barrier anywhere he wishes, instantaneously. He will do anything to persuade Huon to greet him and accept his protection. He can also presumably withdraw or destroy any of the above mentioned; he does send a magic rod to divide a river (the Moses and Red Sea motif) which Huon wishes to pass. Furthermore, Auberon can transport himself and his men instantaneously anywhere on earth. Thus he follows Huon in the forest and appears three times with an army—at Tormont, Babylon, and Bordeaux. In the last city he will also reveal Gaudisse's teeth and hair, which Gérard had hidden, and with equal swiftness will hang the traitors from a gibbet.

As for knowledge, Auberon sees with perfect clarity the past, present, and future. On first meeting Huon, he is immediately cognizant of the young man's identity and past history—his father's death, his trials at court, and the terms of his exile. For the present, he miraculously sees Huon on his desert island or in chains before the king at Bordeaux. And the fairy king weeps several times at the thought of his protégé's future anguish, the pains he will undergo before the story's end. In fact, despite his claims to the contrary, Auberon appears as a divinity or divinity figure, serving God's will, possessing the secrets of heaven, and assured of one day sitting next to God (vss. 3579–583).[33]

Physically, Huon's protector is said to be only three feet tall. He is by no means pleased with his height nor with the fact he was ordained to be hunchbacked. On at least eight occasions we find the words *nains bocerés* or *nains boçus* directed against him (vss. 3275, 3305, 3523, 5910, 6797, 7168, 10231, 10448). But in compensation Auberon was endowed with extraordinary personal beauty. He is small, says the poet, but as beautiful as the summer sun (vss. 3177, 3239, 3532, 10227, 10238, 10457). The comparison between Auberon's splendor and the sun's, with the concurrent notion that the people who behold him are affected as by the sun's rays, occurs several times.

---

[33] For an interesting analogy with a legendary Christ figure, see Adler, *Rückzug in epischer Parade,* pp. 262–63.

Scholars have interpreted this fascinatingly enigmatic figure in various ways. Auberon goes back, so it is claimed, to a pagan god of light, a Germanic god of the underworld, a Celtic Merlin Sylvester, dwarf King of the Antipodes, or any of the many other hypothetical Celtic prototypes for Chrétien's Guivret le Petit and Wauchier de Denain's *petit chevalier*.[34] With far more cogency, Scheludko points out the analogy between our story and folk tales where an unfriendly demon is forced to give the hero assistance.[35] The demon had posed the hero questions and because of the hero's refusal to answer is compelled to pay a high price for eventual compliance. The defeated god then becomes the hero's servant and helps him in the pursuit of his quest. Among literary examples Scheludko cites Jacob and the angel in the Old Testament, Menelaus and Proteus in Greek mythology, and Sigfried and Alberich in medieval German literature. The poet may have taken some such folk tradition as a source for his poem, transforming it from top to bottom in the process.

Rather than embody hostile forces, Auberon may equally well represent the traditional non-hostile divine agent acting on the hero's behalf. He stands as a protective figure, an outside catalytic character, not unlike Athena, Venus, or for that matter Loki and Merlin. In the words of Northrop Frye (not referring to *Huon de Bordeaux*): "In the analogy of innocence the divine or spiritual figures are usually parental, wise old men with magical powers . . ." Or Joseph Campbell: "In fairy lore it may be some little fellow of the wood, some wizard, hermit, shepherd, or smith, who appears, to supply the amulets and advice that the hero will require."[36] Thus is to be explained Auberon's association with the forest. He is a nature figure, an outsider to society, symbolizing the benign, protective power of destiny. His physical deformities are equally traditional, to be found in all literature.

---

[34] One of the most recent exponents of the Celtic thesis is Vernon A. Harward, Jr., *The Dwarf of Arthurian Romance and Celtic Tradition* (Leiden, 1958).

[35] "Neues über Huon de Bordeaux," pp. 376–77.

[36] Frye, *Anatomy of Criticism*, p. 151; Campbell, *The Hero with a Thousand Faces*, p. 72.

Archetypally, the gifts of power and wisdom are accompanied by a corresponding mutilation or handicap. Samson was blinded, Tiresias was blinded and/or made into a woman, Vulcan had a club foot, etc. Poets teach us that perfection is denied the human race, and any man who achieves distinction in one facet of life must pay a penalty in others. Finally, if the *trouvère* likens Auberon to the sun, it is not because of a sun-god tradition in the *chanson de geste* or the *roman courtois* (there is none) but because, archetypally, his power, wisdom, and beauty are to be compared with the sun's. He manifests the light of day, his presence in the story is that of the sun, blessing and fecundating all it touches. A pattern of oppositions runs through the poem: good and bad, heaven and hell, life and death—light and darkness. The darkness of the forest and of Saracen prisons evokes a static, immobile, deathlike state; in contrast stands a world of movement and light symbolized by Auberon, the sun figure. Light plays almost an anagogic role in this epic, and the *Huon* poet, *mutatis mutandis*, anticipates the archetypal patterns of light imagery we find in such Renaissance masters as Spenser and D'Aubigné.

A problem which has puzzled scholars for generations concerns Auberon, why the fairy king and sun figure feels tenderness for Huon, a perfect stranger, why he voluntarily and thanklessly works so hard on his behalf. One theory claims that in the *trouvère*'s source, derived ultimately from Germanic legend, Auberon was indeed the hero's father and aided his son in a *Brautfahrt;* the thirteenth-century poet, for whatever reason, would have eliminated the family bond from his story. Thus Gaston Paris: "Je pense que c'est notre poète qui a effacé du récit la paternité d'Auberon à l'égard de Huon. Il a eu pour cela des raisons qu'on devine et qui sont bonnes; mais la faveur dont Auberon entoure Huon devient alors assez inexplicable."[37] Although the Germanic hypothesis has been totally discredited,[38]

[37] *Poèmes et Légendes du Moyen-Age,* p. 82; also "Sur *Huon de Bordeaux,*" *Romania,* XXIX (1900), 209–18, esp. 216.

[38] Ruelle, *Huon de Bordeaux,* pp. 68–69.

we can retain the notion of Auberon, not as a real father but as a father figure or father surrogate, i.e., a friend, magician, or old, wise man who acts as father to the hero (often an actual or presumed orphan). This tradition is widespread in literature; it provides inspiration for Dante's *Commedia*, Corneille's *Illusion Comique*, and Balzac's *Père Goriot*. The *chanson de geste* as a whole is grounded on a symbolic father cult, with father figures such as Charlemagne and the older Guillaume and Aymeri assisting their actual or surrogate sons (Roland, Vivien, Gui, Guichard, the young Guillaume and Aymeri). The relationship between older and younger man in these poems is much greater, more affective in emotional terms, than between man and woman.[39] In *La Chanson de Huon* the hero has lost his real father. He is, symbolically at least, searching for a father and has not been able to find one in Charlemagne, the traditional father of his people. Since Auberon, presumably unmarried, has equal need of a son and heir, it should not surprise us when, at the poem's close, Huon "becomes" his son and inherits his fairy kingdom. He will replace his new father and presumably become a father in turn. Furthermore, Auberon is depicted not only as a king but as a kind of god and sun figure. We are aware of the long-standing tradition that ascribes characteristics of the sun to the divinity and, conversely, of a father to the sun. This conception, central to the elaboration of some of the most striking Indo-European myths, gives rise to poetic overtones in our *chanson*.

Huon's most dangerous adventure, the sea voyage, partakes of an archetype we have seen in *Ami et Amile*: death and rebirth. We perceive the young man buffeted by a storm, set adrift on a plank, and left naked and abandoned on a desert isle, how pirates tie the hero's hands and feet and bind his eyes, leaving him blind and naked, how even when rescued by Malabron and placed on shore, he remains penniless and naked. Alfred Adler has written a penetrating commentary on this portion of the

[39] This aspect of medieval literature has been touched on brilliantly by Robert Greer Cohn, *The Writer's Way in France* (Philadelphia, 1960), pp. 83–85, 112–14.

narrative;[40] he has drawn interesting conclusions regarding Huon's existential predicament, his fall to the very bottom of the knightly hierarchy and subsequent right to call into question both the hierarchy and the values it upholds. In our opinion the episode is significant also from an archetypal point of view. We have spoken before of the sea as a barrier and road to fulfillment; the storm at sea is also symbolic of a life and death struggle. Since the ocean receives the hero into its depths, it evokes the notion of death, but as a fount of nature it also evokes life, the eternal mother. Huon's nakedness at sea implies, in Freudian terms, a return to the mother's womb, a movement into the depths of nature and existence. Set down naked but whole on the island (a point of epiphany), "naked as the day he was born" (vss. 6841, 6868, 6909, 7176, 7192, 7405, 7984), Huon experiences a symbolic death and rebirth. The young hero risks dying, even expects to die, but survives to participate in a new life. He has lost what status he possessed in the old world but has been cleansed of the dross, inauthenticity, and less-than-perfect attainment implied in it. This episode of ritual death and second birth must not be interpreted as an accretion adding little to the narrative, introduced merely to please a not overly sophisticated public. Instead, the poet should be given credit for his tempest scene, even if he was not aware of its significance in modern terms. It contributes an important link in the pattern of Huon's initiation. Victory in Paris was not sufficient to prove his exceptional heroic qualities. Victory at Babylon also does not suffice. Huon must come to grips with the most elemental forces of nature and be cleansed of the past before his initiation and apotheosis have been completed.

In so much of heroic literature—the myths of Jason and Moses, the *Odyssey*, *Gilgamesh*, and *Lusiads*—death and rebirth are intimately linked to the notion of withdrawal and return. The protagonist has left home to undertake certain adventures; his victory is consecrated by a triumphant return to the point of departure. Although such is the case in *Huon de Bordeaux*, the

[40] *Rückzug in epischer Parade*, pp. 258–60, 280.

hero's return is complicated by Gérard's and Gibouard's efforts to prevent him from claiming his heritage. The last section of the epic is devoted to this question. But once again we must not consider such episodes to be *hors d'oeuvre*. Even though Huon's triumphs are essential to the fulfillment of his quest, their recognition and public acceptance is every bit as important. Hence a refusal of recognition by villains of the same ilk as the Babylonian heathens; hence the difficult but successful discomfiture of said villains again with Auberon's help.

Huon's return establishes his sovereignty once and for all. He is acclaimed as Duke of Bordeaux, rightful heir to his father's land. The orphan is no longer disinherited, his birthright no longer denied. He finds a place in the community in much the same way as Chrétien de Troyes's heroes or Guillaume d'Orange and Aymeri de Narbonne in *chansons de geste*. Yet the story does not end here; the problems raised in the narrative cannot be disposed of quite so easily. Huon, a feudal baron mistreated by the king, a spiritual cousin of Girard de Roussillon, Ogier the Dane, and Garin le Lorrain, will never be left in peace. The king remains weak and/or unjust. And Huon, for all his glory, remains independent of and dependent on him at the same time. A way exists, nonetheless, for the poet to alleviate his hero's predicament. Huon has achieved status in two realms—the supposedly real domain of the *chanson de geste*, and the patently fictional one where Auberon holds sway. In the end he is offered sovereignty in Auberon's kingdom—and accepts. By returning to the symbolic other world, he chooses to abandon the Carolingian world altogether. Like so many heroes of medieval narrative poetry, he resolves the problems of the day by escaping to a realm of fantasy.

Acceptance and renunciation of political sovereignty extends to the world of finance. In the poem's early scenes Huon is depicted as an extremely wealthy young man. Duke Seguin, the richest of Charles's barons, had regaled the court and served Charles in war practically without remuneration (vss. 253–77). The young duke, who has inherited his father's land, brings to Paris a treasure worthy of Seguin's memory (vss. 535–50). But soon he is despoiled of his riches and exiled. This wealth, for that matter wealth in general, will cause suffering in him and others. We know that both Charles and Charlot are attracted by Huon's fortune and the power of his fief, that they mistreat him to seize it; the emperor does not hesitate to accept bribes from Gérard, "regent" of Bordeaux. Charlemagne is also interested in the Babylonian treasure since one of the conditions for Huon's rehabilitation is that he return bearing tribute. Eager for the same treasure is Gérard, who sacks an abbey to enjoy the spoils his brother has conquered. Even Oede the Renegade, a rich man in his own right, is infuriated by Huon's success in a potlatch ritual. It can be shown that all those possessing fabulous riches (Oede, Orgueilleux, Gaudisse) are eager to increase their wealth. They, as well as Charlemagne, Gérard, and Gibouard, are degraded by *cupiditas*. As in so many *chansons*, including the blatantly comic *Pèlerinage de Charlemagne*, an exotic Oriental world stands as the fount and image both of incalculable wealth and spiritual and moral decadence. The crusaders, admittedly lacking in refinements when compared to their Saracen counterparts, are shown to surpass them ethically. Our *trouvère*'s variation on this theme is to depict most of the Western knights as equally corrupt, equally decadent, equally lacking in spiritual values.

Unlike the others, Huon is not greedy for men's riches. Before the *judicium Dei* he gives so readily to the poor that they bless him in return: "Cil te garisse qui ens la crois fu mis / Et il te laist a joie revenir" (vss. 1500–501). He declines the pope's financial offers (vss. 2607–609). Auberon does not offer him wealth nor will he ask for it. At Tormont he gets into trouble for having humiliated Oede by inviting the city's poor to his table. Naked and suffering, he becomes Estrument's valet, serving him for a bare subsistence, and later rides an old horse into battle. Once strongholds have been conquered, Huon does not retain them for himself. Tormont is bestowed upon Joffroi and Hondré; Babylon is given to Sebille, who marries a noble Saracen convert. Huon even demonstrates a willingness to share his own land with Gérard. He offers to give him the city of Bordeaux but to no avail (vss. 9235-251), and when he receives the call to Auberon's realm, Bordeaux will descend to his friend Gériaume. The theme of renunciation or self-sufficiency is echoed in a particularly touching manner when the sailors who have landed at Aufalerne declare they will transport Huon and his men to a Christian port *gratis* for the love of God (vss. 8648-653).

At various times Huon is said to have fallen into *povreté*—meaning wretchedness as well as poverty (vss. 3751, 4420, 4565, 5299). Uncorrupted by wealth, he is even capable of undergoing and overcoming deprivation. Because he can survive without riches, Huon alone is worthy of possessing them. The final display of treasure in Bordeaux, before Charles's very eyes, is a sign of victory, of release from *povreté*. It also contributes again to the expression of Huon's newly attained sovereignty.

Last but not least, he has attained sovereignty over women. After experiences with several young ladies, Huon finds his true love, marries her before the pope in Rome, and presumably installs her as Duchess of Bordeaux and later Queen of Auberon's realm. His success in wooing her over her father's strenuous objections, in an other world setting, recalls the folklore motif of winning a fairy bride. Huon's conquest in love consecrates a symbolic action, a triumph over sinister, perhaps infernal, forces (a theme of Celtic origin?). His marriage and return to Bordeaux go hand in hand. As in *Aymeri de Narbonne,* winning a fief and a woman constitute acceptance into the feudal hierarchy; the woman and the city are symbols of the hero's achievements and witnesses to his glory. Marriage to Esclarmonde, however, constitutes only one aspect of what we may audaciously call the Freudian element in this poem. We have already noticed how the protagonist is accepted into Yvorin's court after having defeated a woman at chess (his victory due to the girl's love) rather than a man in combat, how he returns to the sea, is buffeted by a storm and thrust naked onto a desert island. His initiation includes a return to the womb, prime image of the death and rebirth experience. Other incidents in the narrative can be understood in terms of an unconscious, though quite real, expression of conflict and/or triumph on sexual grounds.

Such are: the river (female) blocking Huon's path and the rod (male) enabling him to cross; the automatons flailing away at Huon before Dunostre (a castration figure); his entrance into the castle through a narrow opening with a young woman's aid; once inside, the severing of the giant's arms, then his head; Auberon's horn and flask, signifying nature's involvement in the quest. We need hardly mention that the medieval poet was unacquainted with modern psychiatry. Phallic imagery has existed since the beginning of time without men having been conscious of its implications in terms of analysis. The *Huon* poet also gives expression to basic human drives, conflicts, repressions, and wish fulfillments. Images common to Western man enter into the Tristan romances, Rabelais, or a nineteenth-century novel. In *Huon de Bordeaux,* as in these other works, elucidating a pattern of imagery helps us to understand the hero's quest and its formulation in literary terms.

The young Duke of Bordeaux undergoes a series of adventures. The highly stylized form these adventures take causes us to interpret them partially in symbolic terms, as in a Chrétien de Troyes novel. Each episode contributes in some measure to the hero's experience of adventure, initiation, and acceptance. A figure of innocence, he has been accused of terrible crimes, is judged and condemned. Alone in the world, forced unto his own resources, he sets out to vindicate himself and prove his right to a place in the feudal world. Through more than human aid he succeeds in vanquishing the powers of evil that have held him and his society in thrall. He marries a beautiful maiden and returns to his kingdom, justified and exalted, having achieved sovereignty in both the other world and his own. Yet he agrees to set out once more, abandoning his own community in favor of sovereignty in that other world, where he will replace the father surrogate and become king. Thus, although Huon himself is transformed in the course of the narrative, society remains the same. He twice escapes from his community to a realm of adventure. *La Chanson de Huon de Bordeaux* is for the modern reader, too, a poem of escape, where he may participate in a domain of fantasy, where heroes are rewarded, villains punished, and the anguishing problems of secular life may be forgotten. Although the world of archetypes does not always open avenues of escape, archetypal patterns will often reveal, in man's unconscious, the desire for a life adventure based on wish fulfillment. Thus does the *Huon* poet create a world of dreams.[41]

*   *   *

On the last page of his "Über die Quellen des Huon de Bordeaux," A. H. Krappe compares our *chanson* to the *Orlando Furioso*. He has not been the only scholar to do so. It is true, as Krappe points out, that both the *trouvère* and Ariosto draw from a wide variety of literary and folkloric sources to create a synthesis, as it were, of the previous tradition. We may add that both *Huon* and the *Furioso* are works of art, written in premeditated fashion by serious poets. Alfred Adler's criticism testifies to this fact far better than our own. For all its sincere exaltation of the ethos of chivalry, there is much comedy in Ariosto's poem. Such also is the case with *Huon de Bordeaux*. Some scholars have made the error of ignoring the poem's humor, treating it in much the same way as *Raoul de Cambrai* or *La Mort le Roi Artu*. The failure to recognize that romantic and comic elements are expressed simultaneously in the epic's fabric has led to more than a little misunderstanding.

The comic in *Huon de Bordeaux* is manifested in sundry ways. We observe quite a few motifs traditional to the *chanson de geste:*

Porter Humor. Huon must cross four bridges to enter Gaudisse's palace. At the first bridge, terrified by a guard, he pretends to be Saracen. Then, regretting his display of cowardice, Huon brutally insults the second and fourth watchmen ("Fiex a putain, dist il, le porte ovrés! ... Tais, glous, dist Hues, mal ait ki t'engerra!" vss. 5477, 5549), fully aware that Orgueilleux's ring will permit free entry. This episode is a variation on the porter humor we found in *Gaydon*. The epic hero, not the porter, behaves badly, but the impulse to laughter remains the same.

[41] For a different "dream world" hypothesis, see *ibid.*, pp. 285–90.

Anticlerical Humor. The Abbot of Cluny encourages Huon to fight Amauri. If Huon loses, the Abbot promises he will return to his monastery and beat Saint Peter's image till the gold falls off (vss. 1415–421). This absurd sense of devotion is, of course, a parody on the equally absurd Saracens who traditionally destroy their idols in defeat. Yet the very same Abbot is shown to be a coward. When, for all his good intentions, he avoids supporting Huon during the ambush, the youth is moved to resentment: "He! las, dist Hues, com mal paraige a ci!" (vs. 803). Later the monks of Saint-Maurice, terrified at the prospect of violence, will give up Huon's treasure to Gérard (vss. 9403ff.). Further reference is made to the monks' vulgarity in manner of dress ("par nos botes et par nos viés sollers," vs. 9389).

Saracen Humor. Oede and his seneschal are driven to rage by a scarcity of provisions in the market place; they are shown to be jealous of their Christian guests. Emir Gaudisse displays "typical" Saracen impotence when Huon kills his prospective son-in-law and later when challenged by Agrapart; he volunteers to become Charlemagne's vassal, if only Huon will defend him, an offer which brings out his extreme, grotesque pride: "J'aim mix en France estre sers racatés / Q'en cest païs quatre deniers donner" (vss. 6459–460). Agrapart cuts no better a figure when to pacify Huon he offers the young man his hideous sister in marriage: a creature black as ink, taller than himself, and with teeth a foot long! These devil figures indulge in much of the grotesque behavior we associate with the mystery plays.

Disguise Humor. In a scene which partakes of Saracen humor, Gériaume arrives at Babylon pretending to be a Moslem. He swears an oath, ridiculous to the medieval public because it is a Saracen oath and because it uses a Christian formula, that we should expect from a disguised Frenchman (vss. 6080–86). Playing his role to the hilt, Gériaume pretends to hate Christians more than anything else in life, beats the French prisoners, and for a certain time discourages Esclarmonde's love for Huon. Naturally enough the old warrior is cursed by the very Frenchmen he is trying to save since they as well as the pagans do not know his intentions. Even Huon himself does not recognize his companions joined to him in captivity, nor they him. Then in a final variation on this theme (though not particularly comic), Huon and Gériaume join in single combat, on behalf of Yvorin and Galafre respectively, each unaware of the other's identity.

Horse Humor. Previous to his duel with Sorbrin, Huon rides an old, decrepit nag given him by Yvorin. Although the Saracens mock the beast's appearance, Huon has the last laugh by defeating Sorbrin and seizing his young, beautiful horse. The episode recalls similar ones in other epics—*Aiol* or *Renaud de Montauban*, for instance—where heroes triumph in spite of vulgar mounts. Comedy resides in the fact that so great a hero, or for that matter any knight, should ride an impossible horse, and that, even so, the tables are turned and those courtiers who had reacted mechanically to the situation are forced to eat their words.

Violence. Fourteen headless corpses lie in Dunostre. Huon slaughters Orgueilleux by bashing his head in, but not before having cut off his arms. The other giant, Agrapart, has the good sense to yield, once his right ear is severed. When pirates refuse to turn Esclarmonde over to Galafre, he has them killed (all but one) on the spot. For having seized the princess, Galafre is forced to give battle to Yvorin. It doesn't matter what happens to either side, says our *trouvère*, for they are Saracens!

> La veïssiés un fort estor mortel,
> Tante anste fraindre et tant escu troer,
> Tant pié, tant poing, tante teste coper,
> L'un mort sor l'autre trebuchier et verser;
> Que d'une part que d'autre, sans douter,
> En sont doi mile ochis et decopé.
> De chou que caut, se il sont mort jeté?
> Sarrasin erent, Dix les puist craventer![42]   (vs. 8224)

The *Huon* poet is capable of going beyond these rather simple effects to create a more profound, individual comedy of his own.

---

[42] There you would have seen a battle to the death, so many spears broken and shields pierced, feet, hands, and heads severed, the dead dashed down one on top of the other; no doubt about it, two thousand were killed and cut to pieces on both sides. But what does it matter, if they were struck down dead? They were Saracens, may God destroy them!

He indulges, for example, in the ironic mode. Huon refers several times to an enemy castle or prison as a hostel for the night; he pokes fun at his friends' cowardice by proposing a halt at Tormont or Dunostre—because they need rest and the enemy fortresses appear to offer splendid accommodations (vss. 3995–996, 4680–684). The tables are turned, however, when the young duke is imprisoned in Babylon; he cannot help crying, "He! las ... con ci a mal ostel!" (vs. 5868).

Irony is developed with greater subtlety when Yvorin tells Estrument that the latter has made a mistake taking Huon as his servant. In fact, says Yvorin, the youth intends to steal his master's fortune:

> "Il atent tant, par Mahommet mon Dé,
> Que tu aras grant avoir amassé,
> Puis t'ocira a un mal pas paser."[43]　　　(vs. 7419)

This speech is humorous (1) with reference to Huon because we know that he is not interested in the *jongleur*'s wealth, that in fact he is of much gentler blood and finer attainments than Estrument, and (2) with reference to Yvorin, since in the end Huon will deceive and rob not his putative master but the emir himself, his daughter, and Galafre.

Once the Saracens have admitted Huon into their community, he becomes the object of a good-humored joke by Estrument. The minstrel has been richly rewarded after a performance. He calls out to Huon: "You've moved up fast. Yesterday I was your master; today I'm your minstrel. It appears to me you aren't paying attention to me any more. Come gather up these cloaks [I have been given]" (vss. 7864–867). Our *trouvère* has involved Huon and Estrument in a social comedy. On the one hand, the hero has become a poet's servant and, by extension, a poet himself, capable of appreciating music (vs. 7382) and, if he wishes, telling tales of adventure (vs. 9025). His new way of life is by no means beneath him nor does he suffer from it. Conversely,

---

[43] "By my god Mohammed, he is waiting until you have amassed great wealth; then he will murder you at a dangerous crossing."

Estrument will be made one of Huon's companions, the last of the band, replacing Garin de Saint-Omer. The minstrel is exalted, depicted in a good light, shown to be worthy of participating in a military career. Both men (and professions) are contrasted to the wicked, greedy Saracen barons, suspicious of everyone and excessively concerned with material luxury.

An ironic treatment of social and religious themes takes place also in the West. Huon had been told to seek out Garin de Saint-Omer in Brindisi. He finds his cousin but, impressed by the man's looks and accouterments, greets him as the lord of the region, to which the sailor and merchant Garin protests (vss. 2683–696). Once again the practice of rigid social distinctions is held up to mockery. We are led to believe, even though Garin is not a great lord, that he surely deserves to be one and is "noble" at heart. At Bordeaux, on the other hand, men of gentle blood commit deeds unworthy of the vilest peasant: Huon is robbed, wounded, and imprisoned; Charlemagne credits Gérard's story instead of the truth. Thus Esclarmonde observes that Christian Frenchmen act worse than the Saracens she has known in Babylon. She threatens that if Huon perish, she will renounce her new faith and return to idol worship (vss. 9332–333, 10049–51).

In two or three particularly striking scenes feudal manners become subject to laughter. At Dunostre Huon demonstrates a fine sense of courtly breeding by refusing to murder the sleeping giant Orgueilleux. But our hero, for all his technical command of chivalric procedure, awakes and challenges Orgueilleux brutally, in a manner more worthy of a porter than a baron: "Fiex a putain, villiés u vous dormés? ... Grans pautoniers, Dix te puist craventer!" (vss. 5004, 5022). Orgueilleux acts with equal brusqueness and *desmesure*. Benefiting from Huon's graciousness, he runs to put on his armor, even praises the young man, but then boasts of how he will destroy him—a boast, of course, which he will not fulfill. He asks Huon for his name, that he be able to proclaim exactly whom he has killed. Huon, after revealing his identity, then "conjures" the giant to name himself as well. Our *trouvère* is parodying the courtly *roman*, where revealing or acquiring a name occurs only at a key moment in the narrative and contains profound symbolism. Huon acted in courtly fashion by waking Orgueilleux; the giant responds in kind, permitting his guest to try on a magic hauberk which renders its wearer invincible. Our hero now breaks away from the system when he refuses to take off the hauberk as he had agreed to. Instead, he challenges the monster and, aided by the hauberk, kills him. Both Huon and Orgueilleux participate in a display of feudal etiquette. Both indulge in a potlatch, each seeking to outdo the other according to the rules. That a monster should conform to such rules is itself incongruous, but humor is particularly manifest when Huon willfully defies the code— bringing us back to reality, as it were—simply in order to win.

Charlemagne's court embodies the most complete perversion of feudal honor. One of Amauri's hostages chooses to pledge his lands rather than his life for the traitor. Presumably he knows to what extent Amauri's word can be trusted. This man's weakness also demonstrates his cowardice, unfitness to be a hostage in the best of heroic worlds, the cupidity of his family, the court, and implicitly of Charlemagne himself. Indeed, the emperor's own words and deeds provide the most striking justification for Huon's escape from a false, degenerate world. They are presented in ironic terms. The emperor admits Charlot's incompetence but proclaims him his heir nonetheless. He warns against traitors, only to fall victim to their wiles. He believes Amauri's insinuations, turns against him, then believes him a second time. He agrees that Seguin de Bordeaux served him well but can think only of the gifts he received from the late duke, which he will soon accept from the hands of traitors. He declares for Huon, swearing he will avenge Gérard's injury even against his own son, unaware that to fulfill his promise, he must indeed condemn Charlot. In fact, he will make an absolute about-face, retract his decision, and persecute Huon, heretofore an innocent victim. Subject to emotion, not reason, the emperor is easily dominated by others. Duke Naimes is justified in reproving his sovereign for too violent a manifestation of grief over Charlot's demise. Despite his urging, "Laisiés le duel, que trop le menés grant. / Puis qu'il est mors, li deus ne valt noient ..." (vss. 1307–308), Charlemagne will not desist. He can think only of revenge. Having accepted Amauri's story the second time, he backs him all the way, even after the traitor has been proved a liar:

"Tant counois bien le courtois Amaurri
Que s'il eüst le traïsson basti,
Si m'aït Dix que il l'eüst gehi."[44]   (vs. 2226)

Charles goes on to blame God himself for having upheld the wrong side in a *judicium Dei* (vss. 2180, 2229). We know that the emperor ordained the "confession clause" with malicious intent, that if by chance the vanquished dies before avowing his crime, the winner still cannot be adjudged innocent. So Huon is banished. Furthermore, the provisions allowing the young duke to return do not in any way mitigate the injustice of Charles's decision, these terms being so harsh that under normal circumstances they cannot possibly be fulfilled. Huon will probably die if he seeks to fulfill them and, as the emperor gloatingly proclaims, most certainly will be executed if he returns empty-handed. Yet Huon does return. He succeeds in the ordeal, unintentionally disobeys Charles's orders (by stopping in Bordeaux), and even so survives the emperor's wrath. Charles is baffled at every turn. He has sworn Huon would be hanged, yet once again cannot maintain his word. Auberon arrives to confound the half-drunk emperor, reveal his sins, and, in a literal as well as figurative sense, supplant him as giver of justice. In grotesque, humorously impotent rage Charles can only cry: "Naymme ... veés, pour l'amour Dei! / Mien essiant, nous sommez enchantei" (vss. 10191–192).

The feudal system, e.g., the highly stylized, literary feudal system traditional to the *chanson de geste*, is being held up to scrutiny. We are shown the weaknesses of a social order based on the personal relationship of vassal to lord, and on the lord's personal meting out of justice. Central to this form of parody is

---

[44] "I know so well the courtly Amauri that I am sure, if he had perpetrated this act of treason, so help me God, he would have confessed to it."

Charlemagne the emperor. A slave to his emotions, to fixations—his dead son, money, drink—this half-comic figure is unable to distinguish his public responsibilities as king from the private ones of a father. Since he responds to complex situations in an almost identical fashion, the resulting behavior pattern corresponds to the Bergsonian *diable à ressort* we noted in *Gaydon*. And by refusing to desist or to modify his stand in any way, he creates a snowballing situation where not only the young Duke of Bordeaux but his own throne and the future of Christendom are placed in jeopardy.

We have proceeded from traditional comic motifs, found in so many Old French epics, to comedy of character, as manifested in the figure of Charlemagne. A similar comedy of character exerts a strong influence on the hero's *persona*. Although we are made only too aware of Huon's virtues, he often acts in error and out of *folie*.[45] In our opinion these examples of *folie* or *desmesure* are comic, not tragic, in nature. They provide a counterpoint to the protagonist's heroic deeds, a comic rhythm which contributes to the elaboration of a very complex psycho-narrative pattern.

One incongruous trait in so great a hero is physical weakness: specifically, his inability to withstand hunger.[46] Auberon uses the fact that Huon has not eaten for three days as a weapon against him, bribing him with the promise of nourishment. But once the offer is made, Huon will talk of nothing else. He interrupts the sorcerer or answers his questions by asking that dinner be served. It has become a fixation, blocking out all other concerns. Similar manifestations of the hunger motif occur during the young man's sojourn in Gaudisse's prison and on the desert island. In both episodes hunger leads to his apparent undoing; in order to eat, he yields to Esclarmonde's seductions, even at the price of damnation (vss. 5930–933), and becomes the servant of a minstrel after having committed apostasy (he will avow belief in any god

---

[45] Levin, "The *Folie* of Huon de Bordeaux," discusses *folie* and its dramatic function in the narrative.

[46] See Lods, "Le thème de l'enfance dans l'épopée française," p. 59.

Estrument wishes). Huon is driven to further excess because of his appetite for drink as well as food. As a result of having over-imbibed, he will sound Auberon's horn without need and will deflower Esclarmonde. Charles too makes a fool of himself at Bordeaux by drinking too much and is given a tongue-lashing by Naimes (vss. 9692-710). The theme of folly through drink occurs in *Le Pèlerinage de Charlemagne* and *Gaydon* (see Chapter III) as well as in many other epics. It underscores the Bergsonian notion of contrast between the ideal and the actual, between man's romantic or intellectual pretentions and those physical elements which also make up the human condition.

Bound to the physical, and perhaps to some extent derived from it, is a "spiritual" characteristic we can only designate as cowardice. Huon, *puer non senex*, is unduly afraid. He fears the Kumans ("for no reason . . . ," says the poet, "in that they do no harm," vs. 2921); he fears Auberon, in the forest, after having blown his horn, and after the seizure of Tormont; he fears to enter Dunostre and Babylon; once inside both fortresses, he wishes he could leave; at one time or another he lacks faith in the magic horn, hauberk, and ring and either is afraid to use them or tries them out on the wrong occasions. Huon is even prone to tears. He weeps upon leaving Rome (vss. 2657, 2664), after traversing strange countries (vs. 2945), in Auberon's domain (vs. 3226), before Babylon (vs. 5600, 5629), and when he becomes Estrument's servant (vs. 7314), just to mention a few. We know to what extent weeping, symptomatic of a passionately, even violently emotive life, was typical of the feudal period.[47] Nonetheless, Huon cries too much, more than any other protagonist of epic history. Fear, so natural to an ordinary mortal, is unfitting in a hero of his grandeur. In him it is a fault; he does not act in the way the public expects.

The *enfes* is guilty of non-heroic behavior, i.e., refusing to adhere to traditional standards of conduct. As in the case of Gaydon's rustic companion Gautier, the exigencies of a stylized,

---

[47] Paul Rousset, "Recherches sur l'émotivité à l'époque romane," *Cahiers de civilisation médiévale,* II (1959), 53-67.

artificial heroic life are placed in opposition to the demands of common sense. This opposition arouses laughter in the public. In terms of the knightly code of his day, Huon acts in a shockingly irresponsible fashion; his acts demonstrate pride, a disdain for prudence and measure. He is clearly guilty of *desmesure*. Because his folly is comic rather than tragic in nature, however, the author characterizes him by the adjective *legier* (vss. 6677, 6720, 9113). As Auberon says, forgiving Huon his sins: "Car plus preudomme ne poroie trover, / Fors que le cuer a trop legier d'asés" (vss. 6676–677).

This *légèreté* or comic *hubris* is most concretely manifest in the young man's relations with his benefactor Auberon. Auberon orders Huon not to summon him with the magic horn except in an emergency; Huon blows the horn to test it. He orders Huon not to visit Tormont; the youth goes there intentionally. Once again Huon summons Auberon when not in mortal danger. Auberon asks his disciple not to seek a fight with Orgueilleux; Huon visits Dunostre that he may challenge him. The fairy king orders Huon never to lie; in Babylon Huon declares he is a Saracen. He forbids the youth to sleep with Esclarmonde before their marriage; Huon violates her on the ship returning to France. Huon once again lies, this time to Estrument.

On seven distinct occasions Huon consciously, willfully defies his master. He reacts mechanically, immediately opposing whatever counsel Auberon offers, however logical it may be. Even more comic is Huon's state of mind after he has been punished for defiance. Whenever, in accordance with everyday human justice, Auberon properly corrects his pupil, Huon responds with outrage, infuriated that anyone should have dared to rebuke him and then insults his erstwhile benefactor in no uncertain terms. "Ah! Auberon, stinking, hunchbacked dwarf, may He who suffered on the Cross curse you," (vss. 5910–911) he cries in a Babylonian prison; on Moysant Island he uses much the same language (vss. 7168–173), in spite of the fact that Malabron has just come, with Auberon's permission, to liberate him. In fact, Huon threatens to defy Auberon again, by telling another falsehood, if ever he falls into difficult straits. And in Estrument's presence he does just that! He will punish his benefactor by committing additional faults which cannot but place him in a still worse predicament, materially and in Auberon's eyes.

On the one hand, as we have already pointed out, Huon's actions are funny because they are mechanical. Whenever Auberon asks him to do something or not to do something, Huon responds by willing the opposite. This rigid, mechanical defiance causes us to laugh much as did Gautier's objections to courtly love in *La Chanson de Gaydon*. But we also laugh at Huon because his mechanical reaction takes the form of defiance, the defiance of a child against his father or master. Another manifestation of childishness is the way Huon weeps and bemoans his fate. On at least one occasion such behavior is designated as *enfanche* (vs. 2671). Huon's defiance appears childish because of its very absurdity. That he is at fault, has willfully disobeyed Auberon, we the public recognize as much as Auberon does, or for that matter, Huon himself. Although it is wholly illogical and unfair for him to blame Auberon for the straits he gets himself into, he does blame him. This attitude, so typical of a child, elicits a smile from the public.

At the same time, Huon's attitude is not entirely without reason, nor do we cease to sympathize with him. The author leads us to believe that the protagonist's lapses are not as serious as Auberon would have them. For one thing, Huon himself does not condemn his lying, nor does he consider it to be of great import. In spite of some formal regrets, he never really admits the error of his ways. "What I did was not important," he says: "I was influenced by loss of memory or enchanted by the devil. If Auberon is at all a *preudom*, he will forgive me" (vss. 5506–509, 5565–567, 5638–642). We the public are forced to accept, at least in part, the hero's own interpretation of his deeds because, in spite of imprudence, in spite of being punished by Auberon, he always comes out on top. Huon succeeds in the quest, regardless of the obstacles placed in his path, perhaps because of them. Auberon warns his disciple not to go to Tormont and Dunostre. Huon disobeys and seizes both strongholds—either through his own resources or with the help of Auberon, who saves his protégé in spite of the latter's disobedience. Although Gaudisse makes sarcastic remarks about Huon's threats to kill him (vss. 6659–664), the joke is on the emir when Auberon arrives and thereby permits Huon to fulfill his pledge. Huon is a hero of romance, leading a life of adventure and glory. A fictional character in a fictional world, he claims the right not to be mistreated or punished. Since the standards applied to ordinary mortals are not applicable to him, he may disregard Auberon's imperatives. Since his ethos is the only one relevant to the epic structure, in the long run the public will agree with him.

Yet he also defends the world's point of view. One of the reasons the young duke will not conform to Auberon's *dicta* is that by doing so he would place himself in situations normal for a hero of romance but which conflict with everyday common sense. When Huon and Gériaume wander through Auberon's forest, Huon is famished. Gériaume counsels him to live on roots, as he himself did for thirty years. Huon replies: "I'm not at all used to it; so help me God, I can't eat such things" (vss. 3234–235). Another time, beleaguered by Oede's men, Huon is about to summon Auberon; Gériaume objects that his friend has not yet been wounded, is not in mortal danger, and thus would be breaking Auberon's command. Huon replies: "Should I wait until they kill me? I will blow the horn, no matter who gets angry!" (vss. 4507–508). One of Auberon's vassals points out that the magician should not be more strict in meting out justice than God himself, who forgave Adam's disobedience (vss. 7054–64). Huon upholds the position of common sense. Starvation as inner discipline, risking death as proof of heroism—these mean nothing to him. No man must be forced by ethical or moral doctrine beyond the normal powers of human nature.

Huon partakes of and repulses the romance tradition. His nature as a literary character is fundamentally ambivalent; he treats Orgueilleux chivalrously, then in an insulting manner, and adopts successively idealistic and common sense attitudes toward combat. So too with Auberon. Huon chooses the hard road, through the fairy king's forest, then regrets his decision. He ardently desires and willingly accepts Auberon's hospitality but wishes to leave immediately. He claims to have no fear of Auberon but trembles whenever the mighty dwarf appears on the scene. He agrees to whatever request is made but almost immediately thereafter refuses to obey. Huon displays heroism and weakness, prudence and folly, conformity and independence. Each state follows directly the one that has gone before, is structurally and psychologically dependent on it. These sudden yet persistent changes in attitude lack the resilience of human nature at its best, appear rigid and mechanical. Yet the public also finds Huon's changeableness peculiarly sympathetic. Most human beings do, at one time or another, act in a comic, that is, unnatural manner. We identify to some extent with the comic hero, seeing ourselves and all of humanity in him.

Although the comic aspect of Huon's *persona* is brought out most clearly in his rapport with Auberon, the latter does not exist merely as a foil. He too fluctuates, changes, demonstrates an *esprit de contradiction*. How many times he is obstructed and baffled by Huon! Yet, though blustering with rage and quite justified righteous indignation, each time he forgives the prodigal son. He comes to his rescue personally (at Tormont, Babylon, Bordeaux) or through an associate (the Red Sea, the desert). The only valid explanation for Auberon's conduct is the very deep and lasting affection he has conceived for the boy. He first appears as a dreaded, even monstrous figure. Gériaume tells us he has the reputation of destroying those who enter his forest; sure enough, the magician does threaten to kill Huon and his band. But somehow taken with the young duke's personal qualities, he offers him magic gifts and remains true to him ever after. He demonstrates sincere, deeply felt sorrow for Huon's errors and the trouble they involve him in, even going so far as to praise his "loyalty" (vss. 3509, 4519, 4521, 10298). Now, of Huon's many fine personal traits, loyalty, to Auberon, Charlemagne, or anyone else, alas! does not find a place among them. We must interpret such praise ironically, as an instance of Auberon's being blinded by love for Huon and often incapable of seeing him as he really is. I use the term *often* because, of course, Auberon is lucid part of the time. The comic element in his nature springs from a tension between fierceness and good nature, between blindness and lucidity, between the righteous condemnation of a judge and the loving pardon of a friend. He too acts and reacts, back and forth, like a jack-in-the-box.

Auberon and Huon, each a comic character in his own right, interact to form a perfect comic pair. Again and again Auberon will be angry at his protégé. He will rage against the young man's folly, in his presence or from a distance. Huon, fully aware of Auberon's wrath and his own guilt, becomes terribly afraid. Then, moved by the pitiful condition into which the young man has fallen, Auberon will take pity on him, restoring him to favor, giving him another chance. But as Huon gains confidence in himself he ceases to fear Auberon. In response to the latter's affection he will demonstrate indifference and a stronger chafing at his master's domination. When in order to assert independence Huon defies the magician, this act unleashes Auberon's rage and his own misfortune. Both men return to the point whence they began, and the action is unleashed once more. The narrative's internal pattern is thus circular in nature; each comic interlude, having run its course, drives the characters to a point where the same or a similar episode logically follows. Tormont, Dunostre, Babylon, the ship, Aufalerne, are structurally the same. They form what we may call the fundamental comic increment of the poem; repeated and extended, they make up *Huon's* comic pattern.

The pattern is rendered so inevitable, so perfect, so apparently natural, because it flows directly from the two main characters' given personality traits and the initial situation in which the author has placed them. Huon and Auberon prey on each other; neither can exist without the other's assumed existence. Auberon is a great ruler, but childless and seemingly friendless. He seeks affection, a friend, an heir, someone on whom to bestow his favors. He chooses Huon largely by chance, without the latter's deserving such good fortune. Huon, on the other hand, is a rightful heir who has been disinherited. He has already been mistreated by one father surrogate (the king) and must defy and conquer another (the emir). He is proud and independent, a young rebel lacking in altruism, concerned only with his personal quest for glory. Auberon should be the master in their relationship, since he possesses the riches, wisdom, and power without which Huon cannot survive. But Auberon is rendered impotent by the very extent of his emotional involvement with a youth who, indifferent to his patron, defies him, knowing he will be forgiven in the end. In fact, Huon is the master, the dominant figure, in their relationship. He knows it and acts on it. Our *trouvère* has constructed a parody on the traditional father-son relationship in which the father suffers at his son's hands, is held up to ridicule by the son. The insolence with which Huon treats his benefactor is different in style, but not in kind, from that found in the earthiest of medieval fabliaux.

Parodying the father-son relationship implies a variation on the old theme of youth versus age. We discover, as in *Aymeri de Narbonne, Ami et Amile,* and *Gaydon,* the traditional conflict between audacious, admirable youths and cowardly or wicked graybeards. Huon is from first to last referred to as *Huelin* or *Huon l'enfant,* a youth who has yet to prove his credentials, while such villains as Amauri, Gaudisse, and even Charlemagne are shown to be venerable patriarchs. The duel between Amauri and Huon is set in terms of the following contrasts: great versus small, strong versus weak, *senex* versus *puer:*

> Or sont el camp li doi baron entré.
> D'unne part fu Amauris de Viés Mes:
> Grans fu et fors et ricement armés,
> De Huon graindres un grant pié mesuré,
> S'ot cinquante ans par eaige pasé.
> Et Huelins fu jovenes baceler,
> N'avoit encore vint et deus ans pasé ...[48] (vs. 1765)

Of course, we find examples of kindly, well-disposed old men too. Naimes is Huon's benefactor in the Carolingian world, Auberon

---

[48] Now the two barons come onto the field of battle. On one side was Amauri de Viés Mes: he was tall and richly armed, taller than Huon by a whole foot; he was over fifty years old. Huon was a young noble, not yet twenty-two. . . .

in the other world; they are elderly sages. Participating in both
realms and providing a bridge between them is Huon's third
counselor, the onetime civil servant Gériaume. He and Naimes
appear venerable in years; they partake of the physical as well as
spiritual characteristics assigned to the old warrior in *chansons
de geste*. Auberon, on the contrary, enjoys the freshness and
beauty of a child. Nevertheless, as Gériaume informs Huon, this
little child was born before Christ (vss. 3444–447). For all his
power and wisdom, Auberon is a weak old man, weak in that he
needs Huon as much as, if not more than, the young man needs
him. He cannot or will not recapture his hauberk from Orgueilleux or destroy the pagan kingdoms existing in his part of the
world, without first being goaded into it by Huon. Even more
important, Auberon is weakened by affection, a burning desire
that Huon become his son and heir. He must dominate Huon,
impose his prudence and wisdom on the audacious free spirit
inherent in the Duke of Bordeaux. Yet by impinging on the
hero's freedom, he blocks his development, acts against the rules
of romance, and thus must be condemned.

As in *Gaydon*, one conflict between old and young centers on
the issue of love. Auberon and Gériaume each take a conserva-
tive, puritanical stand toward Huon's affair with Esclarmonde.
Auberon forbids the couple to make love before they are married;
Gériaume, after having warned Huon in like manner, abandons
ship, leaving the sinners to their fate. We are also told that
Emir Galafre permits Gériaume to speak with Esclarmonde because he is so old, for never would a maiden seek his love (vss.
7952–957). In these episodes Huon thinks of sex quite differently.
Desiring Esclarmonde on the boat, he enjoys her in spite of
Auberon and Gériaume, exulting in his passion and its sensual
fulfillment. On the desert island, comparing their history to that
of Tristan and Iseut, he encourages his fiancée to make love
again: "Let's embrace; we will die more sweetly. Tristan died
for love of beautiful Iseut. We shall do the same, you and I, in
God's name" (vss. 6848–850). Then, after they have been reunited, Huon must be separated from Esclarmonde for the one
night they spend in the Abbey of Saint-Maurice. If they slept

together, says the poet, Huon would surely have had his will of her and profaned the convent, "Car Hues ot trop legier cuer d'asés" (vs. 9113).

Thus does Huon oppose Auberon and Gériaume. But if the youth indulges in sensuality after having won Esclarmonde, he steadfastly refuses to do so on other occasions. At Babylon, although the Saracen princess makes the advances, he yields only when goaded by hunger. Later he will spurn Yvorin's daughter, who loves him with even more passion than did Esclarmonde (vss. 7501–504, 7517–521, 7555–558). Huon stands in absolute contradiction to himself; from a youth of inflexible principles he is transformed into a bold skirt-chaser, returns to his principles, then once more is tempted by lust. His transformation, comic in and of itself, corresponds to and complements a change on Esclarmonde's part. Although the princess defends her virginity and regrets the sin she and her fiancé commit, in Babylon she had made no less sensual and brutal advances to Huon (with the exception of physical assault) than he does to her on the ship. Inflamed by his kisses to the point of fainting, she declares:

> "Sa douce alaine m'a si le cuer emblé,
> Se jou ne l'ai anuit a mon costé,
> G'istrai dou sens ains qu'il soit ajorné."[49] (vs. 5728)

We cannot justify these transformations on psychological grounds alone. They exist, structurally, for the sake of comedy. On two distinct occasions, in Babylon and on the open sea, a lover desires his mate but his advances are repulsed. Not only is frustrated lust itself often made to appear comic; the notion of a chaste epic hero of the old school yielding to his senses, or a Saracen passionflower suddenly overcome with scruples, gives rise to satire on literary conventions, on the way in which literary characters are supposed to act (see the analysis of *Gaydon* in Chapter III). In this respect we note a contrast be-

---

[49] "His sweet breath has stolen my heart, to the extent that if I can't have him with me tonight in bed, I will go out of my mind before daybreak."

tween Huon's liaisons with Esclarmonde and with Yvorin's daughter. The mistress of Monbranc desires the youth, but her passion is never requited. It remains on the physical level and Huon's attitude drives her to fury. But the Huon-Esclarmonde affair attains comic heights due to a mechanical, artificial reversal of roles, a "switch on a switch." When one character gives in to lust, the other is overcome with scruples; both characters change brusquely and symmetrically but in opposite directions. As a result both are seen to act in humorous fashion and their way of loving is held up to gentle, benevolent laughter.

In love, as in war, Huon defeats old men. He wins the love or pity of beautiful maidens (Sebille, Esclarmonde, Yvorin's daughter) and survives. To do so he must defy the Saracen potentates (Orgueilleux, Gaudisse, Galafre, Yvorin) who guard them. Despite their jailers, however, the young women aid Huon in fulfilling his quest. The four old men, whatever their technical roles in the story, act as fathers or elderly husbands to the girls. They are father or husband surrogates; Huon then plays the role of a young lover who defies their will and wins the girl(s) for himself. He deceives them casually, nonchalantly, in spite of themselves. Youth triumphs over age, nature will have its way— as in so much of medieval and modern literature, from *Floire et Blancheflor* to the theater of Jean Anouilh.

*   *   *

We have discussed *Huon de Bordeaux* as romance and as comedy. If our analysis is correct, may it not be claimed that the poem's romantic and comic elements exist in a state of tension, thus reduce the poem's aesthetic value? More than one critic has declared that comedy, irony, and parody are incompatible with a true epic (or romantic) spirit. Our reply is that comedy and romance do exist together in *La Chanson de Huon*, simultaneously and in a state of tension; the tone is indeed serious and willfully comic at the same time. But the resulting tension provides for an individual texture, a vivid counterpoint perhaps unique in the medieval epic. It must not be condemned *ipso facto* for not adhering to canons of a neoclassical aesthetic no longer considered valid for works in our own time.

Furthermore, the incompatibility between *Huon's* two elements is perhaps not as great as might first appear. Many of the romantic motifs were probably taken, directly or indirectly, from contemporary folklore. There is a vast difference, however, between the world of popular fairy tales (any legitimate *Märchen*) and the fairy tale atmosphere of a poem of the court (Chrétien de Troyes, Ariosto, Spenser, La Fontaine, Musset). *Huon de Bordeaux* is a highly sophisticated poem. Its romantic material, from whatever provenance, is treated in a sophisticated, artistic manner and with courtly detachment. It cannot be considered in any way naïve. There is something in the tone of romance which makes the similar tone of high comedy congruous with it.

From the point of view of comedy, although traditional literary forms and motifs are being laughed at, although certain traditional institutions are held up to ridicule, the humor in this poem is by no means harsh or bitter. Comic catharsis, it has often been said, is achieved by sympathy and ridicule rather than pity or terror. If such is the case, sympathy plays at least as great a role here as its companion. The protagonist is a heroic, Christian adolescent. Although he is guilty of *folie* and *desmesure*, we laugh at these faults. We find them funny, neither wicked nor seriously blamable; we continue to sympathize, even to identify, with the young duke. He triumphs over his world, and the public triumphs with him. In no way do Huon's faults interfere with his heroic stature. The nineteenth-century editors remarked with commendable good sense, "... l'on ne voit pas que ce genre de sottises ait jamais rien prouvé contre les héros de roman."[50] The comedy in *Huon de Bordeaux* is one of rapidity, enthusiasm, and love. It expresses, as so often in the Middle Ages, a sense of the richness and beauty of life, the closeness of poet and public to the realities of existence. In this sense, comedy complements rather than conflicts with the element of romance. Both con-

---

[50] *Huon de Bordeaux, chanson de geste,* ed. F. Guessard and C. Grandmaison (Paris, 1860), p. xix.

tribute to an aesthetic of joy, triumph through laughter and adventure. Sin and death are discomfited; man endures.

The complexity of this poem is manifest in its structure. Does the action naturally fall into four main blocks (Scheludko), five blocks and two *retardierenden Elemente* (Voretzsch), or six blocks (Adler)? We do not know. The narrative unfolds as a series of interlocking adventures, whose precise rapports with each other and with the work as a whole are not immediately apparent. Bewildering are the number of parallelisms and antitheses: between cities (Tormont, Dunostre, Babylon), between characters (Aliaume and Gérard; Charles, Gaudisse, and Auberon; Auberon and Gériaume; Orgueilleux and Agrapart), between episodes (Huon's sentimental adventures in Babylon, on the open sea, in Monbranc; his trials in Paris and Bordeaux). Increments appear and reappear, are repeated, the first anticipating the second, often in a state of progression. Certain episodes, which from a strictly narrative point of view appear to be retarding elements or digressions, make an important thematic contribution. The adventures in Tormont and Dunostre provide Huon with an indispensable supernatural aid (the hauberk), test his manhood, offer material for comedy, and help establish the father-son relationship between the young man and Auberon. The adventures at sea and at Yvorin's court again offer material for comedy, particularly the comedy of love, and establish the central archetype in Huon's career—symbolic death and rebirth. Our *trouvère* recounts a version of the archetypal quest narrative but does so in a carefully worked out narrative pattern and with more than a little subtlety and complexity. He does not hesitate to isolate and amplify one element (atonement with the father, incomprehension on the part of society after having crossed the return threshold), to combine otherwise disparate elements (Auberon as supernatural aid, Auberon as father figure), to reduplicate and repeat still others (fight with a monster, rescue of damsels in distress, aid from an older, wiser counselor). The story depends upon adventure, rapidity and variety of incident. Action is panoramic and scenic rather than dramatic, open rather than closed. Intense moral or ethical problems, psychological profundity, and pathos are absent. Yet this complex linear narrative is also circular. Huon's career begins and ends in France, in the stereotyped, heroic world of the *chanson de geste*. A departure allows him to participate in a world of adventure, but he returns home, only to receive the promise of Auberon's kingdom, i.e., a second crossing of the threshold. The comic pattern is also circular, based on the repetition of a similar comic increment. *La Chanson de Huon* is circular and linear, a romance and a comedy, at one time.

The *Huon* poet draws from many sources and traditions. He straddles different worlds (epic, Oriental, Arthurian, folkloric, bourgeois), bringing them all into his poem. As with the *Orlando Furioso*, epic is combined with romance, comedy with the supernatural, satire with sentiment, fantasy with burlesque. His poem opens up widening circles of experience, manifests breadth and scope, includes so much of the variety and inclusiveness of life. It is a culmination of the tradition of the *chanson de geste*, perhaps the last great epic masterpiece in France before Du Bartas and D'Aubigné. More than most works of French literature, it exhibits a cosmic view of life and embodies a vision all too rare, even in the Middle Ages.[51]

[51] Walpole, "Humor and People in Twelfth-Century France," p. 225: "Joy and pain, alternating in the sequence of time, ever intermingled if time be eliminated as an unnecessary category of the intellect—there we have a truth of human existence revealed by the heart to the mind, a collaboration which, no matter how narrow the mind's horizons, lets us see our great or little world as a whole, not as comic, not as tragic, nor as a mere mingling of both, but as a less definable totality of which tragedy and comedy are but aspects and of which art and literature seek constantly to be the more and more perfect expression. Humor, which is of the heart and the mind, has its share of this creative principle and gives to life proportions which include the infinite. It is charitable and full of hope, seeing truth in dreams and folly in despair."

CONCLUSION

Ernst Robert Curtius has written that the Golden Age of the Old French epic coincides with the turn of the twelfth century—with the reign of Philip Augustus.[1] I hope the four essays which make up this volume have helped to substantiate Curtius' statement. The period extending approximately from 1190 to 1230 saw the creation of many fine *chansons de geste;* the same period gave rise to the novels of Jean Renart and the flowering of the courtly lyric. At least a generation after Chrétien de Troyes, Marie de France, Béroul, and Thomas had written their masterpieces, the extraordinary vitality of epic production continued, in spite of the evolution of new literary tastes and genres.

Aymeri de Narbonne is a "romantic" epic treating the hero's quest for a city and a bride, tokens of honor, tokens of the hero's claim to acceptance by the feudal community; it also manifests a credible representation of reality in such matters as the conduct of war, numerical precision, and the depiction of foreign nationalities. *Ami et Amile* employs a traditional epic framework—the same tradition of realism, delight in glitter and violence—to narrate a story of sacrifice and salvation, of two friends who are tested by God, who succeed in a quest for the absolute because their faith proves to be true. *La Chanson de Gaydon* recounts interminable adventures within a framework of the epic of revolt but also indulges in comedy, particularly the comedy of love and

[1] "Über die altfranzösische Epik II. 1. Garin der Lothringer," *Romanische Forschungen,* LXI (1948), 421–37, esp. 423–24; cf. with Alfred Adler, "Ernst Robert Curtius and the Old French Epic," *Symposium,* XIII (1959), 88–95, esp. 91–92.

war, as manifested in confrontations between a gross, uncouth peasant and the chivalrous, heroic, but artificial aristocrats who befriend him. *Huon de Bordeaux* gives rise to comedy of character and situation similar to *Gaydon's*, comedy centered on the protagonist and his benefactor Auberon; the poet uses humor to set off and adorn an archetypal quest narrative: how the hero departs for a symbolic other world, participates in adventures, wins a decisive victory, and returns with the tokens guaranteeing his triumph.

All four poems are different; each has a distinct form and texture. Together with the various epics of revolt (*Raoul de Cambrai, Renaud de Montauban, La Chevalerie Ogier*), they demonstrate the variety and complexity of epic creation in this period. They also bear witness to the epic's occasional high level of artistic success. In our opinion *Ami et Amile* and *Huon de Bordeaux* are works of art, masterpieces which frequently bear comparison with *Roland, Guillaume, Le Couronnement de Louis,* and *Le Pèlerinage de Charlemagne.* The other two, while perhaps not rising to the same heights, deserve a place in medieval narrative comparable to that of our best secondary novelists (Crébillon *fils,* Alphonse Daudet, Colette, and Simone de Beauvoir).

Equally important from the viewpoint of literary history is the way in which all four poems diverge from the early *chanson de geste.* The tradition of heroism exemplified by the *Song of Roland,* even by *Le Couronnement de Louis,* has been modified in the course of the twelfth century. For all their variety, these four epics tend, to a greater or lesser extent, in the direction of romance. We have discussed earlier in this book, particularly in Chapters I and III, the various historical factors in the second feudal period which help account for what amounts to a radical change in taste. No less significant is the strictly literary influence of the *roman courtois.*[2]

The late epic has become more aristocratic or rather it caters to the evolving, more refined taste of its aristocratic public. We

[2] See Hofer, "Der Einfluss des höfischen Epos auf das Volksepos."

are made aware of the refinements in life open to a nobility that appreciates fine clothes, food and drink, sheen, and luxury (*Aymeri, Ami*). The *trouvères* indulge in more elaborate descriptions of *realia*, exult in precision and the mastery of insignificant detail. Class distinctions come into prominence (*Gaydon*); the peasant is set off against a new kind of aristocrat, a man of elegance and extraordinary personal beauty (*Aymeri, Huon*), capable of acts of chivalry, of delivering speeches, paying court to ladies, and obeying rules of etiquette. The supernatural, both Christian and non-Christian, helps determine the narrative line (*Ami, Huon*). Most important of all, love makes a major contribution. The *trouvère* has his hero participate in erotic relationships, often using a courtly vocabulary and the outward signs of courtly ritual; he may even parody courtly love in its more profound manifestations by fusing it with the older epic tradition, with which it is incompatible (*Gaydon*). The protagonist often sets out on a quest, participates in adventures, is concerned with his development as an individual. In more than one late *chanson* (*Gaydon, Huon*) the *trouvère* indulges in the ironic mode, regarding with a smile the antecedent tradition and his own creation. And although originally composed to be chanted, by the end of the twelfth century the epic is read aloud; it has lost whatever lyric qualities it possessed one hundred years previously and has become a strictly narrative genre.

These characteristics are shared by the *roman courtois*. It is apparent that the later *chanson de geste* resembles the novel and has been influenced by it. Yet resemblance and influence do not imply identity. The major distinctions between *geste* and *roman*, most of which were established by W. W. Comfort in 1904, are still valid today.[3] The *chanson de geste* retains concern for religion and the crusade; epic heroes devote part of their careers

---

[3] "The Essential Difference Between a *Chanson de Geste* and a *Roman d'Aventure*," *PMLA*, XIX (1904), 64–74. See also the brilliant essays by Erich Köhler and Hans Robert Jauss in *Chanson de Geste und Höfischer Roman. Heidelberger Kolloquium*, pp. 21–30 and 61–77. However, some of the characteristics Köhler and Jauss assign to the *chanson de geste* are not applicable to late epics.

to a struggle against Saracens (*Aymeri, Ami, Huon*), while, except for the tales of Perceval and Galahad, Christ is largely absent from the *romans*. The epic gravitates around Emperor Charlemagne and his court in Paris; the *roman* deals with King Arthur and his knights in a mythical realm corresponding geographically to the Angevin kingdom of Henry II. *Chansons de geste* presume to recount history; the novel is more readily accepted as pure fiction. In spite of increased romanticization and individualization, the epic hero remains united to his people and city (*Aymeri, Gaydon, Huon*), thereby maintaining a greater sense of community than is present in Arthurian literature. The lineage of traitors, which becomes an ever greater factor in the epic (*Ami, Gaydon, Huon*), is absent from the romances. Love, taken seriously or as parody, plays a more important role in the *chanson de geste* than previously, but never becomes the dominant motivating force. Although *trouvères* created masterpieces in both epic and romance, the latter genre benefited from more conscious, artistic premeditation; we know the names of many authors of romance, not of epic. Certain epics (*Gaydon, Huon*) manifest an antiromantic spirit, i.e., low style, repudiation of chivalry, satire on ladies and the courtly ethos generally.[4] Most of all, epic and romance differ in regard to form. The *chanson de geste* is a long narrative poem usually composed in decasyllabic and dodecasyllabic lines rhyming or assonancing in *laisses* of unequal length. The *roman* is a long narrative poem usually composed of octosyllabic rhyming couplets.

In spite of an admittedly strong influence of the *roman* on the later *chanson*, the two literary kinds remain distinct, do not at any time merge into one. We may even suppose that many of the elements of comedy and romance which flower in the late epic developed naturally from forces latent within the *chanson de geste*, are thus not absolutely dependent on outside influence. It is then possible to conceive of a parallel evolution in both genres,

---

[4] Margaret Schlauch discusses this trend, though not in the epic: "Realism and Convention in Medieval Literature," *Kwartalnik Neofilologiczny*, XI (1964), 3–12.

which would correspond to similar developments in other arts, especially in architecture and music. We tried to indicate in the chapters on *Aymeri de Narbonne* and *Huon de Bordeaux* that the mythos of romance, belonging to world literature as a whole, cannot be restricted to material of purportedly Celtic origin. In fact, romance as mythos or mode exists on a totally different plane from *chanson de geste* and *roman arthurien* as literary kinds. Romantic elements are present in the *Odyssey* and the *Gerusalemme Liberata* as well as in *Aymeri de Narbonne;* yet all three works remain technically epics. The *chanson de geste* was probably derived from some form of oral poetry. Single poems of heroism were written, then followed by longer ones dealing with other adventures of the same heroes or members of their families. New themes were introduced (rebellion, love, the crusade), and finally all poems were combined into vast cycles. To medieval man *La Chanson de Guillaume, Le Couronnement de Louis, Aymeri de Narbonne,* and *Guibert d'Andrenas* belong together. Do we have sufficient reason to separate them?

It is still possible, of course, to criticize adversely the late *trouvères,* from an aesthetic point of view, for having contaminated the tradition of *Roland* and *Guillaume.* Some modern critics claim that this transformation in contemporary taste, by imposing courtly material onto an epic framework, has produced disastrous results. Such normative judgments, shared by quite a few medievalists,[5] repose largely on a neoclassical aesthetic

[5] For example Robert Bossuat, *Le Moyen Age* (Paris, 1931), p. 59: "Si le talent personnel, s'exerçant dans certains cas, a donné à quelques passages, comme la promesse d'Aimeri [in *Aymeri de Narbonne*] ou le duel d'Olivier et de Roland [in *Girard de Vienne*], un relief particulier, il faut convenir que ces compositions bâtardes se diluent trop souvent dans une insupportable rhétorique. Les procédés employés par les remanieurs, dans le dessein de transformer des œuvres destinées à l'audition en objets de lecture, ne réussissent le plus souvent qu'à les avilir." Jessie Crosland, *The Old French Epic* (Oxford, 1951), p. 295: "One has only to glance at any of the late twelfth or early thirteenth-century poems to realize how completely stereotyped the style has become and how the padding increased as the inspiration diminished. By the time this stage was reached the period of epic poetry in France may be said to be over. Romances with

filtered through the evolutionary theory of genres made famous by Brunetière.[6] According to this view, a genre develops in time much as a living organism: it is born, evolves to a moment of "classical" perfection, then decays and dies. The genre at its culminating point is pure, has eliminated factors which would prevent its attaining its true nature; the reintroduction of these elements can only contribute to the genre's decline. Brunetière's thesis has been discussed in the not too distant past by René Wellek and Austin Warren, who, while rejecting the most extreme formulation of evolutionary genology, do favor the study of genre in terms of historical evolution and the relating of historical process to a value or norm, i.e., historical and even aesthetic judgments made with reference to an ideal, an albeit temporary "aim" or type.[7]

The difficulties created by evolutionary genology are legion. Brunetière, obsessed with Darwin's theory of evolution, was seeking to make literary criticism objective by applying to it the methodology of natural science. Genres would evolve and become transformed into higher genres as do the species in nature. His mania for classification is symptomatic of this obsession. Today we cannot accept the Darwinian analogy except as "little more than a fanciful metaphor."[8]

Secondly, accepting normative values obliges the critic to choose his norm. Even with the ready-made example of modern tragedy, Brunetière runs into difficulties. The moment of perfection, he says, corresponds to the careers of Corneille and Racine, the period extending from 1636 to 1677. We may wish, however, to propose other high points, the tragedy of Shakespeare or of

---

their love-intrigues, their often pointless adventures, and their exploitation of the 'merveilleux' had already taken their place."

[6] See *L'évolution des genres dans l'histoire de la littérature* (Paris, 1890), pp. 1–31, and "L'évolution d'un Genre. La tragédie," in *Etudes critiques sur l'histoire de la littérature française*, (2nd ed.; Paris, 1905), VII, 151–200.

[7] *Literary Scholarship: Its Aims and Methods* (Chapel Hill, 1941), chaps. 3 and 4; *Theory of Literature* (London, 1949), chaps. 17 and 19.

[8] Wellek and Warren, *Theory of Literature*, p. 267.

Goethe and Schiller, areas which Brunetière places under the heading of drama but not of tragedy. Even if Brunetière's rather narrow formulation is acceptable, today we think of Corneille and Racine as belonging to different literary generations and representing different aesthetics. Which do we choose to represent the summit? Both dramatists have their partisans. Brunetière's refusal to choose does not resolve the problem in the least. Furthermore, by viewing modern tragedy solely from a neoclassical aesthetic, he cannot help being unfair to other significant dramatists within France (Tristan, Rotrou, Voltaire, for that matter the elder Corneille himself) who differ from the canon. The question becomes insoluble when we deal with genres illustrated by a large number of recognized masters. Does decay in modern poetry set in after Hugo, Baudelaire, Rimbaud, Mallarmé, or Valéry? Who embodies perfection in the novel: Balzac, Stendhal, Flaubert, Zola, Proust? Or, for that matter, cannot a good case be made for the century of Le Sage and Marivaux, Fielding and Sterne?

Conditions affecting normative judgments for the medieval epic are not essentially different from those attendant on the modern novel or lyric. If late *chansons de geste* are to be condemned for having deviated from the highest standards of epic production, some other *chansons* must be found which, according to sound critical and historical judgments, conform to and indeed determine these standards. The scholar who has done more than anyone since the war to set such standards is Jean Rychner. In *La chanson de geste: Essai sur l'art épique des jongleurs,* he seeks to demonstrate that the *chanson de geste* is a genre of oral poetry, was not composed in conscious literary fashion to be written down but uniquely for and in the process of oral recitation; that each time a *jongleur* recites an epic, he composes it anew.[9] Those epics which have come down to us are but late manuscript copies of such recitations. According to Rychner, we cannot apply to a genre of oral poetry the same criteria we do to

[9] Geneva-Lille, 1955; also, Stephen G. Nichols, Jr., *Formulaic Diction and Thematic Composition in the Chanson de Roland* (Chapel Hill, 1961).

literature. Referring instead to the standards of oral creation, we find that the *Song of Roland* alone conserves the lyricism and strophic structure inherent in oral poetry. Later epics, having deviated from the norm, must be condemned.

Rychner follows the theory of oral epic formulated by Milman Parry and Albert B. Lord for Homer and for Serbo-Croatian folk-singers in the twentieth century.[10] However, even if Serbo-Croatian and other primitive epics were composed the way Lord and Rychner say they were (which we have reason to doubt),[11] it by no means follows that the *chansons de geste* that have come down to us or, for that matter, the *Iliad,* are also the result of oral composition. Rychner's analogy between the French epic in the twelfth century and the Yugoslav epic in the twentieth is not at all convincing. The two traditions resemble each other only to a slight degree. A poem such as *Raoul de Cambrai* or *Renaud de Montauban* will be longer than the majority of Serbo-Croatian songs and will have a far more sophisticated narrative structure; its major characters will appear more complex, more subtly drawn, and will undergo conscience crises unknown in the primitive epic; it will treat a problem of political insubordination, a crisis in feudal society that is more serious than problems found in Serbo-Croatian songs; its pattern of imagery will vary to some extent from work to work and will display individual artistic creation; its tone will be unique, different from those of

[10] See Parry, *L'Epithète traditionnelle dans Homère* (Paris, 1928), *Les formules et la métrique d'Homère* (Paris, 1928), and "Studies in the Epic Technique of Oral Verse-Making," *Harvard Studies in Classical Philology,* XLI (1930), 73–147, and XLIII (1932), 1–50; Lord, "Homer, Parry, and Huso," *American Journal of Archaeology,* LII (1948), 34–44, and *The Singer of Tales* (Cambridge, Massachusetts, 1960). Rychner used other articles by Lord which have since been incorporated into *The Singer of Tales;* Mathias Murko, *La poésie populaire épique en Yougaslavie au début du XXe siècle* (Paris, 1929).

[11] N. Banašević, "Le cycle de Kosovo et les chansons de geste," *Revue des Etudes Slaves,* VI (1926), 224–44, and "Les chansons de geste et la poésie épique yougoslave," *Moyen Age,* LXVI (1960), 121–41; Maurice Delbouille, "Chansons de geste et chants héroïques yougoslaves," *Cultura Neolatina,* XXI (1961), 97–104; Duncan McMillan, "A propos de traditions orales," *Cahiers de civilisation médiévale,* III (1960), 67–71.

other *chansons*. Only from the point of view of language do the traditions meet. In both, style is largely formulaic, a formula defined as "a group of words which is regularly employed under the same metrical conditions to express a given essential idea."[12] These are the famous *chévilles* and *clichés* which frustrate many a student approaching medieval literature for the first time. Lord claims that their presence in poems as disparate as the *Iliad,* the *Song of Roland,* and *The Wedding of Smailagić Meho* is proof that all three were composed according to the rules of oral epic. "Formula analysis, providing, of course, that one has sufficient material for significant results, is, therefore, able to indicate whether any given text is oral or 'literary.' "[13] Such, in our opinion, is not the case. A formulaic style alone does not suffice to neutralize all other criteria used in classifying and judging a work of literature. It may indicate that a particular text is oral, that it is a literary reworking of material once composed and transmitted orally, which retains the archaic style of the original (especially if archaic style serves as an aid to oral recitation), or that it is a popular degradation of once sophisticated material. But we must examine a text from many points of view, as a total work of art, before postulating its mode of composition. That forerunners of the Old French epic composed prior to 1050 were oral, that *Roland, Guillaume,* and *Isembard* still reflect an earlier oral tradition (they themselves being works of literature, however), and that practically all of medieval literature, whatever its provenance and means of composition, was meant to be sung, chanted, or read aloud—this much and this much alone can be inferred from the presence of formulaic style.[14]

Rychner goes even further than Parry and Lord; he insists

[12] Parry, "Studies in the Epic Technique," p. 80; also Lord, *The Singer of Tales,* pp. 4, 30.

[13] Lord, *The Singer of Tales,* p. 130.

[14] So too for Homer, see Cedric H. Whitman, *Homer and the Heroic Tradition* (Cambridge, Massachusetts, 1958), p. 156: "The only function denied Homer by the nature of his medium was, for the most part, novelty of phrase. All the larger aspects of his poetry were his own to form, character, structure, imagistic economy, and above all, point." Needless to say, Lord does not agree.

that central to oral creation in the French epic is not the formula but the *laisse*. According to Rychner, the *laisse* is the basic functional increment in oral poetry, the lyrico-narrative unit without which the epic could not exist. In the *Song of Roland,* narrative development coincides with strophic pattern, the *laisse* achieves maximum aesthetic effect by fulfilling a structural need. In the *Roland* the *laisse* is what it should be: "Enfin, tous les moyens lyriques concourent au dessin de la laisse. Bref, la laisse est l'élément, le matériau élémentaire. Et qui ne voit que c'est là sa fonction? qu'une strophe est, par définition, l'élément' d'une chanson? Que serait-elle, si elle n'était pas cela? Ce qui est fonctionnel est beau! Dans le *Roland* la laisse est ce qu'elle doit être ..."[15] Only the *Roland* attains poetic heights. Those epics whose strophes do not function according to Rychner's definition (*Raoul de Cambrai, Ami et Amile,* etc.) must be considered products of decadence, corruptions of the ideal: "La vraie hauteur épique ne me paraît accessible qu'aux chansons du premier type [the *Roland*], seules capables d'une profonde transposition du récit en chant. ... En somme, conserver à la laisse son caractère de *strophe,* c'est vraiment composer une *chanson;* offusquer ses contours, ne respecter ni le découpage naturel qu'elle devrait imposer à la narration, ni l'ordre qu'elle devrait apporter à la disposition des reprises, l'allonger démesurément, c'est altérer le caractère premier du chant."[16]

In his article, "Les chansons de geste et le livre," Maurice Delbouille objects to Rychner's thesis in the following terms: "On rassemble des oeuvres individuelles sous la définition d'un genre conçue *a posteriori,*—puis on parle de ce genre comme d'un être vivant qui naît, vit et meurt,—puis on identifie, sous le signe du *genre,* des oeuvres qui pourtant diffèrent entre elles par bien des caractères,—puis on transfère des caractères reconnus pour ceux des oeuvres d'un genre encore observable à celles d'un genre

---

[15] *La chanson de geste,* pp. 68–125, esp. p. 124. But in all other supposed examples of oral poetry, the key unit is not the *laisse* but the line or formula. Nichols, *Formulaic Diction and Thematic Composition,* avoids the difficulties Rychner has fallen into and is much more cogent on this point.

[16] *La chanson de geste,* p. 125.

analogue partiellement inaccessible mais identifié arbitrairement au premier. Et, négligeant certains faits qui feraient difficulté, on en vient à professer, bientôt, une théorie générale de la poésie populaire ou de l'épopée vivante."[17] It is clear from Delbouille's remarks to what extent Rychner adopts, consciously or unconsciously, Brunetière's notion of genre. If, like Rychner, we think of *chanson de geste* in terms of lyricism, the functional utility of the *laisse*, freshness of style, religious inspiration, etc., *La Chanson de Roland* must be presumed the high point in Old French epic production. But we are not obliged to accept these standards. If, instead, we judge these poems as to existential commitment to the problems of the day, or power and intensity of characterization, *Raoul de Cambrai* stands out; as to exciting narrative and character development over a period of time, *Renaud de Montauban;* as to romantic adventure and the lure of the supernatural, *Huon de Bordeaux.* Choosing criteria other than Rychner's can easily bring about the positing of a late poem as goal or ideal; then the *Song of Roland* must be considered an experimental *chanson,* a first *ébauche* in a series of *ébauches* leading to the masterpieces composed about 1200. By so doing, however, we would commit the same error in methodology that Rychner does. A literary genre is the totality of the individual works which make it up, not a rigid standard established centuries later in the academy; the medieval epic

---

[17] In *La Technique littéraire des chansons de geste,* pp. 295–407, esp. p. 404; cf with Calin, *The Old French Epic of Revolt,* p. 223: "As Rychner himself admits (and takes great pains to demonstrate), only the *Chanson de Roland* contains a perfect oral structure; only in the *Roland* does the laisse serve as the sole functional unit for lyric and narrative presentation. Of the remaining 100–125 medieval epics, all but the *Roland* lack this structure. In every one . . . the laisse does not coincide with narrative line and is not the basic structural unit. It is difficult for Rychner to claim the *Roland* is the only pure oral epic, an 'atypical example' of the genre, then condemn the other 100 *chansons* for not conforming to the exception. He would have us refuse to accept the majority of epics as literature because they are created orally, and also condemn them because they no longer conform to the oral tradition, i.e., are literature!"

is no more pure or purposive than the modern novel and lyric. It is no more possible to determine which individual *chanson* (or which traits of the *chanson de geste* as a whole) should be considered the ideal than to determine which poet or novelist personifies absolute supremacy in more recent times. The *chanson de geste* develops in time, is truly a living epic, though not in the sense Rychner and his school would have us believe. Poetry is created and aesthetic standards and precedents set, only to be transformed; old patterns are corroded and new ones evolve in their place, not necessarily inferior or superior to the old, simply different. A great literary tradition presumes richness and purity, tradition and innovation, coherence and diversity. Such is the evolution of the French epic from the *Song of Roland* to *Huon de Bordeaux*.

We use the term *epic* intentionally. Maurice Wilmotte chose the title for one of his books, *Le Français a la tête épique*,[18] to deny Voltaire's famous statement on French inaptitude for the sublime. Wilmotte's point was that the absence in France of a great neoclassical poet such as Tasso, Camoens, or Milton is more than compensated by the richness of her medieval output. Even if today the rehabilitation of the Protestant, Renaissance epic (Du Bartas, D'Aubigné) and acceptance into the canon of more recent poets (Vigny, Lamartine, Hugo, Claudel, Saint-John Perse, Aragon) bear witness to a splendid capacity for the sublime, the *chanson de geste* marks one of the great moments in the tradition, perhaps the greatest.

Thus may we posit a current of sublime poetry, extending from Homer to Louis Aragon, in which the tradition of *chanson de geste*, both heroic and romantic, finds a place. True, medieval texts were created in a particular place and time; the thirteenth-century *trouvère* earns a living under very different conditions than apply to Valéry and Eluard. However, once the uniquely historical considerations have been taken into account, and providing that the critic makes use of whatever aid historical scholarship can give, he then has a right to approach a text from within,

---

[18] Paris, 1917.

seeking to determine what makes it a work of art—its structure, imagination, world, tone. This is the principle on which so much of modern criticism rests. Although the external, superficial aspects of literary creation vary from age to age (though not necessarily more for the *trouvère* than for the Greek tragedian, the Roman satirist, and the Renaissance sonneteer), internally, essentially, the work of art remains the same over the ages. If it is worth reading as literature, it can stand up under the most searching critical analysis. The Middle Ages is no privileged domain, exempt from the rules of literature and criticism, nor does it need to benefit from such exemption. The best Old French poetry, like all great poetry, is beautiful; no tools that can help us to explain how it is beautiful should be disdained. The only final justification for our work is that we help render all poetry more accessible and more vital to the reader of today.

INDEX

The Epic Quest
Studies in Four Old French *Chansons de Geste*

William Calin

designer: Edward King
typesetter: Monotype Composition Company, Inc.
typefaces: Caledonia (text) and Goudy Open Face (display)
printer: The Maple Press Co.
paper: Warren's Olde Style Wove
binder: Moore & Co., Inc.
cover material: Holliston Roxite

Chansons de geste is the term which designates the Old French epic poems celebrating the deeds of Charlemagne, his barons, and other feudal lords of the Carolingian era.

An attempt is made in this study to apply the techniques of modern literary criticism to the medieval epic. For this work, the author has selected four *chansons* representative of epic production covering approximately the period 1190-1230: *Aymeri de Narbonne, Ami et Amile, Gaydon,* and *Huon de Bordeaux.* One chapter is devoted to each poem.

The concern of each essay, aside from explication, is to explore the epic for archetypal patterns, comic modes, parody, levels of meaning, aesthetic values, and problems of realism. A concluding chapter discusses characteristics which are shared by all four of the epics and which may be posited for the *Chansons de Geste* as a whole, the relationship between the late epic and the courtly romance, and the question of whether the poems participate in an oral tradition or are chiefly literary.